KILLER

THE TRUE STORY

ON

OF THE MANHUNT

THE

FOR BUCKY PHILLIPS

RUN

by RAY HALL

Foreword by Tage Hall and Tara Hall

GMK

Published by GMK Writing and Editing

GMK

Printed in the United States of America

Produced by GMK Writing and Editing, Inc.
Managing Editor: Katie Benoit
Copyedited by Cindi Pietrzyk
Proofread by Kelly Nutter Clody
Text design and composition by Libby Kingsbury
Cover design by Libby Kingsbury
Printed by IngramSpark

978-1-966981-20-6 Paperback
978-1-966981-21-3 EBook

This work was written, designed, and produced without the use of AI (Artificial Intelligence). Human creativity and intelligence may not be perfect, but they are far better than anything artificial.

This is a posthumous publication. Every effort was made by the author's family and the book producer to ensure factual accuracy and completeness of information. Any errors or omissions are inadvertent.

KILIMANJARO IS A SNOW-COVERED MOUNTAIN 19,710 FEET HIGH, AND IS SAID TO BE THE HIGHEST MOUNTAIN IN AFRICA. ITS WESTERN SUMMIT IS CALLED THE MASAI "NGAJE NGAI," THE HOUSE OF GOD. CLOSE TO THE WESTERN SUMMIT THERE IS THE DRIED AND FROZEN CARCASS OF A LEOPARD. NO ONE HAS EXPLAINED WHAT THE LEOPARD WAS SEEKING AT THAT ALTITUDE.

—Ernest Hemingway, *The Snows of Kilimanjaro*

In loving memory of Ray and Joan Hall.

Dedicated to the brave men and women who serve in law enforcement and those who have lost their lives in the line of duty. Also dedicated to the residents of Western New York and the Southern Tier (the 716) who have nurtured a unique perspective of the state and have provided a wonderful place to grow up.

ACKNOWLEDGMENTS

Thank you to everyone who supported this project, especially Paul Laundry and Jim Walton. An extra special thank you to Joan Hall for your never-ending love and support.

CONTENTS

PREFACE

In April 2006, western New Yorkers were just beginning to reemerge after the long and snowy winter. Birds began to chirp again, the days became longer, and the air smelled different. Spring was most certainly in the air. Nationally, the turmoil in Iraq continued to lead in the press, but in western New York, another story captured the headlines: *Prison Escape: State Trooper Shot!*

The alleged perpetrator was Ralph "Bucky" Phillips, and he was a fugitive at large. Like many others around the state, our father, Ray Hall (who we know as Dad), was reporting on the story. Our dad hosted a daily talk radio show, *The Hall Closet*, based in Chautauqua County. While its focus was mainly political, every subject was discussed at one point or another, and, at the time of the Bucky Phillips escape, there was no bigger local story. Callers eager to talk about Bucky were not in short supply. They called in with a variety of opinions, concerns, excitement, and conspiracy theories regarding the fugitive. As the hunt for Bucky Phillips continued, so did Dad's coverage of the ever-evolving story, and it was through this small-town fame surrounding this case that dad eventually gained access to Bucky after his capture. This is how *Killer on the Run* began.

This book is the story of Bucky Phillips, but it's also a testament to the hard work ethic our father carried with him throughout his life. The youngest of four children and only son to a white father and Cherokee mother, Dad was born and raised in rural Oklahoma, where the impact of the Great Depression and the Dust Bowl had not disappeared and the pains of Native American relocation had long lingered. Money, as well as opportunity, was essentially nonexistent. When growing up in such conditions, life lessons—especially the hard ones—are learned early. Dad was no stranger to both poverty and discrimination. At an early age, Dad also felt compelled to leave in search of something more that life might have to offer. That life's journey brought him through a stint in the Air Force and a move out west to test the allure of California before settling back in western New York. Adventure was most certainly found.

All the paths in our dad's life forged his convictions. Dad always advocated for the underdog and, in doing so, other perspectives seemed to go hand in hand: disdain for those who reign in power, being a voice for the voiceless, exposing corruption, championing equality, and seeking justice. Although our father didn't necessarily agree with actions taken by those who are sometimes on the wrong side of the tracks, through the lens of his own life experiences, he was able to understand them.

It was possibly this understanding that allowed our dad to gain access to people that others may find less than desirable or be apprehensive of, as was the case with Bucky Phillips. Dad was able to create a relationship with Bucky that afforded entry and a glimpse into his world, access that consisted of in-person maximum security prison interviews and continual correspondence between the two.

The Bucky Phillips manhunt was one of the largest in the nation and spanned more than five months. During this time Bucky was placed on the FBI Ten Most Wanted Fugitives list, along with the US Marshall Service's Top 15 list. The manhunt also brought out a circus of bounty hunters, "fans" selling "Run Bucky Run" merchandise, and statewide and national media outlets. Unfortunately, the manhunt proved to be deadly for the state police, as multiple troopers were caught in the line of fire. Eventually, the manhunt ended and, like all places once the fervor of attention dies down, western New York reverted to everyday life. But the relationship between Dad and Bucky continued.

Sadly, Dad passed away in 2011, but not before writing down his unique experience with the Bucky Phillips manhunt, which has turned into *Killer on the Run*. With this book, we have filled in any gaps as best as we can to tell the complete factual story of Bucky Phillips in these pages. This is the story of a fugitive, yes, but it's also an ode to the legacy of a man who never gave up, who worked hard and loved his family, who sought the truth regardless. Thank you, Dad, for always encouraging us to dig deeper. We love you.

~Tage Hall and Tara Hall

INTRODUCTION

On September 8, 2006, at 8:00 in the evening with daylight quickly fading, Ralph "Bucky" Phillips emerged from the dense forest that straddled the New York–Pennsylvania border. Exhausted and overwhelmed, the fugitive stood still in a small clearing with his hands raised high and, without saying a word, surrendered to a Warren County deputy sheriff. That was how a manhunt fueled by anger and fraught with danger, desperation, and death, the longest and most expensive manhunt in the history of the New York State Police, came to an abrupt end.

The story of the search for Bucky was splashed across front pages of newspapers throughout the state, and even made national news. Ralph "Bucky" Phillips was featured prominently on *America's Most Wanted* and became the 483rd fugitive on the FBI's Ten Most Wanted List. Phillips achieved another milestone by being one of only a handful of fugitives simultaneously listed on the FBI's Most Wanted and the U.S. Marshal's List of Most Wanted. Cable news provided around-the-clock exposure and frequently referred to Bucky as "Rambo" or a "Rambo-like" figure, alone in the wilderness, outfighting and outwitting his pursuers at every turn.

In the space of only five months Ralph "Bucky" Phillips gained a permanent place in local folklore and carved a niche beyond a mere footnote in the archives of national crime statistics. During 161 days of nonstop criminal activity, this forty-four-year-old, nondescript, petty thief had stolen nearly fifty vehicles, including bicycles and ATVs, and had accumulated an arsenal of stolen weapons. He brazenly trafficked drugs across three states and ultimately wounded two New York state troopers and killed another while eluding a state police agency that once forced J. Edgar Hoover to restructure the FBI.

The search for Phillips swept across New York's southern tier like a raging forest fire growing its own uncontrolled momentum. The manhunt exposed a state police command possessed by such a controlling parochial attitude that it turned a search for an escaped convict into something that had the look and feel of a military occupation, complete with high-speed convoys and arbitrary roadblocks.

Rippling through the echelons of command, with its unyielding corporate culture, the leadership was so abysmal that after the manhunt was over, the union representing the troopers called for an independent investigation, claiming the search was "poorly organized, poorly led and poorly executed."

Accusations of failed leadership are nothing new to the New York State Police. An independent investigation in the nineties concluded that lax supervision had led to widespread fabrication and planting of evidence in criminal cases by career state troopers.

That unwavering attitude, accompanied by swaggering press conferences, imperiled the safety of troopers on the ground, endangered the public, and contributed to the deadly consequences that followed. The New York State Police became bogged down by appearances, opting for showmanship over substance. A once proud organization was held captive by its own symbolism—a symbolism so deeply imbedded that it ceremoniously burns discarded uniforms as if they were American flags.

Phillips was eventually convicted and ordered to serve multiple life sentences at the Clinton Correctional Facility in Dannemora, New York, for his crimes, but the saga of Ralph "Bucky" Phillips began a long time before this. Bucky learned to hot-wire cars by the age of six and stole his first vehicle by the age of seven. By the time he reached his first year as a teenager he had already stolen dozens of vehicles, including bicycles, lawn mowers, tractors, and automobiles, and had burgled dozens of seasonal cabins, numerous small businesses, and more Laundromats and vending machines than he could remember. He pilfered everything from candy and cigarettes to cars and reveled in being dubbed an "outlaw" by local authorities.

The story of Ralph "Bucky" Phillips is so much more than that of the 161 days he spent on the run. His is a story of a failed social structure that locked a young boy into a life of such abject poverty that he could never see his way out. His story is not unique, nor is it uncommon. He, as countless others have and will undoubtedly continue to do, then entered into a criminal justice system that never gave him the tools to succeed, only the instincts to survive. Very much the same as when he walked out of that forest with his hands above his head, Bucky Phillips learned to do what needed doing in order to stay alive.

His is the story of so many lost souls, and it continues to be the story for too many. It is a story of fear, love, and regret somehow rolled up in a perceived blanket of respect for what is right, true, and just. Bucky Phillips played the main role in a story that is so much bigger than him.

Chapter One

FACE-TO-FACE WITH A COP KILLER

The Clinton Correctional Facility is a maximum-security prison located in the Adirondack Mountains near the US–Canadian border. Established in 1845, Clinton remains New York State's largest maximum-security prison.

Known by prisoners and employees alike as "Little Siberia" because of its cold winters and abundance of fresh air, the prison was once a popular early twentieth-century choice for convicts suffering from tuberculosis. It has housed the notorious and the notoriously rich and famous, including Tupac Shakur, Ol' Dirty Bastard, and the Son of Sam.

Late in October 2007, during a spell of particularly pleasant weather that splashed New York State with a brilliant display of autumn colors, bright sunshiny days, and clear, cold nights, I convinced my brother-in-law Paul, a recent California transplant, to drive me in his RV nearly five hundred miles to the prison. My goal was to see Ralph "Bucky" Phillips, the man who gained notoriety not only for his crimes but also for his unique ability to elude New York's mightiest police force. We were not far into our trip before it became obvious why so many people love New York. Scenery unfolded before us like living calendar pages as we traveled from the extreme southwestern corner of the state to the historic cities of Watertown and Potsdam and through picturesque villages nudging the shores of crystal clear lakes. We passed Fort Drum, the home of the US

Army's Tenth Mountain Division created during World War II.

We continued into an early darkness over lesser-traveled roads and could see the lights of the prison as we crested the lower edge of one of several mountainous ridges surrounding the Village of Dannemora. As we descended into the village, we were abruptly plunged into such darkness on either side of the vehicle that I sat suddenly forward and was restrained hard against the shoulder harness of my seat belt. My eyes adjusted quickly to the darkness, and I immediately saw on the driver's side of the RV an immense wall that stood nearly four stories high and cast a foreboding shadow the length of a football field. Massive towers enclosed in concrete, steel, and glass rose high above the wall at its corners and were occupied by armed guards observing the prison grounds.

Luckily there was a gas station and convenience store with a huge parking lot only a short distance from the visitors' entrance to the prison. The manager gave us permission to park the RV overnight. Temperatures fell below freezing during the night, and I would have been in sorry shape if Paul had not experienced RV overnights in California's rugged, snow-covered Big Sur region. He had wisely equipped the RV with an independent, but safe, heat source and plenty of blankets. Dawn brought a still, hard cold accompanied by a heavy frost that coated the entire area in a sparkling blanket of silence. After a shave (I skipped the shower) and a couple cups of coffee, we were standing in line at the entrance to the prison, fifteen minutes before the doors opened for visitors.

Promptly at 8:45 a.m. the distinctive drone and loud snap of an electric door lock being tripped allowed our entry. Inside and immediately to our right were two uniformed guards, one male and one female, standing behind a wire-mesh enclosure encased in heavy glass and surrounded by steel bars. To our left another uniformed guard sat behind a desk and checked our identification, and, despite my press credentials, kept my tape recorder and reporter's notebook. Our items were stored in a coin-operated locker inside a surprisingly small dressing room as we next walked through a metal detector so sensitive that the metal eyelets in Paul's shoes set it off.

We were ushered through another set of steel-barred doors into a large courtyard. We walked toward an imposing brick building buttressed by two levels of steep, concrete steps. A double set of massive wooden doors opened into a cavernous reception area bracketed on three sides by offices with an enormous workstation in the center. The workstation was erected on top of a raised platform, and two uniformed employees sat behind computer monitors and peered down at all who approached. The entire area was a hub of human activity. Uniformed employees, inmates in prison greens, men in suits and shirtsleeves, and a few smartly dressed women trafficked back and forth between offices or disappeared through corridors that led deep into the bowels of the prison.

An austere, middle-aged, uniformed man processed our passes with an air of institutional indifference acquired over time by repeatedly performing the same task. He rapidly clicked through a series of computer screens before he located one inmate in a population of slightly more than two thousand in the facility. He was actually very helpful and apologized for the nearly half-hour delay before we were ushered through three more sets of steel doors to the visitors' area. Another uniformed guard led us into a large room separated at one end by a steel partition with a thick plexiglass panel extending from the ceiling halfway to the floor. The room was bare except for several plastic chairs haphazardly arranged along the visitors' side of the partition.

I hadn't known what to expect, but the man standing behind the inmate side of the partition was a startling departure from what I had imagined. Although we corresponded frequently after his capture, we had never met face-to-face and the only photographs I had seen were unflattering poses circulated by the state police. I suppose I had expected a frightful man filled with self-pity and loathing, but reality shattered my image. Before me stood a man of medium height with a superbly athletic build that even loose-fitting prison garb could not conceal. His dark, damp hair was pushed back behind his ears and his clean-shaven face revealed the finely sculpted features of a very handsome man.

"I know you," Bucky said, flashing a smile. "I've seen your picture."

Before either of us could respond the guard politely advised us that we would be asked to leave the room for a few minutes when another guard brought a key to remove Bucky's manacles. "We had a glitch with the keys," he said as he smiled and left us alone in the room.

Since his arrival at Clinton, Bucky had been segregated from the general population and placed in solitary confinement, otherwise known as the Special Housing Unit (SHU), the most restrictive living conditions imposed in New York prisons. He was confined in a small cell, a prison within a prison, twenty-three hours a day and allowed only one hour of daily out-of-cell exercise. Bucky had access to an exercise area through a metal door at the end of his cell that could only be opened by guards from a remote location. He was otherwise restricted to his cell except for medical and legal visits and one nonlegal, noncontact visit each week. Items of personal property are severely limited for residents of the SHU and were so for Bucky in particular.

He could only possess five books from the general library and a total of fifteen volumes from the law library. He was deprived of a radio or television and denied commissary privileges with the single exception of postage stamps, provided he had sufficient money in his account. When outside his cell he was required to have his hands cuffed in front and those cuffs connected to a chain fastened around his waist. Even his showers were limited, and the guards remotely controlled the door to the shower in his cell. Although he was never accused of assaulting either guard or inmate, he was considered extremely dangerous and viewed as an escape risk because he was serving two life sentences.

Bucky apologized for keeping us waiting but explained that he was in the exercise run when he was told he had visitors. He had no idea who his visitors were since we arrived unannounced, and he had asked for permission to take a quick shower.

"That's why I was later than usual," he explained.

We had casual conversation for the next few minutes before the guard arrived with the key to his handcuffs and waist chain. We were ushered outside the visitors' room until the manacles were removed and we were given the okay to return. I immediately asked Bucky a few preliminary questions. "How are you? Are you well? Are you treated well enough under the circumstances?" The questions were intended to break the ice and give reassurances that I was there only to get his side of the story.

Bucky leaned forward in his chair, lowered his head slightly, placed the tips of his fingers prayerfully under his chin and stared in my direction under a pair of sharply arched eyebrows. Then he launched into a narrative that dispelled every preconceived notion I ever held about Ralph James Phillips. During our six-hour interview, Bucky was charming, witty, articulate, and presented his case with surprising clarity and candor. Later, when asked by a colleague if I believed Bucky's story, I told him that regardless of whether I believed him or not, his story was believable.

"Look, Ray," Bucky said and raised his hands with palms facing outward, "most people have heard that I hate cops. They believe I'm a cold-blooded cop killer and that I would shoot a cop just for the hell of it. I understand that, but," he said, jabbing the air with his thumb and forefinger to emphasize his words, "it was the other way around." Bucky's voice trailed off and his face paled. "They wanted to kill me. They put out the word that I intended to commit suicide by cop. They put out a hit on me. They did that purposely; they wanted to kill me." He paused to let his words sink in. "If I had wanted a shootout, if killing state police had been my motivation, I had many opportunities."

As I fidgeted nervously in my chair Bucky anticipated my next question. He explained that there were several occasions when he could have picked off state troopers sitting in their cruisers on deserted county roads. He said that on one occasion he was within thirty yards of twenty-five or thirty troopers standing in the open without immediate cover.

"If I had wanted to commit suicide by cop, I could have started a gun battle and they would have blown me away. How many could I have taken down?" Bucky asked the rhetorical question to make his point.

"How did you manage to get that close?" I asked in startled disbelief.

"It was an accident, a close call," Bucky smiled. "I didn't know they moved their command post from Fredonia." Bucky explained that he avoided main roads whenever possible and on that particular day had driven the back roads through the village of Sinclairville and was approaching the Route 60 intersection near an elementary school.

"I almost shit my pants when I saw all those cops standing in that parking lot," he said. "But what could I do? Although I was driving a fairly new pickup truck that had balls, I couldn't outrun them."

"What did you do?" I asked after I managed to recover.

"I knew they would stop one guy in a truck, so I just drove across Route 60 and parked next to the county gas pump."

Bucky's account made sense, because Chautauqua County's Department of Public Works had several fuel tanks strategically located throughout the county for the convenience of county road crews and other county employees. I later verified Bucky's description of the geography and watched two county vehicles—a highway department vehicle and a sheriff's patrol car—fill up with gasoline and drive away.

"I got out and pretended to pump gas," Bucky smiled. "I even removed my gas cap." He said a trooper was watching him from a patrol car across the street. "I was scared as hell," Bucky acknowledged, "but I finally twisted the fuel cap back in place, waved to the trooper and drove away. I didn't look to see if he waved back." Bucky added. "I was too scared." Bucky was convinced that the suicide by cop message was a "shoot on sight" order to every law enforcement agency throughout the state.

For the next six hours Ralph "Bucky" Phillips answered questions and talked about his youth, about his parents, about his reform school years, and discussed his life of crime. He talked about the manhunt and described the New York State Police Troop A Commander Michael Manning as "a prick with ears." Since Bucky was preparing for an appeal, I suspected he would be less than forthcoming, but he responded to every question I asked. There were areas where he avoided details that might implicate others, but he candidly discussed elements surrounding specific incidents and events. He talked freely about the shooting of Trooper Sean Brown that triggered the manhunt, but he was purposely vague about what had brought him to that disastrous rendezvous.

Chapter Two

A HALF-BREED SENECA SON

Chautauqua County is situated on the extreme southwestern corner of New York State and is as accessible to Chicago as New York City. Although not as vast as New York's Adirondack Region, much of Chautauqua County and neighboring Cattaraugus County is mountainous and covered with dense hardwood forests that are as remote as the Adirondacks. Except for scattered hunting camps and logging trails that double as hiking trails in the summer and snowmobile trails in the winter, there are large stretches of rugged terrain and unbroken wilderness in both counties.

Like most of the northeastern United States, both counties slid into tough economic times during the sixties as manufacturing plants began to abandon the rust belt for the allure of cheaper wages in the South. In worsening economic conditions, the poor are always the first and the hardest hit, and the last to recover. That was especially true for the region's Native people, who were already stuck on the lower rungs of the economic ladder. The sixties also brought the completion of the controversial Kinzua Dam that broke the last remaining American Indian Treaty with the Seneca Nation signed by George Washington.

The Kinzua Dam formed the Allegheny Reservoir that flooded American Indian lands and forced more than seven hundred members of the Seneca Nation to scramble for higher ground. Many were relocated to what the government proudly touted as newly constructed, all-electric, gold medallion homes complete with electric baseboard heating, central air conditioning, and modern plumbing. The day Ralph James Phillips was born, many of the gold medallion homes had stove pipes jutting from boarded up windows and some had crudely erected outhouses.

Although Kinzua Dam generates four hundred thousand kilowatts of cheap electricity an hour at peak capacity, the Seneca never shared in its electricity. All of Kinzua's electricity is sold to distant places downriver. Many of the Seneca who moved into all-electric, gold medallion homes simply could not afford commercially provided electricity. Such were the existing economic conditions when Bucky Phillips was born and through which he grew into manhood much too soon.

Ralph James Phillips was born on June 19, 1962, in the month the Senecas call the Berry Moon, to Ralph and April Phillips. He was the oldest of four children, having a brother, Adrian, and two sisters, Elida and Armitty. His father Ralph was a full-blooded Seneca who lived off the reservation but suffered the same or even worse economic experiences as his reservation brethren. Bucky's father was forty years older than his mother, and that age difference exacerbated everyday problems normally associated with marriage. Known by his friends as "Buck," the elder Phillips was a good mechanic who tinkered with small engines and tried to scratch out a living as a tenant farmer.

The family lived in a ram-shackled farmhouse in such cruel and unrelenting poverty that each day became an even more painful existence than the one before. Although modern society is inclined to dwell on the inadequacies of the poor and point out the lack of parenting and coping skills, for the Phillips family, survival was a daily struggle. Every day the family faced difficult and persistent problems, problems that would have challenged even the most emotionally stable and economically viable of families.

Bucky's mother was a kind and gentle woman, but his father was a temperamental man with a taste for alcohol and prone to periodic fits of temper. As a result, the aging Mr. Phillips was ill-equipped for either marriage or parenthood and treated his wife and children with equal derision. Bucky's siblings Adrian and Elida were each born with a different chronic, crippling disease, and both required around-the-clock attention. After they were born Bucky immediately became the older brother and bore the liability of increased expectations. Even before Bucky was old enough to go to school, he helped with chores and attended to his brother and sister who remained in diapers and were in constant need of care.

Although much of her time was occupied caring for two sick children and coping with an aging husband, April Phillips remained attentive to Bucky and Armitty. After the death of her husband, she was left alone with her children and struggled to keep the family together with a roof over their heads. Not many landlords wanted a welfare mother with four kids for a tenant. She moved around a lot and was living in a different place each time Bucky returned home from reform school or jail.

With neither car nor carfare April had to rely on the kindness and availability of friends to get around. When she lived near Fredonia, a reasonably affluent college town, it was not uncommon to see her carrying her thirteen-year-old daughter, still wearing diapers and unable to be left alone, over her shoulder to the grocery store and back. Once she even hitchhiked across the state and back just to visit her son for a day when Bucky was in reform school. From all accounts April Phillips was a strong and determined mother who counted her blessings daily.

It was Ralph Phillips who nicknamed his son "Bucky" and taught him how to hot-wire everything from lawn mowers to tractors to cars before the boy ever put his foot through a schoolhouse door. Looking back, those who knew the Phillips family are convinced that Ralph Philips required too much from his son and frequently lost his patience and temper. Bucky suffered swift and certain punishment if he failed to respond quickly enough to a command from the elder Phillips. Even if he committed the slightest offense, the old man would slap the "living shit" out of "the sorry little fucker" and banish him to the barn until he learned some manners. The first time that happened Bucky was not yet school aged.

From an early age Bucky perfected his innate aptitude for

self-preservation and displayed a propensity to accept elevated levels of risk. Taking risks became a natural condition, and by the time he was six or seven, he deliberately chose the worst of weather to trek into the wilderness. In the beginning his excursions into the backwoods were limited to a few hours of the brightest daylight, but that quickly changed to all-day adventures. All-day adventures soon became overnight outings that evolved into several days at a time until he became completely immersed in the forest and the elements.

The idea of a seven-year-old alone in the wilderness for days at a time with little more than the clothes on his back and a single-shot, .22-caliber rifle today presents a horrifying prospect. But for Bucky and his family such activities were common, unquestioned, and accepted. Bucky's willingness to flirt with danger as early as age seven is revealed in a *New York Times* story. A childhood friend, Terry, and Bucky would spend time together from the age of seven. One afternoon, the two were playing house using bales of hay for furniture and one for a television set.

Bucky became bored and, obviously aware of the danger, crawled through the rails of the barnyard pen and purposely began tormenting a bull so it would chase him. The bull at first seemed docile and ignored Bucky's taunts. Bucky changed his tactics. He ran toward the bull flapping his arms and yelling. His initial foray startled the bull and it whirled sideways and ran toward the opposite end of the corral. Bucky repeated the assault three or four more times but could not provoke the bull. Each time the frightened animal would scurry away from Bucky to another spot in the lot. All the while Terry pleaded with her playmate to leave the bull alone, but Bucky persisted.

Undeterred, Bucky devised a new strategy. He began to walk slowly toward the bull, and when he was as close as he dared, he began to huff and puff and wag his tongue at the bull. The bull stood his ground and would give his head an occasional but vigorous shake sideways as if shooing a fly. Tiring of the game, Bucky gave up and turned his back to the bull and walked toward the gate. Suddenly and without warning, the bull charged, and a horrified Terry clasped both hands to her head and screamed as loud as she could. "Run, Bucky, run!" Bucky immediately hit full stride without looking back. As he scooted to safety under the wooden fence, he could feel the bull's hot breath on his back.

That incident happened about the same time his father's flare-ups intensified and overnight trips to the barn became more frequent. Bucky concluded that he fared better by living in the woods for a few days rather than enduring the rampages of his father. By the time he was ten, Bucky had developed outdoor survival skills far beyond his age. He spent hours alone in the woods where one of his favorite pastimes was tracking animals just for sport. He became so good at stalking that on one occasion he was able to crawl up on a deer laying on a cushion of pine needles in a small clearing.

He spent nearly two hours creeping less than fifty feet on his stomach through a patch of tall grass and weeds. He timed his movements with the wind. He would move only as far as the wind moved the weeds along a small animal trail that extended from the edge of the woods. Down wind and concealed by a heavy cover of golden rod he gently patted the unsuspecting animal on its rump. The startled deer sprang suddenly from its bed and bounded deep into the woods before Bucky could scramble to his feet. When Bucky proudly related the incident to his family, his father bristled that he was telling another lie, and if he didn't shut up he was going to get his "ass whipped."

He once started a fire without matches. He found a small, but curious piece of wood shaped like a tiny, concave bowl. The bowl-shaped piece of wood easily fit inside the palm of his hand, and he decided he would use it to start a fire. He gathered a few strands of dry grass and managed to scrap enough moss from dead trees for tinder. He carefully, but loosely placed the ingredients inside the makeshift bowl. He sharpened the end of a pencil-sized stick and using short, firm strokes rapidly pushed it back and forth under the tinder until it began to smolder.

After an hour of hard rubbing and a few gentle puffs of breath, the tinder ignited in a bright, yellow flame. His right thumb and forefinger had blisters, and he created a blister that was sore for a week across his entire left palm. He never repeated the task, because matches were easier, but Bucky remained confident that if the need arose, he could do it again.

Bucky was content in the wilderness, and he embraced its terms and conditions for survival. He accepted the wilderness with neither fear nor reverence. Although his young mind was unable to process thoughts with adult reasoning, he did find it an escape, a safe place, a place that was uniquely his. In time he became equally at ease in the wilderness during all four seasons and learned to navigate the terrain in the dark of night as well as he could in daylight.

Young Bucky became a detached but acute observer who realized that the wilderness treated man and animal with equal indifference, and he quickly learned its language. Before Bucky reached puberty, he observed that when animals of every kind began to show a heavier coat halfway into summer that it was preparation for an early and especially harsh winter. He accepted with neither emotion nor regret that a rabbit's fate was sealed when it ignored the seemingly random but deadly deliberate movements of a fox.

He identified animals that moved by day and those that dominated the darkness. He once spent three days and two nights alone in the woods during the worst of winter storms and learned that in an emergency he could keep warm by sitting atop a partially snow-covered beaver lodge. Warm air escaping from the creatures inside the lodge diluted the bitter winter temperatures. By his teen years natural occurrences had become so tightly interwoven into his life that his every action became an immediate, instinctive response.

Bucky was actually more comfortable in the wilderness world than in the peopled world. By the time Bucky was in the fourth grade he had accumulated a near encyclopedic knowledge of wilderness denizens and observed that life worked well in the wild. He watched predators of every kind fail more often than succeed in their search for food. In the wilderness, defeat was a natural consequence. However, the wilderness hunter always appeared indifferent to an unsuccessful hunt and would trot slowly away without once looking back. No matter how hungry it was, and with neither frustration nor humiliation, the fox might pause only briefly to lick its paws after the squirrel it was chasing scampered to safety up the nearest tree. People, Bucky observed, almost always did the exact opposite. In the wilderness there was hostility, but hostility without belligerence.

It wasn't that he didn't like people, he did. Bucky was small, but wiry and quick and playful and almost always disarmed his doubters with a smile. He made friends easily at school, shunned confrontations, and wasn't embarrassed by taunts and teasing when he refused to accept a challenge for a playground fight. He never reacted angrily when classmates hurled racial insults or poked fun at his worn and sometimes torn clothing. But it was after a game of marbles when he was in second grade that Bucky first encountered the arbitrary and capricious authority of strangers.

The marble game had been a game of "keeps," where a player draws a big circle in the smooth dirt, drops his bag of marbles in the center and gives his opponent a chance to knock each one out using a taw. A player loses his turn when he fails to knock a marble from the ring. The remaining marbles are scooped up and the other player drops his bag of marbles in the center and the game proceeds with the new shooter. Players get to keep the marbles they knock out of the ring, and the one who ends up with all the marbles is the winner.

Bucky won an entire bag of marbles on his first run, including his opponent's taw. His opponent, a half-blood Seneca living off the "rez" like himself, ran screaming and crying to a male teacher monitoring the playground. When Bucky refused to surrender his fairly won marbles, the playground monitor held him down with one hand, wrenched the bag from his hand, and promptly handed it over to the whimpering kid. Bucky was angry and tried to protest but ended up sitting in the corner of his classroom with his back to his classmates. Bucky recovered from the loss of his marbles but carried remnants from that incident into adulthood.

Before his tenth birthday Bucky had become a prolific thief, if not an accomplished one. He would steal anything, not necessarily for profit but for the fun of it. Bucky was a prankster. He stole bicycles, lawn mowers, tractors, and even cars and hid them in the woods just to watch the police search for them. But for Bucky it was never about personal gain. He experienced the same gratification from pilfering a single bar of candy or a carton of cigarettes that he did stealing a car. But Bucky's life was about to change.

In September 1975 the exigencies of living converged in hostile fashion across the life of young Bucky Phillips. His father died at the age of seventy-four, and at a time when Bucky was on the verge of becoming a teenager. Ralph and April Phillips together had managed to push starvation away one day at a time, but now the prospects for the future were bleak—even desperate. Alone with her children, with little education and possessing few marketable skills, April Phillips had even fewer options.

After the death of his father, Bucky began to skip school with increasing frequency and spent more time alone in the wilderness. Bucky was half past the age of twelve. He could not get a job; even a rural paper route required a car, and those jobs fell to adults who faced the same financial rigors. He did help put up hay in the summer and did odd jobs on the weekends, but he was too young for steady work.

Finally, Bucky did what he knew how to do best. He began to take his thievery seriously. Instead of stealing cars he began to steal car parts, gasoline, and tires. He learned to pilfer Laundromats and vending machines for coin and content and would have jars and coffee cans filled with quarters and piles of coins stacked in plain sight on the kitchen table. Bucky became such a habitual thief that it was no longer useful to deny his exploits among friends and family. With his thievery so public he was bound to draw increased scrutiny from local law enforcement.

The sight of Bucky fleeing through neighborhood back yards with the police in hot pursuit became so common that it attracted little attention. One business owner reported that Bucky once burst through his store with two police officers in pursuit. They handcuffed him in the store's office before he could escape out the back door. Bucky's interaction with the authorities was not typical of most thieves; he may have been a thief, but he was a truthful thief. To Bucky, telling the truth was a matter of personal necessity. Always and without exception, whenever he was questioned about a break-in or theft, he immediately confessed. But Bucky's simple, childlike honesty was mistaken for bravado by the authorities and his admissions were perceived as cocky and offensive.

The prevailing view of the extended society held juveniles as contemptible as adult criminals, and law enforcement officials bristled at the notion that juveniles should not be punished with equal severity. Bucky was a constant reminder of the shortcomings of the local criminal justice system and of their rules governing behavior. In Bucky's case, some were just waiting for the day they could "wrap that little son of a bitch in leg irons and ship his ass off to reform school." Local authorities viewed Bucky as a habitual but dangerous thief who only by reason of age escaped what he deserved—harsh adult punishment.

Police frustration was not confined to Bucky but also extended to those neighbors and friends who seemed to shrug off Bucky's thievery. To the astonishment and anger of some local law enforcement officials, even Bucky's victims were reluctant at times to press charges. One man, a neighbor, was reported to have said that he was happy enough just to get his car back. Another victim claimed to have suggested that Bucky was just full of "meanness" and deserved a "swift kick in the ass." Still another man told deputies he got his lawn mower back and guessed it still worked well enough; he never pressed charges. A woman was overheard explaining to John Bentley, the Chautauqua County sheriff, that the only problem with Bucky was that he was "un-churched" when she accepted the return of her son's stolen bike.

Although Bucky did not live on the reservation as a child, he was inexorably tied to his father's Native heritage in ways that were not immediately obvious, even to him. Many in the white world failed to grasp that, historically, American Indians did not view petty theft as a serious crime. That attitude was deeply embedded in Native culture and proved to be a source of constant conflict since the first Europeans settled among the Native people. Indigenous people routinely allowed domesticated pigs to scavenge for wild nuts and berries before they were rounded up in the fall. White settlers also allowed hogs to forage freely but cut small notches in each animal's ear for identification. But proof of ownership did not deter a Seneca from taking a hog for personal use from a European if his family suffered a mishap and needed food.

A Seneca would not have found it unusual to have his personal property stolen, and it was not uncommon for him to assist his neighbor in butchering a purloined pig. Neither man would have betrayed even the slightest recognition and neither man would have considered it theft. Whites on the other hand, except for the Quakers, viewed such casual appropriations as common thievery, and those incidents frequently resulted in unpleasant and sometimes violent encounters.

While local authorities labeled Bucky a dangerous troublemaker, people in the community, on and off the reservation, considered him little more than a minor nuisance, a likable pest. But even Bucky realized he could not beat the system and that sooner or later he must accept the consequences of his behavior without complaint. Instead of defiance, he purposely devised gimmicks to aggravate and frustrate his accusers. His repeated taunts and tricks eventually earned him a reputation exceeding his intent or ability.

Although Bucky was never convicted, or even accused of a single act of prepubescent or teenage violence, that dangerous label became a lasting, albeit inaccurate, association. Not until Ralph "Bucky" Phillips was connected to the shooting of a New York state trooper in June 2006 was there any record of violent behavior, not even when he was in reform school. But Bucky did go to extremes just to annoy the authorities.

There is a local story that describes the nonviolent but extreme actions Bucky would undertake to aggravate his overseers while still a teenager, but old enough to be tried as an adult. One hot and humid summer evening, two deputies transported Bucky to a rural township justice court for arraignment for breaking into a hunting cabin and making off with a set of carpenter tools. On the ride to the town hall Bucky pleaded with his guardians to let him use the bathroom. He was told to either hold it or shit his pants. It was easy for officers to dismiss Bucky because of his smart-alecky remarks, and his repeated requests for a bathroom stop were ignored.

When the trio arrived at the town hall, they found a packed courtroom.

Although most of the people were there for minor traffic violations, the process was delayed by on-the-spot plea agreements, and, despite a pair of strategically placed floor fans, the room was sweltering. The court was called to order as soon as the plea conferences were over. Bucky was escorted promptly before the town justice who listened as an assistant district attorney read the charges. The judge advised Bucky that he was entitled to a lawyer and that if he could not afford one, one would be appointed.

As the judge waited for a response, Bucky squeezed his eyes tightly shut, clinched his abdomen muscles hard, and emptied his bowels in an explosion of the foulest smelling diarrhea imaginable. It was not until the loose stool began to ooze from his jeans and spill onto the floor that the room filled with such an unpleasant odor that it caused people closest to Bucky to gag. There is some debate whether Bucky's actions were deliberate, but the stench drove people to the nearest exit and the judge recessed court for the evening. Bucky was hustled out of the courtroom and taken to a nearby gasoline station where he was hosed down with a high-pressure water hose. He was stripped naked and washed again before being returned to his cell in the county jail in his wet clothes.

As Bucky grew older, what were once perceived as smart-alecky sass and rebellious pranks were viewed as serious threats. One such incident occurred when Bucky was transferred from the Chautauqua County Jail in Mayville, New York. After the unrest of the sixties and seventies the term "pig" was widely used as a derogatory term for a police officer. Bucky thought it amusing, and left a threatening note in his Mayville cell that he would "splatter pig meat all over Chautauqua County." Local law enforcement personnel viewed that note as a direct threat.

It is difficult to establish the veracity of such accounts, but when myth and reality merge, legend begins. Bucky Phillips never set out to become a legend; he never once thought in those terms, but while he was yet a boy Bucky Phillips unwittingly became a part of local folklore. He was the recipient of a compassionate notoriety that spanned three cultures, two American Indian Nations, and a poor, but predominant non-Indian population. People who knew Bucky understood his plight, or thought they did, and often rationalized his misdeeds as humorous acts of self-preservation. Even when Bucky was well into his teens and his offenses became bolder and his tone more serious, people still shook their heads in disbelief and felt genuine compassion for the individual.

Bucky's introduction to reform schools came at a time when juvenile crime was becoming a volatile political issue across the state. Faced with one of the most flagrant juvenile records in Chautauqua County, local authorities failed to distinguish Bucky's actions from that of a youthful murderer since punishment was essentially the same for both offenders. Declared by local authorities as a "person in need of supervision" this thirteen-year-old son of an American Indian found himself confined with some of the most violent juvenile criminals in New York State. During his time at the Industry Residential Center in Rochester, and his year at Brookwood Secure Center in Claverack, Bucky Phillips was trapped inside a broken system and lived in constant fear. His life became one of torment and frantic desperation.

Chapter Three

A BROKEN JUVENILE JUSTICE SYSTEM

Bucky's introduction to the New York State Division for Youth happened in the seventies when an epidemic of particularly vicious juvenile crimes gripped the state and created public outrage. That outrage triggered a struggle between competing ideologies to reform the entire juvenile justice system. As a result, youthful offenders became trapped in the middle of a rancorous political debate to define the demarcation point between a youthful offender and a youthful, but callous criminal.

There is no dispute that New York's juvenile justice system was in serious disarray in the seventies, and by 1976 when Ralph "Bucky" Phillips entered the system it was approaching meltdown. Central to the issue was whether juveniles who committed extremely violent crimes should be tried in adult courts with stiffer sentences or continue to be processed through family court and the New York State Division for Youth. The *New York Times* accurately portrayed the perplexing mess that was New York State's juvenile justice system in a 1976 article.

That article cited frustrations experienced by victims of juvenile crime and the dilemma of beleaguered family court judges. The story mentioned a writer who sought prosecution of two teenaged purse snatchers but was talked out of it by a family court official. It tells of a mother who sought justice for her son who was beaten and robbed in Central Park. Officials pressured her to drop the charges. She persisted for more than a year before the gang members were found guilty and placed on probation.

The prevailing philosophy at the time was that juvenile delinquency was a disorder—a disease that should be treated instead of punished. Acting out, bad behavior, and even criminal offenses were viewed as symptoms of delinquency, and no one seemed to know where to draw the line between delinquents and criminals. But, as the *Times* article pointed out, that was also the sense of state law pertaining to juveniles.

Extreme secrecy surrounding the juvenile justice system and youthful offenders contributed to an atmosphere of public uncertainty around and suspicion of the Division for Youth. Juvenile offenders fell under the authority of the family court system. A juvenile charged with a crime appeared before a judge who heard arguments from lawyers without juries. The entire court proceedings, including the names of the juveniles and all of the court records were closed to the public. Police were not allowed to fingerprint or even photograph juvenile offenders. To further complicate the proceedings, whatever files and records did accumulate on juvenile offenders were routinely destroyed when the juvenile turned sixteen.

The theory behind destroying the records was that a youthful mistake should not destroy a life. But the *Times* story describes the consequences of such a policy. If the juvenile was not rehabilitated, as was often the case, and returned to family court, the presiding judge, who had no information on the juvenile's previous crimes, may give him a more lenient sentence. The story goes on to say family court became so overburdened that a judge might have, at best, only a few hours to reach a decision in a case that probably should have been deliberated for several days.

Perhaps the most troubling characteristic of the system was that most juvenile offenders never even appeared before a judge. Instead, their cases went to a probation officer who usually gave them a stern warning and placed them in some social service project without follow up. That situation created such bizarre circumstances that even the most ardent supporter of leniency for juveniles became perplexed. It was reported that in 1975 more than twenty-five thousand juvenile arrests were presented to family court just in New York City. Nearly seven thousand of those arrests were for murder, rape, armed robbery, and felonious assault, yet there were only 582 juveniles in custody of the state and even a smaller number were in private, nonprofit homes run by agencies.

Most of New York's reformatories were not "locked down," or secure facilities, but that was by design. The facilities were not intended to look or even feel like a prison by adult standards. The facilities were developed by state mandate, which dictated that the purpose was one of rehabilitation and not of punishment. The idea was sound, but as it unfolded on a daily basis that philosophy clashed with reality. The reality was that the facilities were ill equipped, underfunded, and understaffed.

Many "street-smart" juveniles confounded the system by using fictitious names, but there was a terrifying potential for others to exploit the system in more dangerous ways. Fear spread throughout law enforcement, particularly in urban police departments, that children were being paid by older teens and even adults to commit the most heinous crimes without even the threat of a severe penalty. There were reports that payments for such juvenile acts often amounted to little more than a simple toy or elaborate gadget. The juvenile justice system had become dysfunctional and intolerable even by the most modest standards.

On January 1, 1975, former Brooklyn Congressman Hugh Carey was sworn in as New York's fifty-fifth governor. Early in his first term, Carey became embroiled in partisan efforts by a Republican-controlled state senate to weaken the state's liberal abortion laws and reinstate New York's death penalty. It was also during Carey's first term when the issue of juvenile justice exploded across the state. Political opponents immediately used his opposition to the death penalty and the rise in juvenile crime to attack Carey for being "soft on crime" and blamed him for "mollycoddling" youthful killers.

Carey countered by appointing Peter B. Edelman, who had been legislative director for the late Senator Robert Kennedy as director for the State Division for Youth. The new director opposed hastily prepared legislation that would have led to increased sentences for juvenile offenders, and the governor quickly vetoed the measure. Edelman repeatedly argued against longer terms for juveniles and resisted efforts to have juveniles tried as adults. He skillfully used the state's own experience with adult courts against a growing tide of partisan criticism. The director wrote in a New York Times op-ed piece in 1977 that adult state courts would do an even worse job combating juvenile crime. He pointed to the fact that in 1974 there were fewer than a hundred indictments for felony auto theft in New York City at a time when more than sixty-six thousand automobiles had been stolen. But white-hot political rhetoric made it easy to look for scapegoats, and the focus shifted to the State Division for Youth.

Chapter Four

NEW YORK'S EMBATTLED DIVISION FOR YOUTH

Prior to 1970, juvenile crime in New York State had hardly been an issue, but at the end of 1975, and for reasons yet unclear, violent juvenile crimes skyrocketed. In New York City alone murders by juveniles tripled and rapes doubled. The New York State Division for Youth suddenly took center stage in a statewide drama.

The Division came under harsh criticism for granting home leaves to detainees who in many instances used the unsupervised visits to run away and commit crimes. At any one time nearly 20 percent of the Division's population was absent without official leave. In the span of a single year at Goshen Secure Center in New York, the Division's most secure facility for juveniles, the number of runaways more than doubled. Officials defended the continued practice of home leaves and argued that only an extreme few resulted in terrible crimes.

Prominent among the extremes was the case of the fifteen-year-old boy who was driven to Brooklyn to visit his sick mother. When the counselors returned after three hours, the boy was gone. Two months later that same boy killed a taxi driver in a holdup. The story exploded across the landscape, and the issue became further inflamed when officials from the Division for Youth attempted to explain the necessity for such leaves. Louis A. Marcano, the director at Goshen, conceded to a *New York Times* reporter that every home leave was a calculated risk. But he maintained home visits were essential and suggested that was the only reliable method to see whether a child was ready to return to the community.

While the Division for Youth struggled to find a judicious mixture of rehabilitation for the juvenile criminals and methods to protect society from those juvenile criminals, basic programs such as group therapy and remedial reading were drastically cut back or eliminated. Unprepared and ill-equipped to care for a population surge that included the worst-case juveniles—youthful killers, armed robbers, and rapists—the Division's facilities remained holding centers providing little more than custodial care. The youth facility at Goshen housed some of the state's most troubled boys and was surrounded by barbed wire fences with heavy metal grills over the windows. Goshen was also the only facility that routinely locked its detainees in individual rooms at night.

A story written by Joseph B. Treaster that appeared in the *New York Times* in March 1976 described the conditions at Goshen in stark terms. At that time Goshen had eighty-five youths, with a majority of them being between fifteen and sixteen years old. Approximately 75 percent of the population was Black or Hispanic and more than half came from the city. Treaster reported that most were products of the poorest neighborhoods and came from broken homes. He wrote that many were in the low to normal range of intelligence and often unable to read or write. Perhaps one of the more disturbing conclusions of the article was that the reactions of these youths to problems was physical, not intellectual, and that force was their solution.

By that time, however, political arguments over juvenile crime took a dramatic shift from favoring redemption to favoring punishment. Rancorous political dialogue rose to such a crescendo that in 1978, E. J. Dionne Jr., then a reporter for the *New York Times* in Albany, was prompted to write an article entitled *Only Politicians Have Found Easy Answers to Youth Crime*. In that article Dionne cited a report from the Vera Institute of Justice. The report, authored by Paul A. Strasburg, concluded that "in spite of all the evidence of shortcomings in the juvenile justice system, no obvious solutions to these problems have appeared." Despite hot political rhetoric, despite the best intentions of serious people who held the interests of children uppermost, the system cried out for change.

Change eventually came, but not before the state legislature heard from professional staff members from the Division for Youth. Those who testified before legislative committees often said they felt abandoned and even endangered by a politically sensitive management bent on winning the publicity war instead of helping juveniles. Peter Edelman would eventually leave his post after three years, and ever the pragmatic politician, Hugh Carey would abruptly change his position and support the idea of trying juveniles as adults. He was re-elected. Change came all right, but it was not as a result of persuasive or even rational arguments.

Change came in the form of a juvenile crime wave named Willie Bosket. In his book, *All God's Children: The Bosket Family and the Tradition of Violence,* author Fox Butterfield wrote that Willie Bosket was charming, well read, and possessed an above-average IQ. Butterfield said Willie was a young bully who mugged an old lady before he was eight, openly terrorized his classmates, and intimidated his teachers. By the age of nine, Willie was sent to Wiltwyck, a New York State reformatory near Hyde Park, where he set fires, stole a van, and assaulted children and staff with anything he could lay his hands on, including a nail-spiked, wooden club. At the age of twelve he is said to have strangled a nurse with a telephone cord in the Quiet Room, and in 1974 Willie reportedly left Wiltwyck laughing. Despite all this, Willie Bosket became a poster boy for reformed juveniles.

Those who desired to help New York's troubled youth included a long list of prominent, dedicated, caring individuals who made a sincere effort to reclaim misdirected lives. No one was more prominent in that reclamation effort than Eleanor Roosevelt. After the death of FDR, Eleanor Roosevelt made Val-Kill Cottage in Hyde Park her sanctuary. It was there she entertained world figures and common folk alike. She discussed world and national events with Winston Churchill, Nikita Khrushchev, Jawaharlal Nehru, Adlai Stevenson, and entertained youngsters from the local Wiltwyck School for Boys.

It was Eleanor Roosevelt who began what was to become an annual fundraising event for Wiltwyck. In 1976 the Royal Ballet performed at New York's Lincoln Center for the annual event and featured Vice President Nelson Rockefeller's tribute printed on the program. It read, "When Wiltwyck is able to succeed, the child benefits, but so does the community, which is enriched by the return of a whole and more self-reliant individual." Appearing on the cover of the elegantly designed program was a photograph of a sweet, innocent-appearing child hugging his counselor. The smiling nine-year-old boy was none other than Willie Bosket.

Willie was with Bucky Phillips at Brookwood in 1977, but Bosket was placed in a special vocational program approved by Peter Edelman. Despite a propensity for violence Willie was touted as a model for Brookwood's rehabilitative efforts and recommended for release to a halfway house in the community. Before he was released, Brookwood management convinced a PBS documentary filmmaker to "meet this kid Willie." The PBS filmmaker pegged Willie for being manipulating and deceitful. In retaliation Willie slammed the camera into the filmmaker's face. It was reported that Willie laughed and walked away.

Hardly a year would pass before now-fifteen-year-old Willie Bosket would kill two men and wound another in a short span of days. Seventeen-year-old Herman Spates, Bosket's cousin and accomplice in one of the murders, pled guilty to manslaughter and was sentenced to eight and a half to twenty-five years. His underage cousin Willie, the triggerman and guilty of at least two murders, received a lesser sentence as a juvenile, a maximum of no more than five years. The likes of young Mr. Bosket were not an anomaly among the populations of juvenile detainees. Intimidation, threats, bullying, assaults, and even killings among detainee populations within the Division for Youth facilities were not exceptions to the rule.

If the political debate over juvenile crime was rancorous, the debate within the Division for Youth would be worse. Years of rampant political patronage that extended from the highest positions to the lowest entry-level job had created a workforce ill-prepared to confront complex issues associated with juveniles and juvenile crime. An atmosphere of anger and bitterness led to recrimination and created a dangerous workplace.

Juveniles like Willie Bosket were front and center in the internecine warfare between professional staff and the politically sensitive leadership within the Division.

Behavioral problems were common throughout the system. Every facility had its own cast of unruly characters who required enormous amounts of time and attention from an overworked and often undereducated staff. Director Edelman was forthright in his assessment that at any one time, six to seven dozen children in state custody, although not necessarily violent, were in need of full-time psychiatric care. Few youth facilities had a full-time psychiatrist and with the exception of a newly created twenty-bed, secure unit in the Bronx State Hospital, the neediest detainees had no place to go and frequently remained at the mercy of chance.

It remains an easy argument to say that local officials in Chautauqua County law enforcement overreacted to the thievery of twelve-year-old Bucky Phillips. Shipping a boy who was a nonviolent thief to a reformatory seemed an unconscionable act, but there were few other options at the time. Child protection services were slowly evolving across the state without permanent guidelines or funding, or even a clear statement of purpose. In the end, and by default, local officials equated the seriousness of Bucky's crimes with the frequency of his acts and tragically defined his future.

Chapter Five

ESCAPE FROM INDUSTRY

Juvenile records in New York are sealed, including those of Ralph Phillips. But we know his first extended state confinement occurred in September 1976 when he was placed in the Industry Detention Center for Boys in the small, rural community of Industry in Monroe County, New York. Industry boasts that it is the longtime site of the State Industrial School, a reformatory for boys. At that time the detention center at Industry was the largest detention center in the state under the New York State Division for Youth.

To claim that Industry was professionally staffed demeans the term. Most of the employees were from the local area and possessed little more than a high school education. What professional staff there were, counselors and state-certified social workers, was stretched to the breaking point, and they could expect little cooperation from the rest of the staff and even less at the state level. Industry was little more than a state-operated warehouse for problem children.

Life at Industry was a frightening experience for Bucky. For the first time in his life, young Bucky Phillips was locked in an environment that was foreign and fearful. At the age of fourteen, he was thrown into the company of young men and boys from the meanest streets and neighborhoods across New York State. Bucky cringed in fear as fights broke out daily and over the most trivial offenses. The staff at Industry was of little help and could often be found playing cards, especially at night in one or another of the offices used by the day shift. As a result, they were slow in responding to any commotion and found only the remnants of mayhem when they arrived on the scene. Bucky learned quickly that every boy had to fend for himself.

He had been there hardly a week before an older boy, probably fifteen or sixteen, threw him on the floor and kicked him in the groin. He rolled across the floor doubled over in pain and was hit hard across the face with a broom handle. Luckily, that was all it amounted to, and by the time staff arrived only Bucky remained curled up in the corner. His injuries were superficial. His lip was swollen, and there was a small cut at the bridge of his nose. He physically recovered in a few days, but Bucky's survival instincts took over.

Bucky had never traveled beyond the Tuscarora Reservation in the Niagara Falls–Lewiston area of Western New York. He was unfamiliar with Rochester and Monroe County and had no idea how the facility where he now found himself confined fit in the overall landscape. But he knew he had to leave. Bucky spent the next few days by himself. He spoke to no one without first being spoken to, and he ate his meals in silence. He observed his surroundings and watched the staff come and go during shift changes.

His eyes soaked in every detail and action of that process. Each employee would punch a time clock in a small alcove off the corridor and then stand in front of a window with sliding glass panels and sign a log sheet. Bucky was surprised the place was wide open. None of the outside doors were locked and people came and went without restrictions. But Bucky learned quickly that thievery was universal at Industry. Inmates routinely stole from one another and from the staff, and Bucky was amazed at the amount of food purloined by employees.

The pilfering was so obvious that at first Bucky did not believe it was thievery. One employee might depart with a large tin of coffee wedged under his arm, another would have a gallon-size can of corn or green beans. A middle-aged, matronly looking woman might leave with a large paper bag crammed tight with loaves of bread. Once, Bucky watched in silence as one of the professional counselors carried out what appeared to be a very large ham. Bucky quickly learned it was the better practice to limit his possessions and to sequester valuables, especially money, in obscure hiding places.

Miraculously Bucky survived for nearly a week without suffering more than minor jostling and a few hard shoves, but the verbal threats and taunting intensified. Three, maybe four days after his initial beating, Bucky happened to notice a tall, heavy-set, red-haired man who worked the swing shift. Bucky first noticed the man's massive forearms freckled from the sun and covered from wrist to elbow with reddish hair. He approached his shift like everyone else, but Bucky noticed he always left his car keys in his car. Bucky knew the car; he had seen the man drive it into the parking lot one afternoon, and he immediately identified the make and model.

The car was an older two-door hardtop, a white 1967 Ford Galaxy 500 with red leather seats, and was probably equipped with a 390-cubic-inch engine. Bucky knew cars, a talent gained from watching and listening to his father. He knew all the makes and models and what engines were hot and those that were not so hot. Bucky watched as the red-haired man parked the car and took his time getting out. He immediately sensed that the man held a special feeling for the car; he had pride in his possession. The man walked toward the rear of the car, paused briefly then stooped toward the ground. He straightened suddenly upright and went directly inside the compound. Bucky guessed the man hid his car keys under the rear fender and atop the tire and cataloged the entire sequence into his memory.

Immediately after breakfast the following morning Bucky was walking through the dayroom with his roommate, a gangly kid from Buffalo who was picked on as much as Bucky was. Suddenly, three bigger kids suddenly rushed them. Both boys cried out in surprise and yelled for help, but their cries did not deter the intensity of the assault. The boys landed in a heap on the floor in a flurry of kicking feet and pounding fists. They did their best to fend off the attack, but to no avail. When help finally arrived, both boys were sprawled on the floor. Bucky's roommate tried to explain what happened between bouts of crying and curses. Bucky's nose was bleeding and the side of his head throbbed from a kick that had landed solid against his ear. The boys identified the culprits, who were hanging out around the pool table, but the trio denied having been involved and warned their victims to quit lying or they would "get their dicks cut off."

Instead of punishing the offenders, the staff confined Bucky and his roommate to their room, after a trip to nurse's office, until lunch. That was it for Bucky. He confided to his roommate that he was going to run, and the boy became a willing companion. They waited until the call came for lunch and joined the crowd heading for the chow line.

Despite a rigid, orderly routine in the chow hall, Bucky and his accomplice used the occasion to slip inside the kitchen pantry and sneak out the back door. They simply cut across the back lawn and past the softball fields to Rush Road. By 6:00 p.m. that day, both boys had been picked up and returned to the facility in the back seat of a sheriff's patrol car. They were placed on punishment roll and denied all privileges for two weeks. That initial escape would be only the first of five during the year Bucky spent at Industry. On another occasion, and after another beating, he and two companions managed to walk out of the front door and were returned late in the afternoon of the next day. Walking away from Industry was his only reprieve from the daily barrage of threats, assaults, and racial slurs that plagued his existence and made his life a living hell.

Bucky spent as much time as he could by himself. He often sat alone and pretended to read a magazine as he listened to detainees who bragged of past crimes and how they had "outwitted" the dumb cops and "juvies." Bucky wanted to ask them if they were so smart why were they in jail, but decided for his own safety that he should resist the temptation. After listening to the failed exploits of his fellow detainees, he decided that if a crime required more than one person, it was a crime not worth doing. It was during this period at Industry when he reverted to the rules of the wilderness. Wilderness rules were based on the simple principle of survival. Confined to his room and curled up on his bunk, Bucky accepted with certainty that his most pressing problem at the moment was survival.

He knew that for every day he was in jail, his life was in jeopardy. He acknowledged that those entrusted with his care, either by choice or circumstance, were powerless to protect him from the diabolical deeds of a determined few. He had to learn how to shun confrontation and violence. Avoiding violence became a matter of self-preservation. The wilderness taught him that prey seldom confronted the predator; when faced with the choice of flight or fight, flight was almost always the answer.

Bucky walked away from Industry two more times during the next three months. Once he hitched a ride with a milk hauler and made it to downtown Rochester. He hadn't planned his escape; it was instead an opportunity of convenience. He had been left alone to weed flowers along the fence and simply hitched a ride with the first vehicle that drove past. Despite road signs warning drivers not to pick up hitchhikers, the driver offered him a ride as far as Rochester.

Once downtown he spent the better part of an hour gazing into store windows trying to figure out how he could get home or to the Tuscarora before nightfall. Then he suddenly realized he stood out like a sore thumb. The very presence of a fourteen-year-old boy walking the streets on a weekday morning during a school day was bound to attract attention. He was right, and in less than an hour he was being returned to Industry, riding alone in the back seat of a Rochester police cruiser.

Bucky was afraid. He literally feared for his life, and although he had never thought about it before, he felt embarrassed and ashamed of his heritage. His Native roots were not beneficial to his survival; his Indigenous blood actually posed a greater threat. He was a fourteen-year-old "half-blood," one of a kind in a diverse population, and he quickly became the lone oddity. Although his fifth and final flight from Industry may have created greater hardships for Bucky, that flight may have also saved his life.

A beating did not trigger his last flight from Industry. Actually, Bucky had survived for more than a week without an altercation, or even a confrontation, with his usual antagonists, but it was their uncharacteristic behavior that so troubled him. He could not precisely describe his feelings other than a sense of foreboding looming heavy in the air. He felt it whenever two or three of his rivals were gathered together and ignored him, or when one would cast a furtive glance in his direction without a word exchanged. The ringleaders spoke in whispers whenever Bucky was within earshot or would abruptly stop talking if they chanced to pass in the hallway.

He had a strong feeling they were up to something, and he was frightened. His suspicions would later be confirmed.

Confined to quarters as punishment for his latest run, Bucky ate meals alone in his room and was denied privileges. He was prohibited from the dayroom, which meant no television or radio, and from the game room, which meant no foosball, no pool, no table ice hockey, and no shuffleboard. That really didn't matter to Bucky. The television was nearly always turned to programs for the favored few, and on the rare occasion Bucky tuned the radio to a county music station, the immediate uproar made it impossible to hear.

No one even bothered to play shuffleboard. The sticks had all been broken and lay in a pile as ready weapons. The pool table only had three cue sticks with end tips and a cue ball substituted for a missing eight ball that someone had probably stolen from the rack. Despite posted rules declaring that players must rotate turns, the most dominant gang held sway over the foosball and pool tables while lesser members in the pecking order engaged in less popular activities.

That was Bucky's life at Industry. Every day was punctuated with threats, and it was a good day if he was not a victim of some random act of violence. Bucky realized that escape was easy, but he knew that another escape on foot was pointless. Walking and hitching rides in such close proximity to the reformatory was obvious, and from his experience was "iffy" at best. He must improve his odds. He must put as much distance between himself and Industry in the shortest possible time, but that meant that he must steal a car. Bucky waited patiently for an opportunity. He did not have to wait long.

A cold front moved down from Canada at the same time warm, moist air was moving in from the south, and the two opposing weather masses collided over Monroe County. But all Bucky knew was that early one Tuesday morning the approaching dawn was delayed by heavy skies interrupted by brilliant flashes of lightning and loud crashes of thunder. Gale-like gusts whipped rain in sheets against the building in a rhythmic cadence and cast an eerie quietness over the entire compound. By mid-morning the lightning and thunder had subsided, and the winds had died down, but the rains continued in a steady downpour for the rest of the day. Bucky knew the time had come for him to move.

At 2:45 p.m. the rain had brought everything outside the complex to a near standstill and created a quiet, stark dreariness that reached inside the compound. There was very little movement inside. A few boys were seated around the dayroom watching television or listening to the radio, but most of the residents stayed in their rooms. Bucky deliberately positioned himself at the far end of the dayroom where he had a good view of the front entrance.

The swing shift, the 4:00 p.m. to midnight crews, created a brief flurry of activity, and Bucky watched them sign in as they reported for work. A faint smile formed on Bucky's lips as he watched the red-haired staffer park his 1967 Ford Galaxy in his favored parking space, lean slightly forward at the front fender, and then hurry inside and out of the rain.

Bucky did not return to his room. He took nothing with him except his money, fourteen dollars that his mother had managed to send in her last letter. He sauntered past the counselors' offices and made his way to the kitchen pantry. He paused briefly and glanced inside the chow hall. Two staffers were having coffee at one of the tables and another was preoccupied with a crossword puzzle. One of the coffee drinkers gave Bucky a casual glance but quickly returned his attention to his companions' animated conversation.

Although Bucky's movements appeared casual, they were deliberate and carefully calculated not to arouse the slightest suspicion as he eased open the outside pantry door and quietly slipped outside. He tried to stay as close to the building as possible, but by the time he made it around to the side nearest the parking lot, he was soaking wet. Undeterred, he walked directly to the driver's side of the 1967 Ford Galaxy. He reached his hand under the front fender and slid it across the top of the tire. As he expected, his fingers touched a set of keys on a round leather fob.

Bucky let out a sigh of relief as he drove unnoticed from the parking lot onto the main road. His original plan was to wait until dark to take the car, but the unexpected downpour improved his chances of achieving a greater distance from Industry before being discovered. With the best of luck, Bucky thought, he would not be missed until the 10:00 p.m. bed check, and even then, the counts were hit and miss. Even when his absence became apparent, no one would suppose he had stolen a car, and the owner would not miss his car until his shift changed at midnight.

The Galaxy drove like a dream. The engine had great acceleration and it pushed the car forward effortlessly. The gas tank was three-quarters full. Bucky pointed the car south toward Avon and by 3:25 p.m. he was on Route 20 headed west. If everything went as expected, Bucky guessed he would be home by 6:00 or 6:30 p.m. There was hardly any traffic on Route 20, and in slightly less than two hours Bucky was well south of Buffalo. The rain had turned to a drizzle, but the skies remained dark and overcast.

He continued on Route 20 and, a few minutes before 6:00 p.m., made it to the Chautauqua County line at Irving, New York. The small community bumped against the Seneca Nation, and finding himself in familiar surroundings, Bucky loosened his grip on the steering wheel and relaxed for the first time since his odyssey began. When he saw the flashing neon sign on the Irving Diner, he was suddenly very hungry. He parked the Galaxy between two vehicles at the rear of the diner in a place not immediately visible from the main road.

Bucky chose a stool at the far end of the counter, three seats away from two men who sat closest to the cash register. An older couple occupied a table along the wall, and a young woman with a little girl sat in a corner booth at the rear. He was hungry and he knew what he was going to order. He craved a juicy hamburger with french fries and a piece of coconut cream pie. The Irving Diner was famous for its cream pies, and coconut cream was a winner for Bucky, but he knew from past experience that he wasn't likely to get a piece.

Cream pies, or an altercation over the temperature of cream pies between a county health inspector and the owner was indelibly etched in Bucky's memory. He allowed himself a trip down memory lane.

Ralph Phillips had allowed Bucky to tag along when he had business on the "rez," and the Irving Diner was always one of his first stops. Cream pies and the Irving Diner were both favorites of Ralph, and he timed his visits to coincide with the pies coming out of the oven. Ralph was not the only customer with a preference for warm cream pies. The woman who owned the diner would remove three or four cream pies every morning from the oven. Each pie was piled high with a lightly browned meringue and left uncovered on the back counter. The pies sold first come, first served, and most of the time they were consumed before the lunch crowd ever finished eating.

A county health inspector had previously cited the owner for serving unrefrigerated cream pies. She was ordered to cease the practice or install a special refrigerator. On that particular day she tried to explain for the "umpteenth" time that even if she removed the pies from the oven and immediately placed them into a refrigerator they would not cool down before they were all sold. Young Bucky sat next to his father and was eating his coconut cream pie with a spoon while this conversation was taking place.

Even as a youngster Bucky was aware of his surroundings. He watched and listened as the conversation between the owner and the inspector took on more strident tones. Finally the owner broke down in tears and threw a sugar container at the health inspector. The health inspector was a frail sort of man, but he dodged the missile, and it crashed through a plate-glass window on the far side of the diner. That was enough to get other customers involved in the ruckus and the health inspector luckily found his way to the front door and fled. Bucky was accustomed to yelling and screaming and even a measure of violence, but for some reason that episode frightened him, and he began to whimper.

By the time the place quieted down, young Bucky was sobbing and shaking uncontrollably. His father tried to console his son, but quickly lost his patience and threatened to give him something to cry about. In the meantime the owner had regained her composure and, prodded by her nurturing instincts, immediately walked around the counter and snatched young Bucky from his father's clutches. She pressed the boy tightly to her breasts and told him she was sorry for the fracas and that nothing serious had happened.

As now-fugitive Bucky sat at the counter of the same diner, he was on edge. He thought the owner might recognize him by sight if not by name from past visits. The owner, a slender woman beyond middle aged was busy at the grill and did not immediately acknowledge Bucky's presence. He did not know the two men sitting at the counter, but recognized both as being from the area. The owner turned from her work at the grill and asked Bucky if he wanted to see a menu. He shook his head and ordered a burger and fries, but as he expected, he was too late for cream pie. Bucky waited for his food and calculated that he had three or four days, a week at best, of freedom. He knew the staff at Industry would expect him to be returned in a day or two and might not even link the stolen car to his disappearance. But he realized the car was his immediate and most pressing problem.

His first thoughts were to hide it in the woods, but he could not bring himself to do that. Like the car's owner, he had come to appreciate the automobile. He felt big and important behind the wheel and the leather seats gave him a sense of luxury. He knew he couldn't take the car home; it would be too obvious, but he did not want to part with it so soon either. He pondered his dilemma as he ate his hamburger and finished the last of his french fries. He felt obligated to leave the car in a safe place. He was still thinking about the car when he walked to the cash register to pay his check. He really should wash it, he thought, but decided that might be too risky. Bucky handed over four one-dollar bills to the owner who punched the sale into the cash register.

The woman handed him a few coins in change. "Thanks, Bucky," she said with a broad smile and added, "you be good now." Bucky was surprised she remembered him but felt confident that even if she knew he was running she would not be the one to turn him in to the authorities.

Bucky drove from the diner, made his way back to Route 20, continued through the village of Silver Creek and past the grape vineyards and truck farms at Sheridan to the village of Fredonia. Before he knew it, he was on the road to his home in Stockton. That's when he remembered his childhood friend Terry. He had not seen her for a long time, and he knew she would be impressed to see him driving such a fine automobile. He soon found himself sitting in her driveway. He decided against honking the horn and opted to go to the door. Terry's mother warmly greeted Bucky and told him Terry was not at home. Bucky's invitation to take the family for a ride in a stolen automobile was politely refused.

Bucky realized that it was time to ditch the car, but he was reluctant to part with the vehicle. He accepted and understood that his friends or relatives would never turn him in, but neither would they lie nor shield him from the authorities. He concluded that under the best of circumstances and regardless of the vehicle, it would only be a matter of time before he was returned to Industry. Firmly in command of his situation, Bucky pressed down on the gas pedal and the car glided smoothly down the country road toward Fredonia.

Overcast skies allowed darkness to descend earlier than usual and that darkness allowed Bucky to drive unnoticed through the Village of Fredonia. He realized the risk but deliberately took the longest route. He drove past the State University on Temple Road to the place where Route 5 embraced the Lake Erie shoreline. Bucky traveled east on Route 5 for a short distance and turned into the tree-lined drive of the Chautauqua County Home and Infirmary. The parking lot was deserted except for several cars parked near the rear entrance designated by custom and convenience as employee parking. Bucky parked the Ford two spaces removed from the nearest vehicle and took his time getting out of the car.

Even though he knew it would be a few days before the car was found he shared the same sense of pride as its owner and made sure that he had not left it in a mess. He was even careful to place the leather fob that held the keys in plain sight atop the drive train hump. Concerned that someone might be inclined to break a window to get at the keys, Bucky checked each door to make sure they were unlocked. Next, he strolled confidently toward the rear entrance of the building and walked through the dense pines toward the main highway.

In less than ten minutes he had made his way through the woods and was on the main road near the entrance ramp of the New York State Thruway. He walked into the first convenience store he found and confidently ordered a large Pepsi and asked for change for the telephone. He put a dime in the telephone and got the operator. He gave her a number and she instructed him to deposit twenty cents for the long-distance call to a cousin who lived less than a mile from his home. When the phone was finally answered Bucky recognized his cousin's voice and after exchanging a few pleasantries asked him to pick him up. Bucky sauntered through the store, bought a Butterfinger candy bar, and waited outside for nearly thirty minutes before his cousin finally arrived in a beat-up pickup truck.

Bucky spent eleven days near home before the authorities finally paid a visit and returned him to Industry. But they were a fabulous eleven days. His mother embraced him through a veil of tears. Aware that his presence placed his family in a difficult position, Bucky spent as little time as possible at home. He searched out old acquaintances, visited the Seneca Nation, and even spent three days with friends on the Tuscarora Reservation. He camped alone in his beloved wilderness for four days.

But then the day he knew was coming arrived, and he and remembered vividly the two sheriff's deputies knocking on the front door.

Bucky's mother was in the kitchen when she heard the knock. April Phillips laid a dishtowel on the kitchen table and, with as much courage as she could muster, answered the door. When asked if she had seen her son, April did not say a word but nodded her head and slowly moved aside. Bucky emerged from the background, gave his mother a hug, whispered, "I love you, Mom," and was led in handcuffs to the patrol car. As the trio drove away Bucky could see tears streaming down his mother's cheeks, a mother who could do little more than wave goodbye to her son.

Bucky could not hold back his tears. In that moment and for the first time in his life he was overcome with regret. But, like other attributes improperly ascribed to Bucky, even tears for his mother were incorrectly assumed to be a selfish act and provoked laughter and derision from his escorts. He wanted to scream. He wanted to tell them to shut up and leave him alone, but handcuffed to a chain around his waist and with his legs in shackles, he resisted the urge. Instead, he sucked the inside of his cheek between his teeth and bit down until he tasted blood.

Bucky was relieved a half hour later when he was turned over to a pair of state troopers waiting at the county line at Silver Creek to transport him the rest of the way to Industry. Although Bucky had silently suffered the indignities from the deputies during the ride to the county line, one deputy, the one riding shotgun in the front seat, was particularly scornful. The uniformed deputy turned sideways and gripped the wire mesh separating the seats with both hands and gave him a parting shot.

"We bought you a jar of Vaseline," he said with a sinister smirk. "You're going to have so many peckers shoved up your ass that by the time you get out you can shit basketballs." The state troopers seemed unamused and removed Bucky's leg irons and handcuffs. He rode the rest of the way to Industry in the back seat of a state police cruiser. The two troopers didn't say much to each other and hardly spoke to Bucky for the remainder of the trip.

Chapter Six

RETURN TO INDUSTRY

On the ride to Industry Bucky supposed he would return to a familiar routine, confinement to the wing, no off-grounds visits, no game privileges, and meals in his room. He actually looked forward to the restrictions. His confinement would temporarily isolate him from his usual antagonists and afford him a period of peace until conditions forced him to run again. He was certain he would run again, but he was equally certain that future flight would be made more difficult now that he had stolen a car to facilitate his escape, especially a car that belonged to one of the staff.

He arrived at Industry early in the afternoon, but instead of being processed directly into the population Bucky was delivered to the administrative wing. He was led to a sparsely furnished room with only a small bed and a single straight-backed chair. For nearly an hour Bucky alternated between sitting on the edge of the bed and on the chair. Finally, a male staff member brought him a food tray with a sandwich and a paper container of milk. Bucky wolfed down the sandwich. He was still hungry but was even more puzzled by his reception.

After nearly two hours Bucky peeked into the hallway and recognized a female social worker. She was talking with two men in her office directly across hall. She smiled at Bucky and immediately summoned him to join the trio. Bucky took a seat near the door. One of the men, the one who wore a suit and tie, was occupied reading a file and flipped back and forth through the pages several times before he finally laid it on the desk in front of the social worker. He removed his thick, black-framed glasses with one hand and tapped the earpiece against his chin.

"Are we agreed?" he asked without once looking toward Bucky. The social worker and the other man nodded in agreement.

"I'll sign off on it," the man said and got up and walked out of the room. He paused briefly at the door and shot Bucky a quick glance. "Make the arrangements," he said and disappeared into the hallway.

Finally, Bucky became the center of attention. "Ralph," the social worker turned to face Bucky. "You are being transferred to a more secure facility."

At once Bucky was filled with uncertainty. Before he could open his mouth, the social worker explained to him that he would be transferred to another facility operated by the New York State Division for Youth. The move was necessary, she explained, because of Bucky's inability to adapt to the simplest of rules, but more particularly by his repeated escapes from Industry. Bucky's protests were quickly brushed aside by the other party in the room who had until that point remained silent. He reiterated that Bucky's behavior at Industry was a clear signal that more intense observation was called for and that Bucky was being transferred to the Brookwood Center for Boys.

Bucky had never heard of Brookwood and had no idea where it was located. The social worker spread a map across her desk and pointed to Brookwood. It was located at a place called Claverack in Columbia County, about thirty miles south of the state capitol at Albany. When the staff finished the briefing, they asked Bucky if he had any questions. His first concern was for his mother. He was advised that his family would be notified of the move and provided instructions for visitation and communications. Bucky knew it had been difficult for his mother to visit him at Industry and that it would be next to impossible for her to travel across the state.

Bucky was returned to his room and provided with a towel and a washcloth. He was approached by a man dressed in white pants and a white

T-shirt, a man he had never seen before, and was escorted to an isolated part of the wing. He was guided inside a locker room that was connected to a series of showerheads installed against a tiled wall. He was ordered to take a shower and leave his clothes in an open locker. When Bucky came out of the shower, he was surprised to find new clothes, including underwear neatly folded and placed on a wooden bench.

Bucky was escorted back to his room. A small table had been brought in to accompany the food tray that contained Bucky's supper. Bucky was one of the few inmates at Industry who never complained about the food. It was at Industry where he was first introduced to three meals a day. He liked the food. He particularly liked the Sunday noontime fare. Sunday was cold cuts. Baloney, ham and salami, and sliced roast beef and turkey with an assortment of other meats that Bucky was unfamiliar with were all laid out for the taking. There were white and yellow cheeses and pickles and olives and ketchup and mustard and something called horseradish that Bucky learned to take in smaller amounts after his initial exposure.

This evening, a steaming slab of meatloaf was pushed to one side on his plate while Bucky ate mashed potatoes and gravy that he mixed with green beans and corn. He always saved the best for last and shoved the scattered remnants of the meatloaf into his mouth using a slice of bread to sop his plate clean. He even ate a wiggly square of red Jell-O and scraped clean a paper cup filled with vanilla ice cream. He finished his milk and neatly arranged his plate with the empty food containers and utensils. But Bucky was in for another surprise.

The same staffer that led him to the shower returned for the empty tray and informed his ward that he would be spending the night right where he was. He instructed Bucky to leave his door open and advised him that it was "lights out" at nine o'clock. He told him he could not leave his room except for a toilet break. He pointed to a bathroom at the end of the short hallway and informed Bucky that if he had to use the bathroom, he should do it before the lights went out. Bucky remained stoic but was obviously disappointed.

He was anxious to return to the main wing. He wanted to find the red-haired staffer and apologize for abandoning his car in Chautauqua County. He wanted the man to know that he appreciated the qualities of the car and wanted to reassure the owner that he had taken good care of the Ford Galaxy. He wanted him to understand that he purposely left the car in plain view and in a safe place where it would not be stripped or damaged.

The lights went out in Bucky's room precisely at 9:00 p.m. The corridor lights dimmed at the same time and cast eerie shadows through the open doorway and against the wall above Bucky's bed. Bucky spent a restless night. He accepted the reality of his pending transfer to Brookwood and assumed he would be leaving the following day, but he remained unsure and confused. It was obvious that people were treating this differently than his other escapes. Before, he had been returned to his same wing and although he was placed on restriction, he was allowed to interact with his acquaintances.

Being returned to the population after an escape was one of the bright spots of Bucky's time at Industry. That was the only occasion when he was shown a measure of respect by his peers and he even earned a bit of admiration from those who bullied him. But on this night, he was awakened several times by the beam of a flashlight shining in his face. Bucky was under constant surveillance and although it was not exactly frightening, it left him with the strangest of feelings and he remained uneasy.

Promptly at 6:30 the next morning, Bucky was awakened, invited to use the bathroom, and herded back to the locker room with only a bath towel girded around his waist. He was ordered by another attendant to strip bare, and then told to bend over and cough. When he straightened upright, his handler ran his fingers through his hair and had him open his mouth. The aide stood outside the open shower with his arms crossed and watched him shower. Bucky was curious that he had to have another shower, but he kept his mouth shut. When he finished his shower, he was handed a towel by his guard and obeyed when instructed to wrap it around his waist. He was accompanied back to his room and told to dress.

Bucky did not know how long he sat in his room, but there was never a time that he was out of sight from the guard who sat across the hall. The wing was abuzz with a steady progression of commotion from employees reporting for work and the sounds and activities of an institution being awakened from a sluggish sleep. Bucky absorbed the sounds and movements of the morning. His eyes followed an older woman as she wobbled from side to side carrying a tray he supposed was his breakfast. A dark hair net covered her short-cropped, gray hair and sagging folds of flesh swayed back and forth in perfect cadence from her biceps as her arms kept pace with her steps. Her short, stubby fingers were clenched tightly around the sides of the tray, but her dour appearance was betrayed by a broad, cheerful smile as she handed the tray to the guard.

The guard wheeled the food tray in on the same table that held Bucky's supper the night before and without saying a word returned to his post. Bucky ate scrambled eggs with two bacon strips and two slices of buttered toast on which he smeared a packet of grape jelly. He ate a bowl of oatmeal that was overcooked and too lumpy for his tastes, but he made it more palatable by covering it with two packets of sugar and about half of his milk. He had not finished eating before the social worker he had seen the day before entered the room and sat on the edge of his bed. "Ralph," she said with a smile, "have you ever flown on an airplane?"

"No," Bucky replied and twisted his head in her direction.

"Good." She smiled and rocked slightly backward and pulled a brown file folder tight against her chest. "Today will be a first. You will fly all the way to Albany."

Bucky was at once excited, but apprehensive. He was not looking forward to being relocated to a strange place, and he was thrilled and frightened at the prospect of flight. He did not remember the social worker's name but scooted to the edge of his chair to better listen to her instructions. She explained that he would leave before noon and would be accompanied by Robert, the other social worker from the day before. She told Bucky the flight would take about two hours and that he would be picked up by Brookwood personnel and driven to the facility. She tried to dispel any uncertainties he held about the trip—worries she knew he possessed even though he tried hard to suppress his anxiety. She reassured him that

Robert would ride all the way to Brookwood with him and assist in getting him settled in his new surroundings.

She went through several housekeeping procedures with Bucky, including an inventory of his possessions and the articles of clothing he would take to Brookwood. She tried to explain what he should expect at the new facility and encouraged him to follow the rules and keep away from obvious troublemakers. She pointed out that if he were well behaved, he would likely have a home leave over the holidays and encouraged him to make that one of his goals. She asked if Bucky had any questions. He could not think of any but made up one because he felt obligated to ask something just for the sake of making the woman feel better about her efforts.

"What kinds of seats are on an airplane?" Bucky mumbled and tried to sound serious. He could not remember what she said, but she tried to answer the question and told Bucky to sit tight until Robert came to take him to the airport.

The flight to Albany was not at all what Bucky supposed. He and Robert were driven to the airport in Rochester in an Industry station wagon before noon. The state plane had not arrived. They walked around the airport and finally Robert took Bucky inside the main building, and they sat at a lunch counter with the driver. Bucky ate two hot dogs and a bowl of chili. Robert paced nervously back and forth and after several calls learned the plane had not left Albany. When the plane finally arrived, it was nearly 4:30 p.m. Bucky watched as the plane touched down and flowed gracefully down the runway. A lanky, smartly dressed man in tan slacks and a yellow pullover emerged from the plane and disappeared inside the building. He reappeared a few minutes later and walked toward the plane.

Bucky remained in the vehicle with the driver and was glad when Robert returned to tell them the plane would refuel and take off right away. Finally, the driver took them directly to the small blue and white plane with two engines parked on the edge of the concrete runway. "New York State Police" was emblazoned across the tail section of the aircraft in bold, blue letters and "New York Thruway Authority" in smaller black letters appeared directly above the state emblem. The man in the yellow pullover stood by the wing and talked for a few minutes with Robert before entering the plane.

Bucky boarded the plane and held a brown paper bag with his personal belongings that he had brought from Industry. Robert took the bag and placed it in a small compartment behind the rear seat and pointed Bucky to a seat near the window. Bucky had to struggle with his seat belt and when he finally got it fastened, he was surprised to see another man who was obviously the pilot sitting at the controls in the cockpit. The man in the tan slacks sat next to him and the two exchanged a few words that Bucky could not make out as the engine nearest Bucky coughed and sputtered and suddenly sprang to life. Before he knew what was happening the plane had taxied into position on the runway.

As the pilot waited for clearance, he revved both engines so fast that the entire plane shook. Bucky was astonished at the roar of the engines and was pushed hard backward against the seat as the plane plunged down the runway. Bucky could feel the power but was unaware of the speed until he looked from the window and saw the ground rushing past in a blur. He gripped both armrests and held on for dear life. He felt the plane abruptly snap from the runway and turn left almost in the same motion. Suddenly the roar of the engines changed to a muted drone, and he seemed to be floating without any sense of speed. The grass and shrubs and trees quickly disappeared into the haze and the buildings appeared squat and flat as the plane gained altitude.

Robert explained to Bucky that the plane from Albany could not make the trip for some reason and the state police brought this one in from Buffalo at the last minute. Aside from that conversation they remained silent for most of the trip, and Bucky kept his head twisted toward the small window. He marveled as they rode above clouds that reflected brilliantly white from the sun.

The flight went quickly. It seemed hardly any time had passed before they were landing in Albany, but it was nearly dark. Bucky's legs felt wobbly, and his steps were uncertain as he walked from the plane and followed Robert through a hangar to a waiting van. Bucky turned for a last, wistful look at the plane and realized that, however briefly it might have been, he had soared with the eagles. The driver placed Bucky's paper bag in the back of a gray van that had "Brookwood" and the markings of New York State painted on the doors. The trio rode in almost total silence for the thirty-mile trip to Brookwood, which was billed as one of the more secure facilities in New York State Division for Youth.

Although Bucky could not have known this at the time, that sense of foreboding that made him run from Industry may have saved his life. Seven months after Bucky had been transferred to Brookwood, a thirteen-year-old Indian boy named David Smith had been bludgeoned and stabbed to death by detainees at Industry. His body was discovered four days later. It would be later alleged that the staff was playing cards in the cottage while the murder was being committed.

Chapter Seven

BROOKWOOD

Brookwood was not at all what Bucky expected. He had been told that it was a more secure facility than Industry, and he envisioned a building surrounded by high fences and patrolled by armed guards. Industry was much larger, but with that exception there was little difference between the facilities. People always left early on Fridays at Industry to get a jump on the weekend, and the same practice was evident at Brookwood.

It turned out that the driver who picked them up at the Albany airport worked in the maintenance department and had to look for someone to find Bucky a bed.

Finally, a tall, gaunt man with bony hands and a deeply furrowed brow came in and grumbled something about a problem in Wing I. Despite his initial reaction, the man was patient and understanding and, with Robert's assistance, got Bucky signed in. He was even thoughtful enough to ask if Bucky had eaten and when Bucky said he hadn't, the man told him he would try to find him something from the kitchen. When Bucky was settled in his room Robert shook his hand, wished him well, and left.

Bucky spent Saturday and Sunday observing the detainees and actually met several he liked. He and a boy named Brett, who was from Buffalo and had been in Brookwood for six months, immediately struck up a friendship. Brett filled him in on the procedures of Brookwood and pointed out the detainees who could be trusted and warned him of those to avoid. He advised Bucky about the staff and social workers on Wing II and told him about the ones he liked and those he disliked. He told him that Ed and Sylvia were in charge of Wing II and that they were okay.

On Monday he was interviewed by Ed Davis and was told that he would be temporarily assigned to Wing II. Davis laid down the ground rules: get up at 7:00 a.m. five days a week (exceptions could be made for weekends), march in groups of three or four to the bathroom (no horse-play), return to your room, and get dressed (jeans, shirt or T-shirt, and sneakers). Breakfast began at 7:30 a.m., and there was absolutely no screwing around. Immediately after breakfast, the boys would return to their rooms, make their beds, and tidy up the premises. Classroom work began at 8:15 a.m., and they were expected to be there.

The procedures were not unlike those at Industry, and Bucky could easily accommodate the demands, but adapting to procedures was not his immediate problem. His immediate problem was how to avoid three or four of the real bad asses; he had not been there two days before one such bad ass named Gene threatened him for no reason other than he was standing in the same chow line.

Monday had been uneventful; most of the day was spent processing in and becoming familiar with his new surroundings. Tuesday morning started out well enough, and after he had finished breakfast, he met his social worker for the first time. It wasn't a lengthy meeting; she had just stopped by before school to say hello and formally introduce herself.

"Good morning, Ralph. My name is Sylvia, and I will be working with you." Sylvia Honig held out her hand and flashed a warm smile. "We'll talk later." With that she turned abruptly and left the classroom.

Ralph was speechless. Sylvia Honig was a stunningly beautiful woman. She had wavy black hair and a soft, creamy complexion with sparkling eyes and a vibrant smile. From Bucky's standpoint she may have been the most beautiful woman he had ever seen. Although taken by her beauty, it wasn't her looks alone that so impressed Bucky. He at once sensed that she seemed to be the nicest person, male or female, he ever met.

Sylvia Honig could never have been mistaken as one of the stereotypical do-gooders who bore the brunt of political criticisms and were accused of wrecking the juvenile justice system. She was the daughter of a farmer, a small-town country girl who still lived within three miles of the house where she was born. She grew up in a Jewish household. Neither of her parents had much in the way of formal education, but they valued education and instilled the desire for learning in their children.

Sylvia earned a bachelor of arts degree from New York University, Washington Square College and majored in English literature with a minor in philosophy. She taught junior high school English in a school district near her hometown in Upstate New York for four years. She ultimately made her way to the State University of New York at Albany on a scholarship and graduated at the top of her class with a master's degree in social work. As part of her scholarship, she was required to work in juvenile prisons for at least two years. Two years turned into thirteen with Sylvia's last three years being spent at Brookwood Center for Boys.

Brookwood had previously been a school for delinquent girls, then became a co-ed institution that miserably failed before it was finally converted to a maximum-security youth facility for boys. Sylvia recognized that Brookwood housed some of the most incorrigible and dangerous children in the state. They came from the hard streets of New York, Buffalo, Albany, and Rochester, and were mixed with the so-called "bad" kids from upstate and far western counties of the state. From the standpoint of crimes, the rural kids were mostly burglars or car thieves, but many of the streetwise city kids faced a daily struggle for their very existence and were more aggressive and difficult to reach.

Sylvia was a professional. Demanding in her work yet fair and never condescending. She had earned the respect of her peers and clients, yet she was at odds with management from the director of her facility all the way to the office of the state director for the Division for Youth. Few people can describe the chaotic conditions inside the walls of the state's youth facilities better than Sylvia Honig on the day when Bucky Phillips was shipped from Chautauqua County to a state training school.

"We had our successes," the long since retired social worker's mind flashed back to the names and faces of young men and women who left the system never to be heard from again. "But," she said as she smiled wistfully, "the system surrendered to the really hard cases." She explained that upper management wanted so much to show spectacular results that mandatory education and other structured training programs were often marginalized to accommodate the most difficult cases at the expense of the other children.

Ms. Honig experienced firsthand the fallout from management deliberately relaxing the rules to mollify troublemaking teenagers. When she transferred to Brookwood, she was assigned to a wing that housed twelve boys. Three fifteen-year-old boys were known troublemakers and responsible for creating chaos in the wing. All three boys were illiterate, physically well developed, and very hostile. They were the only black residents in the unit, and their repeated intimidation created constant fear among the other boys and spread racial dissention with detainees and staff.

The boys she called Wilson Cole, Leroy Harkins, and Stewart Jackson, all fictitious names to protect confidentiality, remained in bed nearly every day until lunch was called at noon. When Sylvia questioned the practice, she was astonished when a staff member told her: "Niggers don't go to school in Wing II." The other residents, including Bucky, hated school, but they were in class by 8:15 a.m., relieved to get away from their tormentors.

Ed Davis, her cosupervisor, either by duty or design was often absent from the wing, and it was left to Sylvia and others to confront the boys and ultimately suffer their defiance and verbal abuse. It was of no use to complain about the boys missing school to Tom Pottenburgh, Brookwood's director, because he had personally granted Willie Bosket the exclusive privilege of skipping school entirely to work in the maintenance department. Sylvia knew her wing was in a critical state, and she was nearly overwhelmed by the gravity of the situation.

The boy Sylvia referred to as LeRoy Harkins, despite having the most explosive temper and the nastiest demeanor of the three, was granted a forty-seven-day home visit. Sylvia strongly suspected the extended home visit was actually a management attempt to dump him back into the community, but LeRoy ran afoul of the authorities and returned to Brookwood more unruly and defiant than before. Shortly after he returned, he saw a small, slight, light-skinned Black boy wearing a green workman's coverall, a yellow hard-hat, and a tool belt with hammers and screwdrivers. It was Willie Bosket, quietly and efficiently doing his maintenance tasks.

LeRoy demanded a job like that and complained loudly and bitterly to staff and even to the director, but his demands were ignored. The next couple of months turned into a nightmare for Sylvia. Returning from a day off, she learned that Wilson Cole had viciously attacked a night staff employee for no apparent reason. The tall, gentle, fifty-year-old man was accosted in the hallway and beaten so badly that the floor was covered with blood. The man was rushed to the nearby Columbia-Memorial Hospital emergency room and treated for a large gash on his forehead.

Sylvia was astounded to learn that the entire staff had apparently been too frightened of the young attacker to immediately discipline him. Instead, a disciplinary hearing was scheduled for later in the week, but Director Pottenburgh postponed that meeting. Sylvia confronted Wilson Cole directly and informed him that he was in danger of court action and held out the possibility of a transfer. Wilson, confident he would escape punishment, threatened Sylvia with physical violence. After several uneasy weeks, the disciplinary hearing took place. Despite protests from the professionals on staff, Director Pottenburgh only gave Cole what was viewed as a slap on the wrist. He delayed Cole's next home leave for a short time and held out the possibility of a transfer. It did not take Cole long to revert to his previous habits of terrorizing and assaulting the other boys, who became even more frightened, and he raised his level of threats toward the staff.

Afterward, LeRoy Harkins exhibited emotional bouts of rage with increased intensity and frequency. Sylvia was satisfied she could no longer influence his conduct or exercise control over his behavior. His violent tantrums disrupted the entire Brookwood program. His episodes of rage were interspersed with spells of wrecking furniture, spewing obscenities, and having occasional but long periods of uncontrolled sobbing. The episodes became so violet that at times it required up to a dozen men to subdue him and lock him in a stripped room until he calmed down, and on several occasions, he had to be placed in handcuffs.

Chapter Eight

THE JOURNALS OF SYLVIA HONIG

During her years at Brookwood, Sylvia Honig kept careful notes as a supervising social worker. She documented events at Brookwood in seventeen notebooks or journals that she organized into volumes. She used the information to support her efforts to change policies and improve conditions in all of the facilities operated by the New York State Division for Youth. A single entry is in Honig's notes regarding Bucky's arrival at Brookwood.

Tuesday, September 28, 1976: Friday night (September 24) we received our new boy, Ralph [Phillips]. He's fairly quiet. I didn't get a chance to talk to him yet except to say hello.

Bucky maintained a low profile and despite the disorder that reigned daily throughout the facility, he managed to avoid conflicts with other detainees. Bucky was up by 7:00 a.m. every morning, even on weekends, and he made his bed and swept his room immediately after breakfast. Although Bucky did not like school, he was promptly at his seat in the classroom by 8:15 a.m. School was a real drag, but he agreed with Brett that it was a better alternative than dealing with the bad asses who slept until noon. Brett had told him if you were "Black and mean" you could get away with all kinds of shit at Brookwood.

The pair often discussed how they would be punished immediately for the slightest infraction and Wilson Cole could beat the shit out of a staffer and wasn't even called into Pottenburgh's office until a month later. But, as Bucky had learned to accept that life in the wilderness was what it was, he learned to accept life at Brookwood for what it was as well, and hoped he could avoid the worst of it.

Thursday, October 14, 1976: I took Jeff, Dave, Brett, and Ralph to the rec room at 1:30. We were supposed to stay until three, but two other boys barged in and refused to leave. Louis got mouthy. I then asked my four boys to leave with me. There is hardly any recreation program planned for our boys.

Honig's October 14 entry alludes to systemic problems that pointed directly to the inefficiency—even gross incompetence—of the State Division for Youth. Management abysmally failed to support staff recommendations led by Sylvia and others for consistent discipline and she, her colleagues, and the detainees suffered the consequences of the absence of structured recreational programs. There was no softball, no organized basketball, even though there was a large gym, and no track. Arts and crafts were hit and miss, but there were no music programs or theater. There was nothing to occupy young minds and provide outlets to exhaust pent-up energy. To fill the recreational void, the staff improvised with supervised shopping trips or local community excursions, and sometimes they even made the hour-long round-trip drive to Albany.

Bucky fared reasonably well in his first month at Brookwood. He lost a physical confrontation with one of the detainees who was bigger and stronger, but Bucky's willingness to engage in a ferocious defense despite overwhelming odds proved to be something of a temporary deterrent. But the region was about to be faced with the fifth coldest winter in the past two hundred years. As record-breaking low temperatures accompanied by gusty winds, freezing rains, and snow descended over the Great Lakes and gripped the Upstate region of New York, the residents of Brookwood were confined to their respective wings. Closer confinement coupled with limited activities were twin disasters that proved punishing for staff and detainees alike.

Honig's notebook entry details just how bad things were.

Thursday November 11: Gene got mad because we (staff) refused to drive all the way to Albany. Gene began using racial slurs—Jeff began supporting him. Staley Keith was in the wing at the time. It didn't seem serious, so Staley left. Suddenly Gene began punching Brett. I took him to Ed's office and asked him to behave or I would have to call for men to assist. He stormed out of the office, went into Ralph's room, and began punching an astonished, frightened Ralph who was lying on his bed. I shouted at him and called Billie Ann (staff) to get help. He (Gene) went into the lounge and punched Brett again. I ordered Brett and Mike out of the wing. They fled. Then he went into Randy's room and began punching Randy who was lying on his bed. I yelled to Billie Ann to get help. Jeff was with me and kept telling Gene to stop, but Gene paid no attention. Randy was crying and his nose was bleeding. Also, his face was bruised. He and Ralph asked me to lock them in their rooms, which I did.

Bucky stayed in his room for the remainder of the day except for joining the parade to the chow hall for supper. Fortunately, Gene was absent—probably confined to his room—and Bucky, Brett, and Randy ate together without threats. But they were angry. Randy wanted to know why in hell they had to be locked in their rooms for getting the shit kicked out of them by a bad ass. Brett agreed and so did Bucky, who made a generous contribution of nasty comments to the conversation but was secretly glad to have been locked in his room. He had come to accept that Brookwood, like the wilderness, had its own set of rules. Like the wilderness it could be harsh and unforgiving, and like in the wilderness he had to do what he had to do to survive. If that meant that he was locked in his room alone, that was okay.

After the confrontation with Gene on Thursday, Sylvia was really pissed off. She was angry at the system, she was angry with the trouble-makers, she was angry at Gene. *What a stupid shit,* she thought, *for even suggesting that the staff drive him to Albany in two feet of snow.* But most of her anger was toward Pottenburgh, the oversized Director of Brookwood. Here was a man who stood six feet nine inches tall and weighed more than three hundred pounds, but at times he seemed scared shitless of the children—the troublemakers, especially if the troublemaker was Black and from the streets.

She was even angrier when she got home because the town snowplows had covered the entrance to her driveway with at least two feet of hard, frozen chunks of snow. She had to park on the road and climb over the icy embankment to retrieve the snow shovel she had hurriedly tossed in the general direction of the house on her way to work. As she straddled the embankment sideways, her left foot slipped off a chunk of ice and her leg suddenly plunged to the knee in snow and ice. "Shit, shit, shit," she swore as cold, wet snow filled her boot down to her ankle. She laboriously dug out a path just wide enough to get her car into the garage and dreaded the prospect of digging her way out again in the morning. But after taking a hot bath and donning warm jogging pants and a sweatshirt, she was comforted by her dogs and a bowl of hot tomato soup complemented by a grilled-cheese sandwich. Her anger dissipated and she decided she would take the boys Christmas shopping in Hudson on Saturday, even if it meant she had to make the trip on her own time.

Her notebook entry shows she did just that.

Saturday, November 13: At 4 p.m., I took Jeff, Dave, and Ralph over town (Hudson) shopping at Fairview Plaza.

As fate would have it, the unusually cold winter occurred during observations of the nation's two busiest holidays—Thanksgiving and Christmas. Even under normal weather conditions Thanksgiving and Christmas were troubled times for the people at Brookwood. It was a time when families wanted to be together, and it was a time when employees at the Division for Youth scurried to provide "skeleton" coverage system wide; Brookwood was no exception.

College interns returned home for the holidays and even what passed for classrooms were all but abandoned by instructors and students alike. Although it was not formal policy, the unwritten but widely practiced policy was to schedule as many home leaves for detainees as possible during November and December. That was about the only policy that worked well, Sylvia concluded. Except for the most misbehaved detainees, nearly all looked forward to Thanksgiving and Christmas leaves and few would jeopardize leaves by seriously misbehaving.

Honig's notebook entries show what was happening.

Thursday, November 18: I took Gene and Ralph off campus when I drove the new volunteer student, Debbie, to the train station tonight.

Wednesday, November 24: I took Ralph to town (Hudson).

Thursday, November 25: I took Jeff, Mike, and Ralph to Warren Street (Hudson) for an hour from 11 to 12.

Friday, November 26: After lunch I took Jeff, Mike, and Ralph to Hudson and we walked up and down Warren Street for an hour.

Saturday, November 27: I took Jeff, Mike, and Ralph to Warren Street from 11 to 12. Addendum: We were so short staffed over Thanksgiving and there was so little to do at Brookwood; very poor planning.

In its earliest days Hudson, New York, was a bustling port city strategically positioned on one of the more magnificent stretches of the Hudson River. Whaling ships and steamers overflowing with whale oil and passengers made frequent visits and unloaded cargo destined for emerging communities to the west. Today, Hudson and its more than seven thousand residents boast of only a two-hour commute by car or train from New York City or Boston and less than an hour from the state capitol at Albany. Historic Warren Street accommodates trendy shops, a gourmet restaurant, and a few others that make that same claim. Hudson has become something of a mecca for antiques traders who traffic in everything from rare, foreign antiquities to the more common but popular articles of local life and commerce.

Brookwood staff, including Sylvia, often escorted detainees on shopping trips to Hudson if for no other reason than to provide them with a change of scenery. She and other staffers would sometimes roll their eyes when some "big shot" from the Division dropped in and raved about how good it was to expose Brookwood boys to local history and give them a shopping trip as a positive reinforcement. Hudson was steeped in history, but most of the boys from Brookwood did not care one whit about whale oil and seal skins, and they hardly ever had enough money to buy much more than a candy bar.

The reality remained that everyone in the community knew the "Brookwood Bunch," and merchants watched them closely whenever they walked through a store. Experience with Brookwood taught local shop-keepers to keep smaller items of merchandise behind the counter or in closed glass showcases. When Brookwood was an all-girls facility, Hudson merchants suffered losses in lipsticks, nail polish, lip balm, undergarments, blouses, candy, and any other item that could be easily concealed under loose fitting clothing or small enough for pocket or purse. Small pieces of jewelry, rings, earrings, even small bracelets could be slipped between teeth and cheek and under the tongue.

After Brookwood converted to an all-male population the thievery continued, only the selections changed and along with the boys came the added element of competition. Boys preferred to pilfer the more expensive battery-powered items like radios and other such toys and trinkets. Cigarettes proved to be a favorite among the boys, single packs were acceptable, but cartons were preferred. Depending on quality, quantity, and kind, some products were judged automatic winners by peers back at Brookwood. A boy who returned undetected with a single carton of cigarettes earned more respect than two boys who brought back five packs each, but a radio or tape player always trumped cigarettes.

Despite common thievery, not every kid pilfered, and the trips were worthwhile diversions for detainees and staff even if the outing amounted to nothing more than a stroll down Warren Street. Given his propensity to steal, it remains hard to imagine that Bucky Phillips could have resisted the temptation to be among the most opportunistic thieves when it came to off-campus shopping trips. But there is not a single reported instance of him ever lifting so much as a candy bar on any shopping excursion.

Physically Bucky did not fare any better at Brookwood than he had at Industry—if anything, Brookwood was even more violent. But Bucky had an epiphany of sorts at Brookwood. One of his favorite pastimes at Brookwood was to lie on his bed and listen to music from his record player, a gift from his mother. He would often lie on his bed and drift away in music and memories. His first fight at Brookwood was fresh in his mind.

That attack had been so unexpected that Bucky intuitively struck back with all his might. His response had been an automatic reflex and totally uncharacteristic. He bit and scratched and kicked and clawed and cried, not from fear, but from forces he did not understand. His attacker landed the harder punches but broke off the assault when it became more difficult to sustain. It was only later, after the fight when Bucky was licking his wounds that he felt pain. It was odd, he thought, that during the combat he did not feel the blows.

On that day, lying on his bed and allowing the music to transport his mind beyond the confines of Brookwood, Bucky remembered the wilderness. He suddenly realized that even the most fragile creatures in the wilderness, the smallest and the weakest, all shared a common trait. When cornered with no apparent escape, and regardless of how badly overmatched, even the most vulnerable of creatures put up a ferocious fight. He had observed that sometimes—maybe even most of the time—the predator easily carried off the prey, but at other times, it had only been after the fight that the prey surrendered.

At some point the prey seemed to realize, seemed to sense they had nothing left to lose. He once observed a rare sight. At the edge of darkness one summer evening Bucky watched a barred owl swoop from a tree and grab a small animal from the forest floor. The owl had not made a clean catch and was barely grasping the animal's rear by one talon. Bucky was absolutely awed by what happened next. As the owl struggled to control the erratic movements of its prey, it pumped its wings in powerful strokes to gain lift to a favored roost in one of the taller trees. Before the owl could ascend to its desired altitude, however, it suddenly tumbled to the ground in a clump of feathers and the small critter scampered from its grasp. Bucky cautiously picked up the quivering remains and discovered that its head was nearly severed from its neck. He did not know what its prey had been—a weasel he supposed, but faced with extreme danger and in a nearly hopeless situation, whatever it was had fought back and survived for another day.

Going home for Christmas was on Bucky's mind too. But he was worried that his leave might be in jeopardy. Sylvia had told him she would approve his leave, but that she would run it past Ed Davis first. A trip home over Christmas would be a real treat, but Bucky could sense that he put some of the staff members off for some reason. He did not know what it was—no one was in his face or anything like that, but he could feel something was wrong. Instinctively, Bucky kept a low profile and tried to avoid situations that would put him in conflict with the staff. Bucky decided to bide his time and wait for the opportunity to discuss the matter with Sylvia privately. He did not have to wait long. Honig's notebook entry explains more.

Saturday, December 11: In the log, the staff wrote that they were disgusted with Ralph Phillips for telling Jeff the truth that Ralph's phonograph was in working order. The staff had taken Ralph's phonograph away from Jeff, who uses it all the time and told him it was broken. They told Ralph not to tell Jeff the truth, as Jeff plays it too loud, blasts our eardrums and refuses to obey staff when we tell him to lower it. I often yell at him and go into his room and lower it myself. Jeff nagged Ralph so much about when the phonograph was going to get fixed, Ralph finally told him the truth, and the staff felt they had to give Ralph's phonograph back to Jeff. They are afraid to confront Jeff. They got angry with Ralph and told him he shouldn't have told Jeff the truth. I yelled at Jeff today because he didn't lower the phonograph when I told him to. I went in and lowered it myself while he was in the room, and then closed the door to lower the noise and told him to keep it closed as long as it was ok. He obeyed. Betty (staff) and I took the van and four boys over town: Ralph, Randy, Gene, and Mike.

Sylvia reassured Ralph that the flutter over the phonograph would not interfere with his Christmas leave, and in fact, brought even more exciting news. Arrangements had been made for Bucky to fly roundtrip from Albany to Buffalo for Christmas leave. Of course, Brookwood would need reassurances that his family would pick him up at the airport, but Bucky knew that would not be a problem. He would leave Albany on the morning of the nineteenth and return to Brookwood on the twenty-eighth. Bucky was walking on air. The bad asses could beat the hell out of him, and he would not utter a single complaint. He could hardly wait.

Honig's notebook entry shows she was trying to keep the boys occupied.

Saturday, December 18: I took Mike, Randy, and Ralph off campus for an hour today. We shopped on Warren Street.

Bucky was nervous all day Saturday. His trip home was too good to be true. He just knew something was going to happen that would cause him to lose his leave. He spent the afternoon in Hudson, but he could not remember, except for Sylvia, whom he was with or what they did. He made a point to stick as close to Sylvia as he could—even to wait in the hallway just outside the ladies' bathroom until she came out. He hardly looked at any merchandise and did not buy a single thing. Sylvia and Betty bought them pizza on the return trip to Brookwood, and he was sorry when Sylvia left for the day.

Bucky skipped supper and stayed in his room all evening. He thought about playing his records but decided that might attract one of the bad asses. He did not want to take the chance of an unwelcome encounter and pretended to be sleeping on his bed.

After a fitful night, Bucky got up early, made his bed, and sat in his room waiting for the call to breakfast. By the time he left the chow hall he could not remember exactly what he ate. He ate something—eggs or toast or oatmeal or corn flakes—he saw them all on the serving line, or maybe he ate them all, he really could not remember. By 8:30 a.m., Ed Davis came to his room with two new pairs of jeans, a couple of shirts, and an athletic bag in which to carry his clothes and personal belongings. Ed told him he would drive him to Albany and that his plane would leave at 1:00 p.m.

Ed drove the Brookwood van up Route 9 to Interstate 90 and breezed around Albany to the airport. Ed was in unusually good spirits on the ride to the airport. He made idle but sometimes interesting conversation about the scenery and talked a lot about history and the prominent role the Hudson River and the Hudson River Valley played in the Revolutionary War. He rattled off four or five historical sites that would be worth an all-day field trip and questioned aloud why staff had not thought of that before. Bucky, on the other hand, was not thinking about the Revolutionary War or the Hudson River or the Hudson River Valley, or even Brookwood. Bucky was thinking about his flight home.

The Albany airport was not crowded, and Ed found a convenient parking space near the main entrance. He guided Bucky to his departure gate, obtained a boarding pass at the counter, and waited with him. When the flight was called, Bucky carried his athletic bag down a long corridor that led outside and boarded the plane with the other passengers. A very pretty woman happily directed him toward his seat and even helped him place his bag in the overhead. The plane was a big plane with two rows of seats on each side. Although Bucky's ticket was for an aisle seat, seat selection did not matter because the plane was not crowded, and Bucky was able to sit by the window.

His seat was over the wings near the front, he had a great view of the cockpit, and the engine was just outside his window. He stared, open-mouthed at the array of instruments and gauges and blinking lights that filled the space directly in front of the pilots. He watched awestruck as one of the pilots stood up in the cramped cockpit and removed his black jacket with silver trim. Next, the pilot leaned slightly outside the door, hung the jacket on a rack and placed his black cap with its brilliantly polished bill on an overhead shelf and took his seat at the controls to prepare for takeoff. The pretty woman walked briskly down the aisle making sure all the passengers were buckled in and that all bags and luggage were secured.

Bucky stared at the jet engines attached to the wing and estimated that they were twice as big as the propeller on the smaller plane that had delivered him to Brookwood. The engine did not cough or sputter to start like the previous plane either; it whirred in a high-pitched whine, paused momentarily, and suddenly sprang to life. Bucky had been so preoccupied that he failed to notice that the other engine was already running, and the plane was quickly moving into position for takeoff.

Bucky could feel his body being pushed against the seat as the plane seemed to smoothly glide down the runway and gently lift into the air. He did not realize they were airborne until he saw the concrete runway sinking below the wing. The engines began to pull harder as the plane entered a long, steep climb. Bucky likened the sounds of the straining engines with that of a heavily loaded truck making its way up the "three-legged hill" near his home on Route 60 between Fredonia and Cassadaga. Once the plane leveled off and began to cruise through the skies, Bucky was in for another surprise.

The pretty woman had donned a bibbed apron and was pushing a heavily loaded cart down the aisle. It became immediately obvious that she was passing out food and drinks. She approached Bucky's seat and lowered a tray-like table from the back of the seat in front of him and asked him if he wanted chicken or Swiss steak. Bucky was suddenly embarrassed and for reasons that those who have never been really poor simply do not understand. It is embarrassing, even humiliating to be poor. The common myth that children do not realize they are poor is just that—a myth. If anything, children have a greater awareness of their poverty than adults.

His first impulse was to decline the food, but he was hungry. "How much does it cost?" He stammered in a whisper so the other passengers would not hear. He was humiliated to even ask, but he would have been even more humiliated for the other passengers to know that he did not have enough money to purchase food. He had a few dollars that Ed Davis had given him to come home with. Five dollars to be exact, but he had hoped to keep as much of that as possible to buy his mother something for Christmas.

Immediately sensing his predicament, the pretty woman leaned forward and whispered. "Don't worry. It comes with the ticket." She straightened up and spoke in a more normal voice. "May I recommend the Swiss steak?" She placed the plastic container of food on Bucky's tray and helped him remove the foil cover. Once again, Bucky was surprised. The small, compact container held a lot more food than he had supposed. The main section held a gravy-drenched piece of meat with mashed potatoes, and one section was filled with peas and carrots. In another section was some kind of dessert that Bucky did not immediately recognize, but it was really good and tasted like apple cobbler. Bucky finished his meal and slipped a cookie in his shirt pocket for later.

Bucky was mystified at how much and how little of the earth could be seen from a plane at the same time. Looking out his window at twenty thousand feet he could see vast expanses of geography, yet he had no sense of speed, and rivers looked like tiny streams. Standing on the ground next to majestic maples and hemlocks and pines that stretched more than one hundred feet to the sky gave a person a sense of proportion. Walking from the crest of one ridge to another in the wilderness might take an hour, or even a day, but that magnificence was lost when both locations could be seen from above at the same time. Although Bucky was taken at once by the majesty and glamour of flight, he had never felt so terribly helpless. As a result, Bucky developed an unshakable fear of flying and would never of his own accord ever again travel by air.

Chapter Nine

HOME FOR THE HOLIDAYS

Winter continued its assault in the Albany region, and Buffalo and all of Western New York were unable to escape. To many people the snow and cold were just the usual Western New York winter, but the worst was yet to come. The first snow of the winter tracked by the National Weather Service was recorded on October 9 at the Cheektowaga, New York, weather station. Throughout the region lake effect snow had begun to accumulate; by October 21 more than a foot of snow was already on the ground, and by the end of the month the water temperature of Lake Erie was forty-eight degrees, the coldest it had ever been on that date. By November the air temperature in Buffalo was the coldest in nearly a hundred years, and by the end of the month nearly three feet of snow had fallen in November alone. The month of December would remain cold and snowy, posting a record snowfall of more than five feet.

Bucky's mother, his sister Armitty, and a cousin who lived on the Seneca Nation met Bucky at the Buffalo airport. The air was bitterly cold and filled with blowing snow; the forecast predicted worse weather ahead. Armitty was concerned about the driving conditions. A lake-effect snowstorm was hitting Chautauqua County hard to the south and although the roads were still open, all unnecessary travel was discouraged. The family decided to spend the night at the cousin's house on the Seneca Nation and drive home the next day.

The next morning and despite continued snowfall, plows were running around the clock and none of the main roads were closed. Bucky noticed an immediate difference when they arrived home. From the road and despite being shrouded in a thick blanket of snow, the house looked more rundown, desolate, and cold than when he had last been home. They parked the car on the road because the snow was too deep to get in the driveway. Bucky jumped out of the car and wearing only a heavy sweatshirt and sneakers tromped through knee-deep snow to retrieve a scoop shovel from the barn. He used his feet to clear snow from the sweep of the barn door and was forced to tug on the door several times with both hands before it opened enough for him to slide in sideways.

He was struck immediately by the smell of the barn as familiar odors filled his nostrils with the scents of cows, hay, and manure. Although the barn had seen neither cows nor hay since his father's death, the smells lingered, though they had grown stale with time.

Bucky walked down the center aisle of the barn with empty stanchions on both sides and clean gutters that were once filled with manure that had to be shoveled twice a day. He stopped about midway down the aisle when he caught a glimpse of something on a ledge where the hay was dropped from the loft to the barn floor. That was the place where he spent long winter nights sleeping on loose hay surrounded by hay bales when he was banished to the barn as punishment. He stepped across the gutter and had to pick up a stanchion hame that had fallen on the floor. He remembered when his father had whittled the piece out of a sapling.

His father told him to look for a sapling about two inches around and about four feet long. Bucky found just the right piece almost immediately. It was a lone sapling that took root at the edge of the meadow behind the barn and was bent from the wind. Bucky spied it earlier that spring and it stuck in his mind because it was so odd and lonely. There was not a single branch below the dozen or so branches that bushed out at the top. He also remembered it well, because it was one of the very few times when he actually pleased his father. The old man did not say much, but Bucky knew he was pleased. He took the stick from Bucky.

"This will do just fine." The old man smiled and patted Bucky on the head and began immediately to fashion the piece.

Failing to find a more suitable tool, Ralph Phillips used a hacksaw to cut both ends of the sapling to the desired length and used his pocketknife that he kept razor sharp to shape the ends. Bucky watched his father's long, slender fingers manipulate the knife back and forth in short, quick movements until the piece of wood almost magically formed into the desired shape. He attached metal clamps to both ends and fastened a short piece of chain to each end with a snap. The handmade hame was one of two long supports that fastened around a cow's neck and kept the animal fettered to the platform. The stanchion was secured at the top and bottom of the manger and allowed the animal enough neck movement up and down and sideways to eat and drink with its head in the manger.

"Yup," the old man chuckled as he snapped the hame in place, proud of his handiwork. "This will work just fine," he said and smiled at Bucky.

Bucky ran his fingers back and forth on the inside of the hame where constant movement of an animal's neck had worn away the smooth bark and exposed a long gash of bare, polished wood. The snap that fastened the hame at the top was missing, but Bucky managed to loop the short chain to the manger with a piece of old baling twine that must have served the same purpose at an earlier time. Next, Bucky turned his attention to the object that caught his eye in the first place.

He removed a small, concave piece of wood that he had once used to hold tinder to start a fire. He remembered when he placed the odd-shaped piece of wood on the ledge in case he might need it again. After a closer look he found the pencil-sized stick that he had used to ignite the tinder. Suddenly Bucky's attention was diverted when he heard his mother loudly calling his name from the porch. He had been so absorbed in his thoughts that he did not know how long she had been trying to get his attention. He quickly shoved his fire artifacts back on the ledge and went to the door. He saw his mother standing on the porch holding the scoop shovel that she had stuck in a snowbank near the kitchen door before traveling to the airport to pick up her son.

Despite the cold and snow Bucky shoveled for a good half hour to get the driveway clear, and carved out a wide path to the mailbox. Once inside, his hands were so cold that his fingers ached, and his feet were numb. He removed his shoes and socks and stuck them in front of an upright heater.

Christmas day fell on Saturday that year, and the cold and snow put a damper on travel throughout Western New York. People awoke on Christmas morning to a severe snowstorm that prevented all but the hardiest of souls from venturing forth. Bucky spent Christmas day with his mother and Armitty, and he felt badly that he had no gifts to offer but no one seemed to notice. His mother had hung Christmas stockings for her children, each with an orange and an apple, some chocolate candy, and a few suitable trinkets. His sister and mother each exchanged several gifts, and both had gifts for Bucky. The gifts were useful items. Armitty gave him a pair of leather gloves, a shirt, and a Timex wristwatch. A cousin gave him three model car kits. His favorite was a 1957 Chevrolet.

His mother gave him underwear and a western belt and buckle. She told him she had put a Carhartt jacket on layaway at the New York Store in Dunkirk but didn't have enough to pick it up until she got her check on the third of the month. She told Bucky that she would call Brookwood to see if she could get his furlough extended to the first week in the New Year. Bucky agreed and suggested she call Sylvia Honig.

Bucky had a great Christmas. Family and friends were glad to see him, and all encouraged him to make the best of it. His mother made Bucky feel really good when she refused to take the five dollars Ed Davis had given him at Brookwood. She told Bucky that him being home was the very best Christmas present she could get. She was encouraged that Bucky's time in training school might do him some good. He might even learn a trade and make something of himself. The Family Court judge that sent Bucky to reform school thought that too and told her so.

"It'll do him good, Mrs. Phillips," he said when he sent him away. "He'll learn a trade."

After breakfast Alice Phillips started Christmas cooking. In anticipation of Bucky coming home for Christmas Alice had been frugal with what little money she had and clipped food coupons and watched supermarkets for in-store specials over the holidays. She had even bought a frozen turkey immediately after Thanksgiving and kept it on the back porch wrapped tightly in foil and covered with a basket. She had plenty of food on hand.

A man named Herman Swanson, a local dairy farmer in the Stockton area had stopped by on Thursday afternoon and left off a big box of food. He said it came from the church. Alice suspected it came directly from Mr. Swanson.

He actually delivered three boxes and as many grocery bags; one contained a ten-pound bag of white potatoes and a five-pound bag of sweet potatoes. Another box was filled with cans of green beans, peas, corn, and cranberry sauce along with two big cans of raw pumpkin for pies and two cans of chili with beans. There was a big bag of rice, a bag of marshmallows, a three-pound can of mixed nuts, a box of powdered milk, two cans of evaporated milk, two boxes of Corn Flakes, and two boxes of Raisin Bran. A frozen turkey was in a plastic bag by itself, and the third box held ten pounds of flour, a big can of Crisco, ten pounds of sugar, a bag of oranges, and another of apples. Alice Phillips was grateful for the food and despite the weather, she was happy and determined to have a good Christmas. The family ate around 4:00 p.m. and Bucky ate so much that he felt uncomfortable. It was nice, he thought, to eat and just sit around without being threatened by a bad ass.

On Sunday the snow relented, but it remained bitterly cold. Bucky was occupied all day Sunday and Monday with friends and relatives who either could not make the trip on Christmas day or otherwise spent the day with their own families. Gifts were exchanged again on Monday and there was plenty of food, but Bucky was growing increasingly restless and impatient. By Tuesday his weather-induced house confinement was wearing thin and his only remedy was to return to the wilderness.

On Wednesday Bucky began to systematically gather his necessities for several days alone in the wild. His sleeping bag was rolled up where he had left it in a back room that was usually closed off during the winter and used mostly for storage. He retrieved a box that held his survival gear, which he ha found buried under a pile of discarded clothing and blankets. He spread one of the blankets on the cold floor and sat with his legs crossed beneath his body and began a methodical examination of its contents.

Everything seemed to be just as he had left it. The first item he retrieved was a small, amber container that once held prescription medicine. Bucky had converted the discarded pill bottle to a waterproof container for matches. He would not have thought of using the discarded pillbox for matches if his mother had not been busy one summer canning strawberry jelly. She filled small jars with hot jelly and before it cooled, she poured melted paraffin into the mouth of each jar. An airtight seal was formed when the wax hardened. She had accidentally over filled one jar and hot wax ran over and spilled on top of the kitchen table.

Instinctively Bucky had run for a dishrag to wipe the spilled wax, but his mother had stopped him and told him if he waited until it set and hardened, he could simply slide it off the table; otherwise, any attempt to wipe it off would result in smearing the wax all over the table. As Bucky had sat at the kitchen table waiting for the wax to harden, he'd picked up a match and began poking it around in the pool of cooling wax. He discovered that the wax coalesced around the head of the match. Bucky realized the importance of keeping matches dry in the wilderness and the hot wax gave him an idea.

When his mother was ready for another wax pour, Bucky grabbed the empty pill bottle and shoved several matches tip first inside the bottle. April initially refused to pour hot wax over the matches, but Bucky nagged until she relented. As soon as the hot wax solidified around the matches Bucky pulled one from the bottle and struck it against the match box. The match ignited in a flash, and Bucky knew immediately that he could start a campfire in the wilderness in wet, cold weather with dry matches.

Bucky brought himself back to the present and pushed aside a roll of waxed string about the size of a baseball that was tightly wrapped and covered in tin foil. He found the string useful for a variety of tasks in the wilderness. He had used it to erect a temporary shelter and to hang small animals to roast over an open fire. Once, he even used it as a belt when his belt buckle had broken and rendered his leather belt useless.

The next item Bucky pulled from the box was a flat, green and white "Half and Half" tobacco tin. The tin was one of several he had filled with tiny shreds of newspaper mixed with pine shavings that he whittled from a discarded piece of a two by four. He had soaked the mixture overnight in kerosene and packed it into the tobacco can, being careful to leave enough room to seal the top with wax and snap the lid shut. Dry matches were essential to start a fire, but dry tinder ignited damp wood easier.

Over time Bucky experimented with "tinder boxes" using different materials mixed with the hot wax. Each experiment worked, some better than others. He'd even filled an ice cube tray with match heads and covered the entire tray with melted wax. The wax-cubed tinder worked, but he abandoned the idea because it was difficult to remove the cubes from the tray and they were too small to burn really hot. He'd even immersed paper matchbooks in wax, but that too proved impractical.

He found he could make tinder bricks by lining a small baking pan with wax paper and pouring in a mixture of shredded paper, wood shavings, and melted paraffin, but they were slow to ignite. He had once emptied powder from a shotgun shell into the tinder mixture. The gunpowder burned much hotter and was especially effective on damp wood, but a shotgun shell was too expensive to waste. In the end, the tobacco tin proved the most practical, but in time he would discover that the tinder worked as well without soaking it in kerosene.

There was a jackknife in the box and a Case pocketknife that belonged to his father. A thin, cotton rope was coiled around a metal hand axe that had a three-inch blade inside a folding metal handle. The axe, like the knives, had a razor-sharp blade that could easily cut through wood or shave hair from his forearm. The metal hand axe was acquired by theft. Two years earlier Bucky had removed a window in broad daylight from a hunting cabin that had a sign hanging on its porch that read "Forty and Eight Club." Bucky did not know what the sign meant, but he was attracted to the cabin that was in a secluded area well off the main road in the town of Ellery.

The cabin was big by hunting camp standards and had three rooms.

Bucky entered through what was obviously a bedroom that had four single rope beds built against the walls. Another room, half again as big, had a fireplace and a kerosene kitchen stove. Cupboards were fastened to the rear wall and around a heavy porcelain kitchen sink that stood on rough-hewn legs near the back door. A long wooden table occupied the center of the room with a heavy, but well-worn butcher's block shoved against one end. The other room was much smaller and looked like it was added as an afterthought. Judging from a beam that ran across the room just below the ceiling, Bucky guessed it was used to hang deer carcasses.

Several fishing rods hung on the wall, and a tackle box sat open on the floor. Bucky examined a single-barreled, twelve-gauge shotgun that was leaning in one corner. He could not distinguish the manufacturer, but it was an older gun with a split stock that had been wired together with smooth wire. Bucky spent nearly an hour examining the cabin's contents. There were several items he wanted, but he was on foot and could not carry a portable camp stove and what looked like a new Coleman lantern. He would have missed the hand axe had he not revisited the open tackle box.

Bucky picked up the tackle box and rattled it around to get a better look at its contents. The box was filled with fishing plugs, lures, fishhooks, lead sinkers, and three rolls of fishing line. There were the remains of a fishing reel. At first, Bucky thought the metal axe was just a long piece of cotton rope wrapped around a piece of metal. When he examined it closer, he discovered what it was. The small axe had a hook on one side of the folding handle that allowed it to hang from a belt. Bucky did not know what the cotton rope was used for, but he guessed it might have been used to drag freshly killed deer to the road.

Bucky kept the hand axe and replaced the tackle box where he found it. He walked out the back door and used the hand axe to pound nails back in when he replaced the window. Bucky left several gouges in and around the window, but even if the owners suspected a break-in they would not find anything missing. He reasoned it would be some time before the loss of the hand axe was discovered, and the owner would probably believe he had left it somewhere.

Bucky dressed lightly, but appropriately for the cold weather. He slipped on the top half of a pair of insulated underwear and a loose-fitting flannel shirt. He wore his regular jeans with a wide leather belt and pulled on a pair of felt-lined arctic Pac boots over a thin pair of socks. His father had bought him the Arctics two sizes too big for his ninth birthday. Experience taught him that wearing heavy socks only made his feet sweaty and cold and that wearing too much outer clothing not only made him perspire but also severely limited his movements.

With a baseball cap pulled low over his eyes, Bucky shoved a stocking cap inside his blanket-lined jacket together with a pair of thin, brown, cotton gloves. He slung his Mossberg single-shot, bolt-action .22 over his shoulder, and hung a rolled up sleeping bag from his other shoulder. The rifle had been another gift from his father, but the compact snowshoes attached to his sleeping bag had been pilfered from an isolated hunting cabin together with an army canteen hooked on a web belt and an army surplus mess kit.

Snowdrifts always accumulated behind the barn and at the edge of the gradually sloping meadow. But this winter was different. Bucky could tell from the way the snow had drifted across the meadow that the prevailing winter winds had been directly from the west instead of the usual southeasterly direction. That was what prompted him to stop at the barn and strap on his snowshoes. It was a good thing he did, because the entire meadow on the downhill side was packed with snow all the way to the top of ridge. He stood upright and waved to his mother who was watching from the front porch. Even though she had grown accustomed to Bucky's forays into the wilderness, she was always nervous and worried about him being alone in the woods.

"How long will you be gone?" she had asked, her voice barely audible as she clutched her sweater tightly under her chin.

"I don't know. Two, maybe three days," Bucky shrugged, "no more."

"Don't be too long," April Phillips cautioned. "I'll call Brookwood Friday."

"Don't worry." Bucky gave his mother a reassuring wave as he turned to go. Bucky did not want his mother to worry, but he had already made up his mind. He had no intention of voluntarily returning to Brookwood. Even the bad asses had figured out the worst penalty for going AWOL was a temporary loss of privileges and an ass chewing from Davis or Pottenburgh. Although Bucky would put up a protest over his punishment and mope around and look sullen, he actually welcomed being confined to his room and the loss of rec time. At least, he thought, he would have less contact with the bad asses, and that would not be all bad.

The snow was so deep on the meadow side of the barn that Bucky had to climb the slope sideways, even with snowshoes, until he was halfway to the crest. The snow had drifted so deeply across the lower half of the meadow, and it took him longer to get to the top of the ridge than he had supposed. He thought about removing his snowshoes before entering the woods but left them on when he decided to walk an abandoned logging trail instead of cutting directly through the trees. Although the thick woods kept snow from accumulating in huge drifts across the forest floor, tree branches strained from its weight and pushed lower hanging branches to the ground.

About thirty strides into the woods, Bucky paused on the trail and looked around. He had become so familiar with wilderness areas that he had even given trees individual names. The "Bee Tree" was a tall ash hollowed at the fork that had once held a hive for a swarm of honeybees. In another part of the woods there was the "Lightning Tree," a gnarled maple that bore an ancient scar from a lightning wound that stretched the entire length on one side. The "Turkey Tree" was a tall hemlock in the midst of a stand of hemlocks that was a roost for a rafter of wild turkeys. Bucky could not discern what made that particular hemlock different from the others; they were all about the same height and looked the same, but it was a perennial favorite of the turkeys. In another area there was the "Gum Tree" aptly named for the gum-like substance that oozed from its trunk and was sticky enough to attract and hold insects.

In addition to naming trees, Bucky either named, or often referred to entire areas using familiar names like "state lands" that were vast expanses covered with nearly identical pine trees. The trees were all planted in orderly rows and stretched for several miles across state lands. Bucky did not know exactly when the trees had been planted or who planted them. His father had told him members of a CCC camp—whatever that was— had planted them as seedlings and that the government should never have done away with the camps.

To the west of Chautauqua Lake toward the village of Sherman, there were places that were not identified on any maps, but locals knew the locations as "Little American" and "Slab City." "Charlotte Center" in the center of the county was neither a village nor a post office, but people referred to the area as if it were. Designations like "Bone" or "Little Bone," or "Old State Road," or Old Chautauqua Road," or the "Three-Legged Hill," or "28-Mile Creek Road," were commonly known, but would hold little meaning for strangers. But to Bucky and many of his friends, all such names identified specific locations.

Standing alone in the middle of a long-abandoned logging trail Bucky surveyed his surroundings and realized that what should look so familiar suddenly looked strange and unfamiliar. Nothing looked the same; the entire landscape presented a weird and wonderfully eerie spectacle. The brilliance of the undefiled snow, barren of tracks from bird or mammal, made everything look dark and dismal, and Bucky was captured by its stillness. There was not a sound. Nothing was stirring, not a bird, not an animal, even the wind was still. It was like the snow had absorbed all the sounds and movements of the natural world. Bucky proceeded along the logging trail until he arrived at a demarcation point where all signs of man vanished, and the woods turned into wilderness. The logging trail became only a trace, a barely discernable path traversed only by animals and the occasional hunter who ventured off the beaten path.

Bucky turned slightly sideways and began a slow, but steep descent. He picked his steps carefully. With the snow so deep, it would be easy to trip over fallen tree branches or slip on a snow-covered rock. Bucky was not as fearful of falling and breaking something as he was of being thrown against a tree and jarring it hard enough to rid its drooping branches of heavy snow in a sudden avalanche. Normally, he would not have been concerned about a tree dumping its snow all over him. He had been snowed under before and had once made a game of crawling beneath a tree's low hanging branches and pulling a single snow laden limb toward the ground.

When Bucky released his grip on the snow-laden branch it quickly snapped hard upward and against the next higher branches. That movement created a chain reaction from one branch to the next and in an instant all the snow jarred loose from the tree and covered Bucky from head to foot. Until now, the worst thing that happened was the discomfort of getting wet and cold. Regardless, Bucky remained cautious. With such a heavy snow—heavier than he had ever seen—he was unsure of the consequences. He remembered once getting hit hard on the head by a big plop of falling snow. He was not hurt, but the blow had knocked him to the ground.

About halfway down the hill, Bucky almost stepped on a rabbit snuggled under a small pile of brush. The rabbit scampered away kicking snow high into the air without a sound. A potential meal was out of sight before Bucky could get his rifle from his shoulder. Bucky finally made his way down the animal trail to a small valley wedged tightly against a more imposing peak on the opposite side. Here, the trees gave way to dense underbrush that was higher than a man's head and would have been impossible to navigate except for the well-defined animal trail that led through the thicket. A taller person would have had trouble with the tangle of snow-covered branches overhanging the path. Bucky had to bend low to the ground and even crawl on his hands and knees at one point to get through.

Bucky knew where he was going, and when he emerged from the thicket the valley widened into a sprawling panorama of marshes and wetlands. The wetlands had been created over a number of years by a series of beaver dams that proved to be a nuisance for county road crews when a well-traveled county road was repeatedly flooded. The county claimed that the offending beavers had been relocated and blew up the dams, but the beavers kept returning year after year.

Bucky continued on but was growing uneasy. The weather was changing. Out in the open, the wind whipped tiny crystals of snow and ice through the air in sharp bursts that stung his face and made his eyes water. Suddenly, and for reasons he could not immediately grasp, Bucky felt a sense of urgency.

He decided he would make camp on the edge of the wetlands just inside the tree line. The sooner the better, Bucky thought as another burst of snow whirled around his head. He quickly found an ideal spot in a stand of tightly clustered hemlocks and pines that jutted from the wetlands and spread across a gently sloping knoll behind what appeared to be an active beaver lodge. Luckily, there were two large hemlocks in the center of the stand. The trees were too large for Bucky to reach around and the ground beneath the trees remained remarkably free of snow. Bucky leaned his rifle against a tree and dropped his sleeping bag at the base of the same tree.

For the next hour he was busy preparing his campsite. He used his small hand axe to cut two saplings, each one about five feet long. He had to search to find a near mate to the first one he cut, but he found another that was nearly identical only a short distance from the beaver lodge. He carried them back to the site and set out to find a longer pole that he could lash between the two hemlock trees.

That search required more effort. Ideally, he needed a pole at least eight feet long and one that was about the same size on both ends. Finally, he chose a low hanging tree branch from one of the smaller hemlocks that was about the right size, and he hoped it was long enough. Back at the campsite he used his jackknife and hand axe to trim all the branches from his collection and whittled a sharp point on the largest end of each sapling. Next, he hurriedly fashioned a loop on one end of the pole with his piece of cotton rope and tied it securely to the tree about five feet from the ground. Then he coiled the rope in large loops around the entire length of the pole and fastened it as tightly as he could to the other tree.

Satisfied that the pole was secure, Bucky shoved the pointed sticks into the ground and let the tops lay against the center pole at an angle. He spaced each sapling about a foot from either tree and shoved the tips through the cotton rope looped around the center pole. When he had the frame secured, he stepped back to survey his handiwork. When he looked at the framework it became obvious that the distance between the trees was farther than he expected, and he would need another sapling for additional support. He soon found one, then another, and finished the framework for his lean-to. The framework was critical but covering it with branches was the most time consuming.

For the next hour Bucky gathered hemlock branches filled with long, green, pine needles and lashed each branch with heavy twine to the lean-to framework. He even went to the trouble of weaving the boughs together with small, green twigs to give the structure added strength. When he had the framework completely covered, he began the process all over again. This time he used the branches to fill in any bare spots. He guessed it took him nearly two hours to finish the lean-to and his hands were sore from the sharp pine needles, but he was pleased with his work. The lean-to, covered on three sides, was not waterproof, but it would provide some protection against the snow and would help break the wind.

Bucky checked the watch his sister had given him for Christmas, it was half past noon. Bucky's next chore was easier. The twin rules of surviving in the wilderness are always the same—stay warm and dry. Bucky had to gather firewood. He found a ready supply of branches on trees that had succumbed to the wetlands or the beavers, or both. He gathered several armloads and made two piles of firewood on either side of his lean-to. He even found a good supply of tinder using small, dead twigs from the hemlock trees. Bucky carefully placed the tinder under his sleeping bag. He had his shelter, for what it was, and he had his firewood, now he must turn his attention to another matter.

He had eaten a big breakfast at home, but if he wanted food for supper, he was going to have to find it by his own cunning. If he had been better positioned, he might be eating rabbit for supper, but hunger was not a stranger to any of the wilderness creatures, including Bucky. He decided he would probably have better luck hunting around the edge of the watershed and along the tree line. The best he could do, he thought, was to kick up a rabbit.

Once again, luck seemed to be with Bucky. He carefully zigzagged from the edge of the wetlands back and forth to the tree line when a grouse lifted off on his third pass. He did not see it at first, but he immediately recognized the telltale flutter of wings peculiar to a grouse. He caught a glimpse of the bird flying into the tree line only a short distance away. Bucky had hunted grouse before. He knew its habits. The birds would fly only a short distance and look for cover. At other times, instead of looking for cover, a grouse would run on the ground for a long distance without ever becoming airborne. Bucky had his rifle ready. He had developed a bad habit, a habit cautioned against by nearly everyone; he always hunted with the gun safety off. That allowed him to get a shot off quicker, and sometimes that extra blink in time made the difference.

Bucky cautiously walked around the remains of trees that had died natural deaths and left jagged stumps as stark reminders of their former existence. He inched toward a tree at the edge of the tree line that had been uprooted by the wind and peered cautiously over its root ball. There, not ten feet away, a speckled grouse was standing stone still among the scraggly ground pines with its head cocked slightly sideways. The bird's body blended perfectly with its surroundings, and if Bucky had not been looking for it, he would have walked right past it. Bucky had observed that same peculiar behavior before and immediately realized that the bird detected a threat.

Thirteen-year-old Bucky Phillips read the signs well. The grouse had assumed a posture that signaled imminent danger. Bucky instantly knew that the grouse was not concerned with a human being; the bird was not looking in Bucky's direction. Guided by instinct, Bucky instantaneously assumed the same posture as the grouse. He pushed his nose against the moss-covered root ball and the only part of his body that remained visible was his eyes and his baseball cap. Bucky remained motionless except for his eyes. His eyes darted back and forth, but his head was perfectly still. He was searching for the slightest movement, but it was his ears that first provided the payoff.

His ears first caught the extreme leading edge of a nearly imperceptible rustle. But that sound was enough to instantly draw his eyes in its direction. He waited. Finally, he heard it again. This time it was closer, but he still could not see what had so riveted the attention of the grouse. When he heard the sound again, a faint smile pushed at the corners of his mouth. He only heard a scratch, an unmistakable scratch that trailed off into a slight rustle of leaves. He slowly raised his rifle and rested it atop the root ball in anticipation. He heard it again. This time the scratch was well defined, and a telltale "cluck" accompanied the rustle of the leaves.

Suddenly, a charge shot up Bucky's back and he blinked his eyes hard several times to make sure they were not playing tricks on him. Bucky could not believe what he was seeing. In a totally uncharacteristic and unbelievable moment two hen turkeys came into full view scratching for food as if it were a calm summer's day. Both seemed unconcerned, oblivious to the weather; one would scratch first one way then another while the other seemed to stop and observe. They both moved forward nodding their heads in perfect rhythm, pausing only to randomly scratch and peck at the ground. Bucky's eyes snapped quickly to the grouse. It remained perfectly still. He counted to ten under his breath and waited for the "tom" that might be lagging behind. The hens were alone.

Bucky kept both eyes open and lined the turkey nearest him in his rifle sights. He had been taught well. The object of his aim was blurred, but the front sight of his rifle was in sharp focus. His father had taught him that technique. His finger pressed softly on the trigger and his breathing was measured. He gently squeezed the trigger. In that instant, and before the sound of the gunshot subsided, several things occurred simultaneously, and Bucky saw them all unfold in explicit detail. His target never flinched but fell face forward in a single motion without the slightest flutter. The grouse, frozen in place, exploded instantly into full flight, and Bucky saw every movement of its wings as it disappeared above the treetops. The surviving hen achieved flight on a low trajectory in the opposite direction with the first complete thrust of her wings. Bucky watched it all happen within the sound of a single gunshot. Then silence, diminished only by the wind filtering through the trees; silence once again embraced the wilderness and returned it immediately to its natural condition.

The hen lay outstretched on a cushion of snow-covered leaves with not a single feather out of place. Bucky held her upside down by the feet. She was heavy. He did not know how much she weighed, he was not very good at guessing weight, but she was meaty. On other outings he had killed grouse, rabbits, and squirrels; he killed a duck once; and one time he had even killed and eaten a Blue Jay, but never had he ever killed a wild turkey. Bucky was content to know that he could get several meals from the turkey. Next would be the tedious task of cleaning the bird. Bucky had never cleaned a turkey before. He had watched his father pluck a chicken after it had been submerged in boiling water to soften its feathers. Once the feathers were softened, it was easy to pluck them out by the handful. Here in the wilderness, a tub of scalding water was not an option.

Once he had returned to his campsite, he noticed that snow had already begun to accumulate on the backside of his lean-to. That was good, he thought, because it would help insulate him from the wind. Bucky had to test his work. He stretched out within the confines of the lean-to on a cushion of soft pine needles and leaves that he had scattered across floor. The air remained cold around him, and he could see light through the boughs, but the lean-to succeeded in blocking the wind and blowing snow. Although the pine needles and leaves fell far short of being a mattress, and a little dampness clung to his bedding, Bucky found his conditions comfortable. He was pleased he had gone to the extra trouble of weaving twigs through the boughs to make the lean-to more secure.

Bucky knew what he had to do next. He had to start a fire and clean the bird. He had not taken the trouble to build a fire pit using rocks. Instead, he dragged and pushed and rolled a short piece of log about four feet long and as big around as his waist into position in front of the lean-to. The log would serve as a backlog and hold the fire in place. Next, Bucky reached under his sleeping bag and retrieved a handful of small twigs he had gathered for tinder. He meticulously snapped each small twig into pieces about the length of his outstretched hand. He arranged each twig in a tight circle no larger than a fifty-cent piece directly in the middle and in front of the fire backlog.

Next, he squeezed the tops together to form a small teepee-shaped structure. He repeated the process several times; each time using slightly larger twigs and sticks until he had created a graduated, teepee-shaped woodpile nearly three feet tall. He left one side open just enough to ignite the smallest twigs in the very center with a match. In less than a minute the entire pile of wood was alive with flames. The woodpile was designed to ignite quickly and collapse upon itself to slow the burn and create a hot bed of coals against the backlog.

At first, Bucky thought he might try to heat water in his canteen cup and pluck feathers in small bunches, but that would take too long. Skinning the bird was probably the best option. It would certainly be the quickest, and he would not have to contend with plucking feathers. He used waxed string to suspend the turkey by its legs from a tree branch and found that skinning the bird was at first awkward but became easier after the skin was pulled around its torso. He used his father's Case knife to cut a circle directly above the knee joint on each leg. Next, he shoved the tip of the knife blade under the skin and simply pulled the skin with feathers intact past each drumstick, over the torso and down the neck. One swipe of the knife removed the turkey's head and it landed with the skin and feathers and blood in a pile on the ground.

Bucky examined the carcass for a bullet hole. He had first considered a headshot, but decided it was too far away to chance. He aimed instead at a point just below where the wing joined the body. His decision about the distance was confirmed when he stepped off twenty paces from his stand to the point where the bird fell. The bullet hole was barely visible; it entered slightly under the spot where the wing joined the body and traveled at a downward angle to exit at the bottom of the breastplate on the opposite side. The shot had been clean, and the meat was not damaged.

Bucky removed all of the innards, but was careful to lay aside the heart, liver, and gizzard. He sliced the gizzard in half and scraped out its gritty contents. He would later melt enough snow to steep the pieces in his canteen cup over a bed of hot coals while the turkey slowly roasted on a spit he carefully erected over the fire.

By the time Bucky got the turkey over the fire, it was well into the afternoon and the snowfall had gained momentum. It remained dark and overcast, and Bucky shivered when he was hit by a cold gust of wind as he stepped away from the shelter of his lean-to. He made sure he dumped the remains of the turkey far enough from the camp to keep whatever might find it at a respectable distance. He gathered another load of firewood before darkness fell and decided to settle down in preparation for a long night.

Back at the camp Bucky hunkered down in his lean-to and found it to be much more comfortable than he had supposed. The fire drove away the cold and the lean-to did a remarkable job diverting the wind and snow. Bucky was actually warm enough that he removed his coat. He even removed his Arctic's, but left the felt Pac's on his feet. He adjusted the turkey over the fire and judged that his organ meat had cooked long enough. He skewered the heart with a pointed stick and waved it back and forth several times to cool it down enough to eat. It needed salt and pepper, and it was chewy, but other than that it was good.

Bucky had a particular fondness for chicken and turkey livers. The liver was lean and tender, and Bucky marveled at how much meat there was in a turkey liver.

Darkness came early during the winter and even earlier in the wilderness. The snow was falling faster, and Bucky could hear the wind whistling through the trees. He watched snowflakes glimmer past flickering flames, and occasionally one would die with a hiss as it landed on the hot coals. The stillness was complete. All wilderness creatures had gone to nest, bed, or burrow to wait out the storm. Even though the storm drove the animals to ground, Bucky was certain the turkey entrails and skin had already been claimed.

It was odd, he thought, very odd about the turkeys. He never supposed for a second that he would have run across two female turkeys casually sauntering through the woods in such weather. Perhaps the pair used a lull in the weather to rummage before an even worse storm hit. Whatever force of nature compelled the turkeys to scavenge had worked to Bucky's advantage, and he never questioned the results.

The aroma of the roasting turkey permeated the campsite and carried on the wind, but Bucky could tell by looking that the bird was not completely cooked. He decided to remove the turkey from the fire lest he fall asleep and have the hen fall into the fire and come to ruin. He would continue the roasting process at first light and proceeded to lash the carcass to the cross member of the lean-to and wrapped it several times with twine to make sure it was secure. Earlier he anticipated eating a drumstick for supper but had to be content with the organ meat. Bucky crawled into his sleeping bag but did not zip it shut. He used his coat for a pillow and lay on his side staring into the fire while gnawing on a very tough but flavorful piece of turkey gizzard.

He would awaken two or three times during the night to refuel the fire. It was times like these that Bucky cherished. He could not have been further from Brookwood if he had been halfway around the world. Although he was less than an hour's walk in any direction from civilization, here alone in the middle of the wilderness in the middle of winter Bucky felt safe. He was safe from the "law." Not a single sheriff's deputy or a state trooper would ever venture out on such a night to find him. The bad asses at Industry and Brookwood would not last the night under the same circumstances, and Bucky took a measure of comfort in knowing that.

Bucky was alone for the night with only his thoughts to keep him company, and he thought about many things, but the idea of God kept popping up. Although he did not know what to make of God, he never once questioned his existence. Bucky naturally assumed that God was real. Nearly everyone believed in God; he did not know of anyone who did not. Even really smart people believed in God. His schoolteachers believed in God, he had overheard them talking among themselves about going to church. Even the judge who had sent him to Industry scolded him and told him that he should ask God's forgiveness first and then plead with his mother for forgiveness for all the grief he had given her.

The way Bucky had it figured was that God either got really mad, or felt very sad when people did something wrong, but aside from that, Bucky never actually knew what else God did. Bucky supposed he should feel badly about his misdeeds and that he should ask for forgiveness, especially from his mother since he saw her nearly every day. But what troubled Bucky most was that he did not feel bad about his sins. Sins were what the family court judge called Bucky's thefts and told him that stealing a package of cigarettes was just as bad as stealing a car in the eyes of God.

Maybe God could not tell the difference, Bucky thought at the time, but nearly everyone else could. Experience had taught Bucky that the "law," including the judge, put up a much bigger fuss over a stolen car. At the time Bucky wanted to ask the judge to explain that a little better, but the judge did not seem to be in the mood. Bucky figured his lack of experience with God was the result of one of two things. Either he was just not smart enough to understand God, or God only dealt with adults. Bucky fell asleep with the rawness of winter whirling about him and thoughts of God and his mother and the turkeys flashing back and forth in his mind.

Morning broke in a fury of swirling snow and howling wind. All that remained of the campfire was a pile of glowing embers. Bucky quickly sat upright and pulled on his Arctics. He stood outside the lean-to shivering in his shirtsleeves. Snow was everywhere. All night, snow-laden winds howled over the top of the lean-to and covered the entire backside of the structure with nearly a foot of snow. Snowflakes that failed to make the hurdle fell to the ground and created a waist high drift between the two hemlocks that supported the makeshift shelter. Bucky had designed his lean-to with that purpose in mind and as a result spent a warm and cozy night directly in the teeth of a severe winter storm.

Snow covered his woodpiles on either side of the lean-to. He picked up two pieces at a time and banged them together to remove the snow and quickly fashioned a teepee of firewood over the embers. The wood finally ignited, but only after he directed several heavy puffs of air over the hot coals. In no time a roaring fire successfully challenged the elements and removed the chill from the immediate area. Bucky knew he must lay low and wait the storm out. He was aware of the danger of trying to navigate the wilderness in the grips of a storm and accepted the verdict without complaint. He had food, the turkey was enough to last several days, and all he had to do for fresh water was melt snow in his mess cup and fill his canteen.

Bucky's stomach was growling. He was hungry. It was time to put the turkey back on the fire. He freed the carcass from its bonds. In a curious surprise, Bucky discovered that the turkey had not frozen overnight. It took him several minutes to get the bird back on the spit and situated over the fire. Satisfied that the turkey was positioned correctly, Bucky stood upright and peered over the top of the lean-to and surveyed the wetlands from his vantage point inside the tree line. He pulled his cap lower over his eyes to deflect the blowing snow and saw snow drifts everywhere.

Snow was piled high atop the remains of dead trees and the root ball of the wind-fallen tree from where he shot the turkey was completely covered and made indistinguishable from its surroundings. Clumps of sedge grasses that spread across the wetlands collapsed under a heavy, white weight and appeared as huge snowballs suspended in water. Snow was everywhere, everywhere except atop the beaver lodge. Even through the wind and blowing snow Bucky could see steam rising from what appeared to be a random scattering of tree branches and brush. He realized there was nothing random about a beaver lodge. Every stick and every twig had been carefully positioned with extreme efficiency. Although he had never seen inside a beaver lodge, he once saw one that supported as many as seven beavers. He recognized instantly that the beavers were home. With nothing else to do, Bucky squatted in the lean-to and heated the remaining half of the turkey gizzard over the fire.

Bucky spent his second full day in the wilderness huddled up under his lean-to, getting up only to relieve himself or gather firewood. He remained warm and dry, and he had water. As long as he met those conditions, he felt comfortable. The wind let up late in the afternoon on the second day, but uncharacteristic of Western New York winters it remained bitterly cold and continued to snow. The creatures of the wilderness continued to lay low waiting for a break in the weather, and Bucky waited with them. To break the monotony, Bucky gathered his snowshoes and tromped a short distance to the beaver lodge.

The snow was deep with a hard pack on the bottom, but it was loose and powdery on the surface. He created large puffs of snow when his snow-shoes came in contact with the loose powder. Bucky removed his snow-shoes and slung them over his shoulder when he reached the near side of the beaver dam. He carefully picked his way through the tangle of sticks and branches to the center of the dam. He could see the full dimensions of the dam more clearly from that vantage point. The dam stretched more than ten feet across and was intricately anchored on both ends. The con-struction was much wider than Bucky could see from land and was fash-ioned in such a way that water flowed through in trickles.

Warm air escaped around his feet and legs as he stood directly over the center of the lodge. But the warm air was accompanied by a strange odor. The smell was not entirely unpleasant, but it had the strong, damp, musty scent of an overcrowded household. Bucky was surprised at how much warm air escaped from the lodge, and aside from the smell, he reasoned he could bed down overnight and remain comfortable and warm. Bucky sat on the dam for a half hour or more hoping to hear or see one of the resi-dents. But, like all the other creatures, the beavers remained quiet.

On the morning of the third day Bucky was awakened by a series of loud splashes coming from the beaver dam. Although the loud splashes were intended to scare away potential predators and to sound as a warn-ing for other beavers, Bucky recognized the sound to mean a break in the storm. The splashes signaled that nature's creatures had left their nests, beds, and boroughs and were searching for food. Bucky quickly and qui-etly picked his way toward the lodge to get a glimpse of the beavers. He saw the wake left by a swimming beaver, but not the beaver. He hung around the lodge for another half hour and even squatted atop the lodge to spy one of the furry creatures, but to no avail. He finally gave up and returned to his campsite and packed his gear, including the remains of the turkey. He made sure every ember in his fireplace was extinguished and removed his cotton rope from the center pole. He was surprised when the lean-to remained standing under the weight of the snow.

He spent the day wandering in an increasingly wider circle making his way home. Unlike his trek into the wilderness, there were plenty of animal tracks in the snow on his return. He even followed a grouse as it strolled, flew, walked, and hopped for nearly a mile before he lost its signs. He saw rabbit tracks and knew he would soon find them paired with the tracks of a hungry fox. Deer imprints were all over the place, and there was one set of tracks he could not make out. Bucky made his way out of the wilderness and walked the last half a mile home on a rural county road. It was only when he saw the enormous piles of snow pushed to either side of the road by snowplows that he realized how intense the storm had been.

Bucky had not yet recognized luck to be a factor in his life, but he knew he had survived an outing that would have been challenging for the most experienced adult under the same conditions. Bucky had no idea that the National Weather Service at Buffalo reported average temperatures for both November and December six degrees below normal and that nearly a hundred inches of snow fell during that same period. He was unaware that the unusually harsh winter forced industries to close or cut back operations and schools that remained open operated on a delayed schedule. He did not know that the National Guard was called out to assist the region in clearing snow-clogged roads and city streets.

Bucky had no inkling of the economic chaos generated by a winter so severe that it forced businesses and factories to close because of critical shortages of everything from gasoline to groceries. Had Bucky known the full extent of the winter storms, he would have become even more determined to challenge the elements with even more daring exploits. A supremely confident fourteen-year-old Bucky Phillips, fully aware of the risks of being alone in the wilderness, survived two days and two nights alone in that wilderness during one of the worst winters in the history of Western New York. Bucky would never speak of his adventure, but he was still very proud of his feat.

Bucky stayed at home and was now AWOL from Brookwood, and he understood and accepted that he would be apprehended and returned. His ultimate return to Brookwood would have seemed to him to be the least likely event to hold anything positive. But, like his flight from Industry where he felt he was in imminent danger, being returned to Brookwood may have been equally providential. By the time Bucky returned, except for scattered snow showers, the winter had released its grip just enough for roads and streets to reopen and for commerce to resume nearly normal operations. People throughout Western New York let out a collective sigh of relief and began to believe that the worst of winter was behind them, but that was not to be.

On January 27, 1977, a low-pressure system crossed Lake Erie and stalled east of James Bay before finally entering the Canadian Maritimes. Snow began to fall early the next morning in the Buffalo area, and by mid-day temperatures had dropped twenty-six degrees in four hours. By that time, the area was in the grips of a full-fledged blizzard with wind gusts of seventy miles per hour and the wind chill falling to sixty to seventy degrees below zero.

Roads and highways became a living nightmare with stranded motorists and abandoned cars. Schools and fire halls and churches and supermarkets were filled with refugees from the storm, and several houses burned to the ground because it was impossible to get fire equipment to the scene. Blizzard conditions continued through the night and for the first time in over 140 years, the *Buffalo Courier Express* did not publish its morning newspaper. Snowmobiles and four-wheel-drive vehicles were pressed into service rescuing people stranded in homes and automobiles and were used to transport food and emergency medical supplies.

The storm played itself out by noon on February 1, but left twenty dead animals in the Buffalo Zoo and was responsible for the deaths of twenty-nine people in the Buffalo area. Many stores and schools and factories remained closed for a week, mail delivery was suspended, and the US Army came in from Fort Bragg to assist with the cleanup. The storm was of such force and magnitude that had Bucky Phillips been home, his natural instincts would have been to challenge the storm and all its intensity. It remains unlikely, even as skilled as he was, that fourteen-year-old Bucky Phillips would have survived the Blizzard of '77.

Chapter Ten

BACK TO BROOKWOOD

Thursday, December 30: Ralph Phillips's mother called to extend his visit until January 4 so that she could buy him something when her check arrives on the 3rd. I granted permission.

January 11, 1977: Ralph Phillips is back. He was apprehended and flown back and returned to Brookwood yesterday.

Life at Brookwood was even worse for Bucky when he returned, even though a couple of the former bad asses had either returned home, gone AWOL, or transferred to Goshen. The threat of being sent to Goshen was always present, but Bucky did not know of anyone ever transferred there. Besides, when one bad ass left, there was always another one to take his place. Often, Bucky had observed, the new bad ass was usually worse than the one who left. There were a couple of new guys Bucky read as trouble and did his best to avoid, spending more time alone in his room working on his model cars.

Bucky managed to avoid the worst of the troublemakers and breezed through January except for a couple of minor altercations with lesser-known detainees. By the time the calendar flipped to February Bucky was really pissed. Some no-good son of a bitch had stolen his watch. Bucky did the only thing he could do and reported the theft to the staff. As Bucky expected, nothing happened until three days later when he returned from classes to find his models smashed all to hell. The 1957 Chevrolet lay in pieces atop his bed and the 1962 Studebaker Gran Turismo Hawk that he had finished only the day before lay on the floor smashed to bits. Bucky was furious and ran immediately to the rec room and grabbed the first bad ass he could find by the collar.

"One of you no-good, motherfucking sons of bitches stole my watch and broke my models." Bucky screamed in a fit of tears and grasped the front of Andre's shirt as he stood at the pool table chalking his cue. The intensity of the sudden outburst took everyone in the dayroom by surprise. Bad ass Andre, who on previous occasions had kicked the shit out of Bucky, was caught completely off guard and dropped his cue stick and stumbled backward. "Hey man, it wasn't me," Andre coughed and sputtered meekly. Bucky loosened his grip and shoved him away.

"You cocksuckers might as well kill me now," Bucky stood with hands on his hips and yelled through a stream of tears. "Because if you don't and I find out who did this, I am going to cut your fucking throat from ear to ear even if I have to do it when you're asleep,"

Nearly every bad ass was in the rec room that day, and they all stopped dead still with mouths agape and watched in wide-eyed amazement as the scene unfolded before their eyes. You could have heard a pin drop as Bucky fled the room, and finally from somewhere in the crowd an unidentified voice that addressed no one in particular softly uttered in an astonished whisper, "Man, that is one mad motherfucker."

Bucky's sudden outburst had taken everyone by surprise, including the staff attendant. There were no written reports made of the incident, but the news spread like wildfire across the Brookwood campus, and by the next day everyone from the director on down the chain was talking about it. Even Dr. Jarrett, Brookwood's part-time resident psychiatrist, a man with heavy jowls and a broad chest, managed to wag a thick, heavy finger in Bucky's direction and made some remark that sent the office secretaries into a spasm of giggles. Bucky returned the gesture with a nod and a smile and kept moving. He had never heard of any detainee ever meeting with

Dr. Jarrett, although Brett once told him that Jarrett was paid over one hundred dollars an hour. Bucky could not imagine anyone getting paid that much, especially Dr. Jarrett, who always seemed to spend his time drinking coffee, eating cookies, and cutting up with the secretaries.

About the only person who failed to respond one way or another to Bucky's outburst was Brookwood's psychologist Dr. Reisman. Some of the Black kids called him "Dr. Goofy," and when any of the kids used his proper name, they invariably pronounced it "Rise Man." He had a wiry build with a razor-like face and shuffled forward in a slightly sideways motion. It was all Bucky could do to keep from stopping and staring at the man as he cascaded right past Bucky in the hallway without ever looking up. Bucky did spend almost an hour talking to Sylvia about the incident, and she warned him that some of the more aggressive boys, Andre in particular, might decide to take revenge. She also told Bucky that she would put the missing watch and his wrecked models on the agenda for the next group session.

An entry in Sylvia's journal:

Monday, February 14: Andre was very rude to me when I started the meeting. After the meeting got underway, Pottenburgh (Brookwood's director) arrived.... Ed started discussing Ralph's broken models and watch, which had been mysteriously destroyed.

After Ed Davis finished his attempts to make an object lesson out of Bucky's destroyed models and missing watch, Bucky remembered the meeting quickly deteriorating. Andre unleashed a series of verbal vulgarities and immediately demanded Ralph be arrested for threatening his life, making a big production of something *he* did all the time. Pottenburgh nervously twisted back and forth in his chair, obviously embarrassed that a scene was unfolding in the presence of a guest.

Ed Davis coughed and sputtered in a feeble attempt to demonstrate that he had control of the meeting, but it took firm and decisive action from Sylvia to get the meeting back on track. She suddenly slammed her notebook down hard on the table and stood up in the same movement.

"Let's get this meeting back on track," she demanded in a firm, but steady voice that for an instant caused the room to go completely silent. The meeting lasted for more than an hour, but all of the adults, except Sylvia, seemed to think Bucky's reaction was worse than the destruction of his models and the theft of his watch.

Bucky's situation did not improve. Andre was a one-man wrecking crew who, on his milder encounters, would walk up to Bucky and punch him as hard as he could in the face. Bucky's nose was sore from repeated assaults from Andre and other bad asses whose behavior seemed mild when compared with Andre. There was not a single day that Bucky was not a victim of assaults ranging from a single fist to the face to more severe beatings. Bucky became such a frequent visitor to the nurse's office that despite his obvious abrasions and bruises she began to question the frequency of his visits. Bucky finally abandoned his visits to the infirmary unless he happened to be escorted by a concerned staff member. He repeatedly begged staff for protection and requested to be locked in his room. He even met with Pottenburgh, but nothing changed. The only person to make an effort to protect him was Sylvia Honig.

Honig began her career with the New York State Division for Youth as a certified social worker in 1965 and almost immediately discovered the Division was more concerned with its public image than in dealing with troubled juveniles. During her thirteen years as a social worker for the state, she remained amazed at how much time and energy was spent on efforts to find the most politically correct name for New York's youth prisons. Frequent consultations with experts led to system-wide meetings, seminars, and brainstorming sessions that resulted in a steady evolution of name changes ranging from "Training Schools" to "Residential Treatment Centers" to the current use of "Detention Centers."

There is probably no other document that makes public the everyday, abysmal conditions of New York State's juvenile prisons and sheds a light on the young, incarcerated life of Bucky Phillips than those terse, spontaneous notations in Sylvia Honig's journals. Honig's work was not her life, but it was a big part of it. At the end of each workday, she habitually stopped by her aging and ailing parents before returning home to her dogs and cats. Almost every night before going to bed, she recorded events in her journal, which numbered over a thousand pages. She never married, but she did have a love affair that lasted for twenty years with a man who was half American Indian and half French. When she was fifty and he fifty-six, she held her lovers' hand in a Troy, New York, hospital and through a veil of tears watched him die from kidney failure. Now retired, Honig continues to live only a short distance from the house where she was born on a rural, dirt road in the town of Nassau in New York's Rensselaer County. She is still a fierce advocate for the rights of those in the criminal justice system.

Honig recorded instances of abuse, mismanagement, and neglect on a daily basis at three institutions, the former Hudson School for Girls, the former Wynantskill Center for Girls, and Brookwood Center for Boys. She accumulated thousands of pages of documentation that paint a picture of a failed juvenile system that routinely kept its failures from public view and deprived the very youth they were chartered to serve. During her thirteen years as a certified social worker in the Division for Youth, Honig railed against those in authority responsible for failed policies that provided little more than custodial care for New York State's incarcerated juveniles. Her natural and unedited notes revealed a workforce plagued by indifference and incapable of providing for the daily health and safety of those remanded to their care.

Although political patronage played a role in the makeup of the Division's workforce, a greater problem was the cultural divide between predominately Black, urban detainees and a workforce drawn from local, mostly white, rural communities. Except for professional staffers, the regular staff was made up primarily of high school graduates, very few had college backgrounds, and a larger number than one might suppose were high school dropouts. Even in the absence of blatant racism, that obvious cultural divide created problems with serious racial overtones that plagued the entire Division for Youth.

That cultural divide was further exacerbated when a Black, urban detainee received what other detainees and staff saw as little more than a mild rebuke for outrageous behavior. It remained obvious that urban detainees, particularly Black urban detainees, frightened the staff. Upper management feared the possibility of even greater disruptions, even riots, over disciplinary decisions and were often reluctant to fully support faculty and staff. As a result, management would frequently and unfairly over-compensate and mete out more severe punishments to other detainees for much lesser offenses. Those actions often pitted mostly rural and mostly Caucasian detainees against urban Black detainees and kept them in a state of perpetual conflict.

Conditions deteriorated throughout the Division, but Brookwood experienced a daily cacophony of obscenities and vile epithets hurled back and forth between staff members and detainees. Group meetings more often than not became angry shouting matches that saw more aggressive detainees controlling the meeting and the intimidation of weaker-willed attendees. Conditions became such a chaotic mess that to maintain order, Brookwood Director Pottenburgh hired a man just released from prison for killing his girlfriend and her mother. Black Hawk San Carlos kept the most dangerous kids in line, but he was a man apparently possessed with great appetites and passions of mind and body and was commonly absent. Conditions at Brookwood frequently reverted to the whims of chance during his carnal pursuits.

The Division came up with what seemed like a good idea. All staff members should teach classes; nearly everyone signed up, but the program died when so few of the staffers actually showed up to teach. As a result, there were no report cards, no homework assignments, and no books to read. Brookwood did not have a library. Then there was the observable thievery. Staffers often walked out with clothing items from supply that were meant for the boys. Coffee and grocery items regularly went missing.

Honig would eventually carry her stacks of documentation to the state legislature and give sworn testimony before select committees. State officials forced the Division for Youth and Brookwood to adopt reforms that worked as long as the state legislature showed an interest, but it was not very long before the place returned to its former condition. It was only after Honig blew the whistle on the treatment afforded Willie Bosket to the New York media that a reshuffling of management within the Division for Youth occurred. But Honig suffered the fate of most whistleblowers. One of Peter Edelman's last acts before resigning as State Director was to transfer Sylvia several hours away to Elmira, New York. As expected, Sylvia refused the transfer because her father was then dying of terminal lymphoma.

The following entries in Sylvia Honig's journals describe conditions at Brookwood and provide a glimpse into the life of Bucky Phillips from the time he was returned to Brookwood until the day he was released. It is worth noting that Brookwood was a secure facility, which meant Bucky Phillips and other runaways were restricted to their wings, or their rooms, or placed in isolation as punishment for misbehavior or for taking flight.

Tuesday, February 22: Ralph Phillips and Jimmy ran Friday night from the Washington Avenue Armory (in Albany) where they were watching a wrestling match. (They were apprehended in Utica the next day or the day after and returned to Brookwood.)

Monday, February 28: Friday night Jimmy, Ralph Phillips, and Brett broke a window and tried to escape, but were caught.

Monday, March 7: Gene broke out of Brookwood Saturday afternoon around 1:30 p.m., taking Jeff, Ralph, and Jimmy with him. They broke out through the rec room door, climbed up the drainpipe, got on the roof, and scrambled down the walls somehow. Ralph was caught going up the drainpipe. Bruce grabbed him and put him in the infirmary (isolation). Brett turned himself in shortly afterward. Probably Brett and Ralph were intimidated into running by Gene, who organized the runaway.

Friday, April 1: Ralph got nasty and wouldn't sign his contract. [Brookwood tried a failing education program, ordering the boys to sign contracts for classes. The entire program failed immediately.]

Monday, April 4: Terry and Ralph Phillips ran from the Crandall Theater in Chatham Friday night. They stole about three cars and were apprehended by police in Rochester or the Buffalo area and sent to Industry. They were returned to us today.

Friday, April 8: Andre got progressively worse—kept putting his hands up in my face—threatening, threatening the white boys—loud etc. I told him he was a punk because he knew he could get away with his threats to a woman, but wouldn't talk to me that way if I were Staley Keith (staff). I told him he was vicious and deliberately behaving wrong. At one point, he brandished a broom around that I ordered him to put down and finally he did. I threatened to cut off his off-grounds if he kept up this threatening talk and sticking his hands in my face. He finally agreed—very angrily—to obey me and then went down to the gym. When he came back, he drew quietly for a while in the lounge and ignored me and I did the same, but before I left, he began wrestling with Jeff and then Dom (staff member) and when I asked him to stop, he told me angrily to "shut up." I challenged his remark with "What did you say?" but he walked away.

The white boys are terrified of him, and some of them—particularly Ralph—are afraid of Jeff. Ralph asked me to lock him in his room after breakfast—which I did. This upset Jeff. I told him Ralph requested it because he was so fearful of Jeff because Jeff has been slapping him around. Jeff felt bad and assured me he would leave Ralph alone.

Monday, April 11: All the white boys in Wing 2 went up to talk to Pottenburgh. They spent at least an hour and a half in his office. He told me they want something done about Andre, who is terrorizing them. He wasn't telling me anything I didn't know. Last night there was major trouble in Wing 3. I hear the boys had a set of keys.

Thursday, April 14: I returned to Brookwood at 11:30 and learned that last night we had three runaways from Wing 2: Randy, Terry, and Ralph. Randy and Terry were caught several hours after they ran, but Ralph is still AWOL. Ed Davis (my co-supervisor) restricted them to the wing for an entire month. I think this is excessive and inhumane punishment in view of the fact that we all know they ran out of terror because of Andre's constant threats, blows, and harassment, and also—because of the close confinement of the wing—the stale smoking, such a punishment is a crime. I think that one week's restriction to the wing is sufficient. But NO ONE asked me, and Ed made the decision. Apparently, Tom (the Director) had no objection.

Friday, April 15: Ralph Phillips was caught last night and is being held in detention in Buffalo. He stole a car (or cars) from this area and got to the Indian Reservation in Buffalo. The field worker called and told me that Ralph was being placed on the plane tomorrow morning and would arrive in Albany airport at 11:05 a.m. Saturday.

Monday, April 18: Billie Ann (staff) had gone out to get three trays (punishment room confinement meals) for Ralph, Terry, and Randy, who are wing restricted.

Friday, April 22: Randy, Ralph, and Terry are still restricted to the wing. They are very bored and disgusted—their behavior is deteriorating. They keep fighting (play) wrestling, rolling around on filthy rugs, spending hours in their rooms. They never get a breath of fresh air or exercise outside of wrestling. They are not doing any schoolwork. Most of Wing 2 staff agree with me that Ed Davis's discipline is punitive and destructive (Ed has top authority in the Wing, although we both have master's degrees in social work, but he got to Brookwood just before I did, and so Pottenburgh made him the top authority in the wing.)

Tuesday, April 26: When I came in at 1:00 p.m. today, Ralph and Brett asked to talk to me in private. They asked me what Pottenburgh was going to do about Andre. They said when the five of them went to talk to Pottenburgh (on April 11) he said he would do something. I asked them, "What did he tell you he would do?" They said he told them he was going to the Board about Andre. They said they are tired of waiting, as Andre keeps hitting them day in and day out. They said they talked to Terry and learned about the ombudsman coming and said they would talk to him also and bring charges against Andre for beating them constantly. They said the staff often see Andre hitting them and yell at him to stop, but he does it anyway and gets away with it.

Thursday, May 5: During the group meeting, I confronted Andre with his intimidation and assaults. Terry got off wing restriction today. The other three: Ralph, Randy, and Brett—wouldn't discuss it in the meeting—no one would be honest—so they are still on wing restriction. We still have locked doors on the wing at all times. All doors are locked at all times—no matter where kids are—in or out of their rooms—in or out of the bathroom etc.

Wednesday, May 18: Billie Ann and Bertha (staff) reported to me that Andre was terrible this morning. He "yoked" Billie Ann, slapped some of the boys, and kept intimidating them all day. I told Ed Davis. He said Andre was good when he was around. I sent a letter to Peter Edelman today (Director of the New York State Division for Youth) making recommendations.

Saturday, May 28: Mike Nugent (staff) took three boys off campus in his jeep. Randy, Ralph, and Terry. Mike left a little after 11:00 and said he would be back in a couple of hours, but by 3:00, he still wasn't back. Around that time, Clyde (Wing 1 staff) called me from up front and asked me to come up. Randy was there with a cut foot. Mike was back too, but he reported that Ralph and Terry went AWOL. They were last seen floating downstream in rubber tubes. As soon as I made all the "runaway" calls, in walked Bruce Kline (staff) with Ralph and Terry who insisted they hadn't run away but were given permission by Mike to meet him at the bridge. (Apparently a misunderstanding.)

Monday, May 30: At around 8:30 I received a call from Reida Koskowski (staff) who reported that Ralph and Jimmy had run. They had been out swimming with Gene Cephas (temporary staff-ex-con) when they took off.

Tuesday, May 31: 10:00 I got a call from Betty Larkin (staff). She called to tell me that the troopers just called; they picked up Ralph and Jimmy in Oneonta. They had stolen a car—but troopers were not pressing charges against Ralph because he's a juvenile.

Wednesday, June 1: I learned that on Monday, Memorial Day, Andre slapped Ralph and Scott—and possibly Brett. Scott cried and he and Ralph asked to be locked in their rooms. I asked Scott about it today and he said it was true. He said Andre hit him for no reason. Ralph and Jimmy ran the same day.

Thursday, June 2: Jimmy asked to be locked up in the infirmary for the rest of the day, beginning this afternoon, after lunch. He is still terrified of Andre. Ralph and Jimmy were taken off wing restriction (by Davis) but remain on building restriction for one month. Andre was threatening and abusive all day to staff and residents. He called Reida Koskowski "fucking bitch—fat bitch—fat hoe," etc., and ordered her out of our wing. (She's the arts and craft staff). She won't speak to him at all. He carried a stick with him and banged on the walls and windows up front. Later he had a metal poker he broke off from somewhere, and carried it around, finally giving it to Dave Watrous (clerical staff)—who pleaded for it.

Friday, June 3: I talked to Tom (Brookwood director) today about the recent events involving my contacting the legislature, my talk with Larry Dye (Deputy Director of DFY, an ex-con) yesterday.

Saturday, June 4: Jimmy came to talk to me today, he wanted to know what we're going to do about Andre, and stated that if Andre returns next Friday, as scheduled, he plans to run, and to keep running. He said that Pottenburgh promised him and four other boys in the wing that he would find solutions to the problem of Andre, but he never did anything. He talked against Ed Davis and Pottenburgh for allowing Andre to continue assaulting boys. He felt I was the only person who was trying to get Andre out of Brookwood because I brought the ombudsman and the assemblymen (to Brookwood). Ralph Phillips also said he plans to keep running away—mostly because of Andre I believe.

Tuesday, June 7: Jimmy and Ralph are still threatening to run before Andre gets back. Reida Koskowski reported to Ed Davis and me that Ralph told her today and he's been saying it openly for days. Reggie (staff) took Ralph and Jimmy to Colliers Farm to clean up the mess they made when they ran last time and broke into Colliers.

Thursday, June 9: Last night all the boys in Wing 2 (my wing unit) refused to go to bed. Ed Davis was called and came in at 10:30 p.m. Finally, all the boys went to bed. Ralph was the first one to go to bed. He thinks he went before Ed got there.

Saturday, June 11: Around 4 p.m., he (Andre) jumped on Ralph and pinned him down in the hallway. Vernon Jeffries (staff) was standing right there watching. Mike Nugent (staff) commented on it. Gene (staff) was there too. I went down the hall and ordered Andre to get off Ralph. He did but flew up in my face—very hostile. I asked Vernon why he allowed it. He said (in front on the boys) "They were playing." Five minutes later Ralph went to his room with Mike Nugent and talked for about ten minutes. Mike reported to me that Ralph threatened to run because of Andre. Mike said he counseled him to "hang on" for another week or so and then things would get better, referring to the new security wing that is in the planning. I then went to Ralph and asked him if he was just "playing" with Andre. He said "No." I told Vernon that in the future he is to stop Andre immediately—even if his victims say they are only playing, as the other boys are too frightened to contradict Andre or incriminate him. I went and told Ralph what I had told Vernon and he thanked me.

Saturday, June 18: Brett and Ralph ran last night at 9:55 p.m. from the courtyard. Mike Nugent had taken them and a couple of others—including Terry—out around 9:30. Just before they went back in, the two went up the pole, jumped on the roof, and took off. They are still AWOL. [Added comment by Sylvia Honig:] Brookwood was supposed to be a maximum secure facility. The boys could take off easily anytime and proved it repeatedly.

Tuesday, June 21: Ralph and Brett were apprehended and returned Sunday. They stole two cars and ended up in nearby Gallentin. They are restricted right now. Their escape and capture made the front page of Monday's *Register-Star* (Hudson's daily newspaper). Brett told me he ran because he was mad at Bruce (staff).

Friday, June 24: "Pop" (John) Grant told me this morning that Willie Bosket and Frank Tiano (maintenance man staffer) came to blows yesterday. He says Willie needs a few days in the secure wing. However, Willie was walking around today, wearing his maintenance outfit, and apparently suffering no loss of privileges. Someone told me he was off campus last night. [Added comment by Sylvia Honig:] On March 17, 21, and 24, Willie James Bosket, age 15, paroled from Brookwood went on a killing spree in Harlem, shooting three men, killing two of them—and became New York state's most notorious killer and most dangerous prisoner; later he stabbed prison guard Earl Porter and [sic] Shawngunk state prison on April 18, 1988.

Today we learned that four boys are being transferred from Industry. Tonight, we heard that Monday, several boys at Industry beat a boy to death and his body wasn't discovered until yesterday. Apparently, the staff assumed he was AWOL. It was David Smith, a 13-year-old Indian kid who was bludgeoned and stabbed and his body hidden in nearby woods. I was told that while the murder was taking place, the Industry staff was in the cottage playing cards.

Saturday, June 25: The four boys from Industry arrived around 11:00 p.m. last night. I talked to John M., he described to me the killing of David Smith at Industry. He said Jeff H. decided, "Let's kill him," because Smith had told on him about something. John M. said he didn't want any part of the killing, but he watched while Jeff H. and possibly others (he was vague about some details) bashed in Smith's head with rocks three separate times. He said he didn't know for sure if Smith was dead and didn't see them bury him under some brush but heard about it later. When I asked John M., "Where was the staff when all of this was going on?" He replied, without hesitation, "In the cottage playing spades."

June 28–July 11: I was on vacation and pass days. I returned on July 12.

Thursday, July 28: Last night Quille (staff ex-con from Attica) lost his keys and was afraid the boys had it [sic]. Also, he said Gardner (staff) suspected some of the boys of smoking marijuana. Ed locked the wing and told the boys the wing would remain locked until they confessed. Eventually, Randy admitted he had brought back marijuana and five boys, including Randy, admitted they had smoked it last night—Bob, John M., Jimmy, Ralph, and Randy.

Monday, August 9, 1977: Over the weekend, a window was broken in the hallway. The kids told me that Willie Bosket broke the window. Terry pushed out some of the glass. Helen Gentile (administrative staff, social worker) told me she asked maintenance repeatedly to fix the window. One of the kids picked up a huge piece of glass and put it in his pocket. Later on, although Quille (staff) warned our boys to stay away from the broken window, Ralph Phillips "went over to bang out some of the glass. He cut his fingers to the bone, possibly severing tendons. He was rushed to the hospital and bandaged. He has lost the use of his hands temporarily. He doesn't know if there will be permanent damage." Today, two or three days later, the glass was still broken in that window with big, jagged shards of glass visible to all. Helen Gentile went and got a hammer and a piece of cloth and knocked out the rest of the glass onto the outside area! I don't know if the window was repaired by tonight. I forgot to look. Willie (Bosket) is still walking around in his maintenance job.

Thursday, August 11: I learned . . . that Charlie, Reggie, and Quille (all Wing 3 staff) did a "jailhouse search," throwing the boys' things all around the rooms. The boys were furious. I learned today that Jim Stone was removed from his job as superintendent of Industry (as a result of the murder of David Smith).

Friday, August 12: Jovita (a young woman volunteer) apologized for her part in the room search. I didn't learn until Ralph told me today that Jovita had torn his room apart. She said she didn't think she was authorized to do it, but the staff told her to "C'mon." The boys accepted her apology.

I called Bill White, Ralph's field worker, and convinced him to request in writing Ralph's release effective before the end of August. Ralph was elated.

Tuesday, August 16: I learned that up until yesterday some staff are putting boys to bed at 9:30—not writing up room confinement reports (regular bedtime is 10 p.m.) and using room confinement as punishment. I explained in group meeting that room confinement for any reason other than "dangerous to self and/or others" is illegal and not to be used.

I learned John B. was angry because Charles Ivery (staff) was strong-arming some of the boys, and Charley and Quille had established a new "rule" that after last bathroom call before bedtime, if any boy wanted to go to the bathroom, he had to do 100 pushups or he could not use the bathroom.

Charles admitted that was the new rule. I told him and the group that the rule had to be discarded and that from now on, any boy could go to the bathroom on request . . . no pushups required. I put it in the log.

Wednesday, August 17: I called Bill White and arranged a release for Ralph on Sunday and a visit for Terry.

Thursday, August 18: I got Ralph's ticket, requested his money, typed up and distributed his department notice.

Friday, August 19: I asked Pottenburgh for $5.00 for Ralph Phillips. He agreed and let Pat (secretary) give it to Ralph.

Saturday, August 20: Someone stole the $2.15 of Ralph's money, which was in an envelope marked "Ralph Phillips $2.15." I had to make it good out of my own pocket. From now on money remains in the safe.

September 6, 1977: I returned to work after two weeks sick leave (sinus infection). Brett and Ralph were released.

Ralph Phillips left Brookwood with the clothes on his back, a new pair of denim jeans, and a new pair of Converse sneakers. He had a one-way train ticket to Buffalo, five dollars in his pocket, and he carried a brown, paper bag with two cotton T-shirts, two changes of underwear, and three pairs of athletic socks. He had thrown away the remainder of his meager possessions except the record player that had once been the subject of much controversy and which he left abandoned atop a cabinet in the mess hall. For some reason he had kept the broken pieces of his model cars that had been smashed by one of the bad asses, but on his final day they too were thrown in the trash.

There were no ceremonies to mark his departure—nothing like a graduation exercise. There were only a few scattered goodbyes to some of the detainees lounging in the wing; several of the weekend staff wished him good luck, and a couple admonished him to stay out of trouble. That's all there was to Bucky's departure, he simply walked from the wing, got in the front seat of Ed Davis's private vehicle, and was driven to the train station in Hudson.

When the car pulled away from the main facility, Bucky looked back one last time. For some strange, vague reason he was momentarily possessed with a feeling of melancholy—a sense of loneliness. He would definitely not miss the place from which he had fled so many times only to be returned, but there was a peculiar finality to this departure. He felt as though he was being expelled. He felt like he was being driven from a place to which he could never return, and indeed he would never again be sentenced as a juvenile. From that day forward, Bucky Phillips would be tried as an adult and would do hard time in adult prisons.

Chapter Eleven

A TASTE OF FREEDOM

Bucky's mother and sister were waiting for him at the train station in Buffalo, and although it was nearly midnight, the trio stopped on the thruway at Denny's for a hearty breakfast. Bucky was actually looking forward to eating at Denny's. On the train ride from Hudson, he had imagined what he would order. He at first thought he would have steak and eggs and pancakes and gravy and fried potatoes and toast and jelly and sausage and bacon, but he changed his mind several times before the train reached Buffalo. By the time he sat down and ordered breakfast he realized that it was not anything in particular he wanted, but it was the idea that he actually had a choice. He ate a stack of pancakes and eggs with bacon and sausage links and hash brown potatoes drenched with milk gravy. He washed it down with a large glass of orange juice followed by a glass of milk and ordered a Coke to go.

April Phillips had enrolled her son in school in anticipation of his release from Brookwood, but school was still two weeks away. Bucky was eager to revisit his wilderness haunts and tramped through the woods for the next several days, returning home each night. He hiked to the beaver dam where he had camped in the worst winter weather he had ever experienced. The remnants of his lean-to remained just as he left it between the two hemlocks except that the pile had become more tightly compacted by the weight of the winter's snow. He closely examined the beaver lodge but did not see or hear its inhabitants. There were fresh signs of their work in the way of newly trimmed twigs and tree branches that had been carefully inserted to expand the dam and push its waters closer to the tree line. Bucky guessed that if nothing happened to the beavers the pond would make its way to the county road a good half a mile away by next summer.

Although Bucky got along well enough in school, the classroom did not hold much attraction for the fifteen-year-old. He liked English literature, loved American history, struggled with math, but excelled in metal and woodworking classes, and was a whiz at electronics. He built a radio that he could tune with a pencil and received an A for creating a simple but useless battery using a potato. He detested riding the bus back and forth to school and after several weekends of hard work finally got his father's pickup truck running. Bucky proved to be every bit as good a mechanic as his father and even had a greater love for automobiles.

The motor on his dad's pickup was seized up, and Bucky meticulously broke the engine down piece by piece. He pulled the pistons, replaced one of the rods, and put in all new inserts. He tore the carburetor apart, cleaned and spread its pieces over a large piece of cardboard, and painstakingly reassembled the entire unit. He ground the valves during an auto mechanics class at school and patched several places that had rusted out along the bottom edge of the doors using Bondo and fiberglass. Bucky fastened an old pair of license plates on the front and back of the pickup and drove it unregistered and uninspected to school, without a license.

It was Bucky's mechanical skills that landed him a part-time job with a local dairy farmer while he was still in school. Charlie Spindler always paid him in cash daily, and Bucky did everything on the farm but milk the cows. Charlie was a slender, gangly sort who always looked like he had a two-day growth of brownish-gray stubble and who always laughed at nearly everything. Bucky liked Mr. Spindler, because it did not matter when he showed up, there was always work of some kind available; one day Bucky might be fixing fence or cleaning out the free stall barn with a small front loader. The next day he might be moving heifers from pasture to pasture or dragging a wagon full of chop to fill one of the farm's silos. If Bucky showed up to work one day and missed the next, that was all right with Charlie, but Bucky also liked Charlie Spindler for another reason. Mr. Spindler trusted him to operate any and all of his farm equipment.

The Spindler farm was a hill farm, a farm more suited for growing hay than corn or other row crops.

That also meant it was a "wet" farm, or a farm that, unlike graveled land, did not drain water very well and was more difficult to cultivate. That did not deter Charlie Spindler. He would simply reinforce the undercarriage on his hay wagons with steel and drag the wagon across wet stretches with large, Ford diesel tractors. Charlie appreciated his farm machinery, but he was not afraid to use it. If one of the hay wagons became mired in the mud, Charlie would flap his skinny arms, yell as loud as he could, and laugh as the tractor driver struggled to move the load.

"Pour it on. Blow it up. If that Ford can't take it, we'll get an International," he would say. His bellows of encouragement could be heard over the din of the tractor as he watched the machine struggle and inch the heavy load ever so slowly forward. When the tractor suddenly lunged forward, breaking the load free, Charlie would slap his knees with both hands and loudly hoot as the wagon rolled easily across solid ground.

On more than one occasion Bucky watched Charlie hook two powerful tractors to a wagon full of chopped corn or hay mired in the mud and cut deep furrows in the ground as he dragged it through the muck. There were times when black smoke from the diesel exhausts would linger at the site for a half hour or more.

By the time Bucky's sixteenth birthday rolled around, he had saved enough money to get the pickup properly outfitted with new tires and had it in good enough shape to pass state inspection and have it registered in his name. He traded in his learner's permit for a full-fledged driver's license, but opted to take his test in Little Valley, the county seat of Cattaraugus County. Bucky dropped out of school before he turned sixteen and parlayed his experience operating equipment on the Spindler farm to a fulltime job with a local excavating contractor. Bucky quickly became a skilled equipment operator. He learned to maneuver a D-4 Caterpillar with the deftness of someone much more experienced and was not intimidated by the largest earthmovers.

The construction season in Western New York is seasonal; a successful season is usually crammed between spring and late fall. But, in the late seventies and early eighties, construction work in Western New York was particularly slow. Much of Bucky's work consisted of excavation jobs or site preparation for building rehabs that might last only two or three days in any given week. Although Bucky was generous with family and friends, he managed his money well and was satisfied with a frugal lifestyle between reservation and nonreservation communities. As Bucky matured, he began to explore and understand the attitude and behavior characteristics that separated these two completely different cultures. He learned that his friends and relatives who lived on the reservation thought and acted differently from those who lived in predominately white communities. Nowhere was that difference more prominently displayed than in political campaigns and elections.

A campaign in the white community saw candidates and supporters going door-to-door handing out pamphlets and scattering signs in yards, along the highway, and in storefronts. White candidates boasted of creating jobs and getting more business and industry to move into the county and cutting taxes; most of their issues were economic issues. White folks would choose political sides early in a campaign and talk about the candidates and, more often than not, express dissatisfaction with their choices. Campaigns on the reservation focused mainly on moral issues, and few people spoke publicly about anything political.

Gambling was always a big issue, but Seneca Nation candidates hardly ever talked about issues except in council meetings. At that time in Bucky's life, casino gambling was a distant wish, but Seneca Nation Bingo was a hot issue. There were campaign signs on the reservation too, but not as many, and most residents of the Nation remained quiet about their feelings on the matter. Their silence was not a reflection of indifference—most were waiting to see where the money was. Directly paying for votes in the white community would have created a scandal of monumental proportions, but accepting money for the promise of a vote on the Nation seemed an entirely practical exchange. In close contests, the longer an eligible voter waited before committing to a candidate or an issue, the more valuable their vote became. For some issues, the going rate for a vote was rumored to have been as much as five hundred dollars.

One time, Bucky participated in a conversation with coworkers after a sudden downpour halted their construction job and drove them inside a local restaurant in Silver Creek for coffee. The topic shifted to the Seneca practice of buying votes and reservation life in general. "That's the difference between being civilized and uncivilized," one white, middle-aged worker boomed and pounded his fist on the counter. "That's what happens when the government gives them everything."

"What does the government give them?" Bucky asked pensively.

"Free health care. They don't care. They run right to the emergency room whenever they get a fart cross way." The man drew a deep breath and bragged. "Hell, I gimped around on a broken foot for two weeks before I ever went to the doctor."

"Why did you do that?" Bucky asked.

"I toughed it out for as long as I could," the man winced. "I didn't just run to the doctor. The doc put my whole leg in a cast, and I was laid up for eight weeks."

"That seems like a long time." Bucky flashed a smile and looked the man directly in his eyes.

"I could've come back in six weeks, but I got the doc to give me another two weeks and a bunch of us went fishing up in Canada. Besides," the man explained, "I earned that, I had it coming, but I sure as hell wouldn't sell my vote."

"Well," Bucky said and leaned on his elbows toward his sanctimonious coworker. "Maybe, just maybe, that Indian on the rez figured out a long time ago that the man with the money always wins." The man had just admitted that he had successfully stolen two weeks of disability payments from the government, Bucky thought, but it was obvious that he, like the Senecas, did not consider all thefts a crime.

Bucky continued to work and, despite scattered instances of petty thievery, stayed out of trouble. He earned a decent wage, and his was not a reckless lifestyle. He helped provide for his mother, lived at home most of the time or stayed with friends on and off the Nation, and he even managed to save a few dollars. Thievery was not essential for his livelihood, but that did not stop him from stealing. Bucky Phillips simply became more discriminating in selection, and for all practical purposes was becoming a professional thief.

He became expert at breaking and entering and at leaving as few signs of entry as possible. He made it a rule to leave a nearly pristine crime scene and resisted the temptation to take more than he could carry outside in a single trip. Gone were the days when a vending machine was pilfered and unceremoniously dumped on the floor or damaged if it had little or no change. It became his goal to make his presence nearly invisible. He chose his targets carefully and avoided stealing anything that could not quickly be moved. He did not study great works of art or great artists, but he learned the difference between oil paintings and prints.

He disciplined himself to ignore a quart jar full of loose change in favor of a piece of Waterford crystal. He learned he could get as much money for a genuine Hummel figurine or a single piece of Lladro as he could get for a pair of premium tires. He quickly realized it was safer to handle smaller items and that he could easily dispose of them out of state. Hooking up with antiques dealers or craft show vendors throughout Pennsylvania, Ohio, Kentucky, and Tennessee had been easier than Bucky had supposed.

Bucky traveled light. He learned that even honest dealers, who would otherwise resist purchasing a van load of merchandise from a stranger, despite obvious suspicions, would quickly snap up a single piece from that same stranger. Bucky became a very good salesman and learned not to be too greedy. He adopted the successful practice of offering dealers and vendors two dissimilar items at a specified price for the pair. One of the paired items was immediately recognizable as being inferior to its mate. The vendor would usually make a counteroffer for the most valuable piece and reject the other. If the true retail price for a cut-glass pitcher was three hundred dollars, the vendor might offer fifty dollars or perhaps seventy-five dollars. Bucky would grit his teeth and rub his forehead. "Gees," he would sigh. "I'd like to, but I've really got to have a $150 to get to Indiana."

He soon discovered it did not take much haggling before he would give up, and in total exasperation exclaim, "Okay, give me a hundred dollars and you can have the pair." That usually worked. But Bucky's favorite venues were gun shows, particularly in Maryland, and Prince George's County especially. People there had discretionary money—the closer to Baltimore and Washington, DC, the better. He could walk through a gun show in Maryland and sell a one-thousand-dollar piece of Lladro for a couple hundred bucks without much trouble. Disposing of three or four good pieces on a weekend was profitable for a young man still in his teens. But the greatest changes Bucky implemented in his modus operandi was to operate as far away from home as he could conveniently travel and to keep his mouth shut. This time around, others may have suspected him of criminal activity, but they never heard it from him—he never bragged of his exploits to anyone.

Bucky may have turned over a new leaf in his criminal activities, but that did nothing to keep local law enforcement from questioning him about various thefts and burglaries throughout the county. Once, he was even questioned by the state police and FBI about a van that had been stopped on the thruway with a load of unstamped cigarettes. Although the Minnesota-licensed van had been followed from Winston-Salem, North Carolina, Bucky was interrogated as if he were a suspect.

He accepted such interactions as a natural consequence of his past, but deeply resented it when the police pulled him off a work site. At least once a month, some agency of law enforcement would place him in the back seat of a patrol car and pretend to question him in front of his coworkers and his boss. They would talk to him about subjects as mundane as the weather or ask him how he liked his job and if he had seen any good movies lately. He knew that his antagonists deliberately intended to embarrass—even humiliate—him, and he knew they wanted him to know exactly what they were up to.

There was nothing Bucky could do except apologize to his boss and accept the aggravation. Bucky was absolutely convinced two visits in as many weeks from the police were the reason one Buffalo contractor fired him. On another occasion his boss complained directly to the County Sheriff about his deputies taking Bucky off a piece of heavy equipment and actually bringing the entire work project to a screeching halt. The sheriff's deputies eased up for a while; the state police continued the tactics, but with less frequency; and the FBI finally stopped altogether.

Bucky continued to work and live his life in such a manner that impressed and surprised many who knew him. He even managed to trade up in cars two or three times, each time getting a better vehicle than he had before. He really did not care what make his cars were as long as they had "balls." Although Bucky was impressed with speed, he was equally impressed by performance. In another time and another place, Bucky might have been a successful racecar driver or employed to test the performance of experimental vehicles for one of the world-class automakers. When he sat behind a steering wheel, he immediately became part of the vehicle. He could feel every vibration and shudder as the vehicle sped down the highway. He could sense the hesitation and feel the torque as a vehicle shifted through its gears. He experienced the "play" in the car's steering as its tires competed to hold a grip on the road surface. There wasn't much Bucky Phillips did not know about cars. But stolen cars would become Bucky's Achilles' heel, his fatal flaw.

When he was seventeen, Bucky would demonstrate his mechanical skills in a most peculiar, but spectacular, way. Bucky was hiding out from the law when he threw a rod in a "piece of shit" car he had stolen between Olean and Portville, New York. He was taking the back roads when the engine suddenly exploded in a loud clatter and stopped amid a cloud of smoke. Undeterred, Bucky crawled under the car right on the shoulder of the highway and drained the oil from the pan into a five-gallon bucket. Next, he pulled the damaged rod and piston from the cylinder through the oil pan and stuffed the cylinder tightly with rags. After he closed everything as securely as he could, the car started and ran really rough, but it churned along well enough to let him limp back to Salamanca.

Although Bucky remained "Suspect Number One" in the hearts and minds of local authorities, he cleverly avoided their intrusions by traveling frequently between two Indian Nations and Chautauqua County. Making friends was easy for Bucky. People were naturally attracted to this gentle young man who was well mannered, charming, and unpretentious. Women liked him and older women in particular were taken by the way he respectfully stood whenever one would enter into his presence. He would hold the door open for women who were complete strangers and would offer to exchange places with a woman in the checkout line at a supermarket.

Bucky had developed into a very handsome young man, but despite his gentle and gracious nature, he was in an awkward place in his life. He was seen frequently in the company of any number of females, sometimes at a movie or a sporting event and sometimes out for a dinner date. But he was an avid auto racing fan, and not many girls wanted to spend an entire weekend watching cars speed in reckless abandon around a dirt track. As a high school dropout, he did not participate in school functions where boys meet age-appropriate girls, and since he was so well known to local law enforcement, he purposely avoided popular hangouts that served alcohol. As a result, Bucky avoided serious or enduring relationships. But that would change before the year's end when a casual friendship became a romantic relationship.

Kasey Crowe had known of Bucky since her preteens but had never talked to him other than to say hello. She was not particularly attracted to him; she was fifteen and had never had a serious date. Bucky was attracted to her right away and purposely arranged his schedule to cross her path at every available opportunity. He saw her several times, but while they enjoyed each other's company, their relationship remained purely platonic until the summer of 1981. When the scales dropped from his eyes, and he gazed for the very first time upon a beautiful, young woman who stood tall and proud, Bucky made his move. He remembered their first real kiss. He said his heart was beating fast, he was having trouble breathing, and without a word he gathered her in his arms. They clutched each other in a silent embrace that culminated in a deep and passionate kiss. When they finally broke apart, they stared at each other in silence for the longest time. The couple would never marry, but nothing seemed more natural than the relationship that developed between Bucky and Kasey. It was if it had been preordained.

Together they produced a daughter—their love child. In 1982 and two days before Christmas, Patrina was born. Although he and Kasey lived apart, it was the happiest of times for Bucky, but in less than six months, life for the loving couple and doting parents would become a train wreck.

One day, by chance, Bucky drove past a construction site and saw a set of air tools complete with several jack hammers and a portable compressor sitting on a trailer.

The equipment was parked behind a newly constructed chain link fence with a gate fastened with a length of heavy chain and locked with a simple pad lock. He recognized the lock as one that could easily be picked by using a ten-penny nail with its head pounded flat. That was another skill his father had taught him. When he was younger, he had made such a key and walked around Dunkirk and unlocked as many of the same pad locks as he could. He never entered the stores or warehouses, but had locked nearly a dozen locks together and left them on the steps of the local police station.

As Bucky drove past the construction site, he hatched a plan. The next day, a little before noon on Saturday, Bucky changed the license plates on his pickup to a single Pennsylvania plate and drove to the construction site. In short order, he had picked the lock, entered the site, hooked the trailer to his truck and pulled it off the site, being sure to chain and lock the gate behind him before driving away in broad daylight with the equipment in tow. The construction site was almost directly across from the state police barracks. Bucky chuckled as he turned east on Route 20 and headed toward the reservation. But his smile quickly changed to a frown when he realized he might have miscalculated.

He had broken one of his own rules that he swore to uphold while he was in reform school at Industry—always work alone. He could not work alone on this heist. Although he pulled the job alone, he had to rely on others to secure the merchandise until he had a chance to find a fence—someone who would buy the entire package with no questions asked. He had stayed straight for almost a year after he left Brookwood, but after that he had parlayed his thievery into a profitable venture. His occasional excavation work netted him two hundred dollars a week, and he made even more when he could break open a basement site or dig a footer for a foundation. He liked that work, because he could always rent or even borrow a backhoe without investing a lot of time and expense.

Bucky padded honest work with what he called "little things" and always had one or two thousand dollars in cash stashed at home. He had learned to pilfer two or three good houses or burglarize a jewelry store and take only a few expensive, but collectible items. He preferred nick-knacks and figurines. That method worked so well for him, and especially in those places, he could break in without leaving much of a trace. And, if he left a few marks on a doorjamb or broke a piece of glass, the owner may not even miss two or three items for a day or two. Even if an item was noticed missing immediately, with nothing else missing, the police would lay it off to a shoplifter and consider a jimmied door a failed attempt at a break in.

There were other times when Bucky spied a valuable item in a store and would simply walk out with it under his jacket or up his sleeve. He found he could easily pick up another three to four hundred dollars a month on a couple of weekend trips down south. His method was actually more profitable and less risky than stealing a car. But the air tools proved too great a temptation, the pickings proved too easy, and in the right hands the tools could easily net two thousand dollars.

He drove directly to the house of a friend who lived on the reservation and asked if he could leave the equipment for a day or two. His friend may have suspected the equipment was stolen but was reassured when Bucky parked the trailer in plain sight and told him to tell anyone who might ask that it belonged to him. Two days later the friend called Bucky and told him a part-time member of the tribal police saw the equipment and asked about it in a casual conversation. Bucky at once supposed he had been made and the law would be looking for him. His only thoughts were to get the hell out of Dodge.

Bucky knew the cops would be on the lookout for his pickup, and he decided to leave it parked in plain sight at his mother's apartment. He reasoned that the cops would drive by the house, spot the pickup, and assume he was still in the area. But Bucky needed a car, and he needed one quickly. He immediately called a friend in Cassadaga and persuaded her to give him a ride to the Salamanca side of the Seneca Nation. She protested that her car was low on gas, but reluctantly agreed when Bucky promised to fill her tank on the reservation and give her an extra twenty bucks for her trouble.

Time was of the essence for Bucky. He knew it would be easier to steal a "rez" car, and he needed to put as much distance between him and Chautauqua County as quickly as possible. An hour later his friend dropped him off at a reservation-owned gas station in Salamanca. He saw several cars in a parking lot behind the Seneca Museum directly across the street. Bucky was in luck. Of the four cars in the parking lot, he opted for an older model Chevrolet. Had he the time to be discriminating, he would have preferred another option, but the doors were unlocked, and the keys were in the ignition. The car appeared well kept and was clean inside, but Bucky only had to start the engine and see a puff of smoke from the exhaust to know the car used oil.

After he had driven less than a block, he knew the engine was losing compression—most likely from a leaky head gasket, and there was a lot of slack in the transmission. The gauge showed nearly a full tank of gas and that was uncommon for most reservation cars. He knew that, for reasons mostly economic, Senecas hardly ever filled up the gas tank. He drove past several gas stations that occupied the exit strip off the Southern-Tier Expressway and made his way west toward Jamestown. Bucky could never have imagined the bizarre sequence of events that would transpire in the next two hours.

He had hardly been on the highway fifteen minutes before he saw two New York State Police cruisers speeding eastbound in the opposite lane.

Now, he thought, sure as hell someone had seen him drive away from the Nation in a stolen vehicle. The state cops did not have their lights flashing, but that only heightened his fears because that was an indication they were not responding to an automobile accident or other traffic-related emergency. He knew he had to get off the expressway in a hurry. He had passed the Onoville exit, which depending on what direction you were going, was either the first or last exit for the Seneca Nation.

In less than ten minutes Bucky slowed down for the Randolph exit but changed his mind when he thought he saw a sheriff's patrol car parked at the exit truck stop. He kept driving toward Jamestown and turned off at the Kennedy exit and drove on the old state road to the outskirts of village of Falconer. He skirted the village, because it was adjacent to Jamestown, Chautauqua County's largest city, and took a less traveled county road. Although a more circuitous route, it would eventually allow him to enter Pennsylvania unnoticed and afford him a place to ditch the car in a remote area.

Bucky had driven less than a mile when he looked in his rearview mirror and saw a police car speeding toward him with lights flashing and siren blaring. Bucky eased off the accelerator and recognized the car as a town cop instead of a sheriff's deputy or a state trooper. He had to make a decision—he could either try to run, or stop and see what the guy wanted. He decided to pull over. The cop car came to a screeching halt right behind him, and the officer quickly got out and walked toward Bucky. Bucky was partially out of the car when the officer suddenly stopped and pointed to him and yelled, "Get back in the car. Sir, get back in the car."

What the hell, Bucky thought and slid back under the wheel. He took a look in the side mirror and saw the officer fumbling to remove his weapon from its holster. "Fuck this," Bucky muttered aloud and floored the accelerator. The Chevy did not suddenly respond as Bucky hoped. Instead, the motor almost stalled but slowly gathered speed. Bucky could see the officer in his rearview mirror standing with his legs spread wide apart. His mouth was agape, and he was staring dumbfounded surrounded by a cloud of dense smoke from the Chevy's exhaust. The officer finally recovered and ran to his car. Bucky took another peek in his mirror and saw him turn, quickly bend down, and retrieve something from the road. *Holy Christ,* Bucky thought, *the guy dropped his fucking gun.*

Bucky had a good lead on the cop, but the car he was driving simply did not have the energy to outdistance the police car. In a matter of seconds, the police car crested a small rise and was bearing down on Bucky. Bucky was driving over a paved, but narrow road and saw that he was fast approaching an intersection, and the intersecting road was gravel. There was little Bucky could do—he could not outrun the guy; he had to outmaneuver him. When Bucky neared the intersection he gunned the engine, cranked the steering wheel hard to the right, and slammed on the brakes. The car was locked in a sideways skid and the air was filled with the smell of burning rubber. The car fishtailed a couple of times but Bucky quickly regained control and watched the cop car slide through the intersection in a screeching trail of smoke.

Bucky punched the accelerator for all that it was worth, but the car did not have the steam to escape his pursuer. The road had a long, steep grade that sapped the strength from the Chevy's engine, and Bucky realized it would only be matter of seconds before the more powerful cop car would be on top of him. Just as Bucky crested the hill, he suddenly slammed on the brakes, gripped the steering wheel with both hands, and leaned back hard against the seat. Smack in the middle of the road at the bottom of the hill was a yellow school bus with its red lights flashing. Bucky was pumping and pressing the brake pedal as hard as he could. There was not enough room on either side of the bus to go around and Bucky was headed right for the front of the bus.

He came to a screeching halt just inches from the front bumper of the bus. The bus driver sat horrified with a front row seat to the events unfolding before her eyes. Suddenly, Bucky heard two fast pops, then two more, and was showered by broken glass. He did not realize immediately what was happening. "Holy shit," he finally screeched, "that asshole is shooting at me." Bucky was already out of the car and running as fast as he could across a small clearing to a clump of trees that lined the road. Once in the safety of the woods, he stopped to gather his thoughts and saw the police officer running back and forth waving his arms around the bus with his gun drawn. Bucky took several deep breaths. "That fucker's nuts," he sighed.

Bucky was in deep shit, and he knew it. He did not know exactly where he was and although he was in a clump of trees the surrounding area was mostly open meadows and farmland. There was no place to hide and since there were so few houses, stealing a car would not be a reasonable option. Whatever he had to do, wherever he had to go, would be on foot. Bucky decided there was little else to do. He found a comfortable tree stump and simply sat down to wait and see what would happen. Nearly a half hour passed before two county sheriff cars, a state police cruiser, and two additional town police cars joined the town cop. Bucky watched everything from his vantage point on the tree stump. He observed one cop car after another stop at the school bus.

In every case, the drivers would get out and walk around the scene; some would board the bus. The front and back windshields had been shot out of the Chevy, and for some reason unclear to Bucky, all four doors were wide open, and the hood and trunk lids were raised. One after another of the officers would walk to the car, peer inside, then walk away. After nearly an hour the bus driver was allowed to continue on her way. She was probably a nervous wreck, Bucky thought, as several police cars jockeyed to one side or the other to allow the bus to get by. He even thought for a moment that waiting in the trees would prove successful, but that was not the case. He decided to make a move. He crushed a cigarette on the ground with his foot and cautiously made his way toward the meadow on the opposite edge of the trees.

"Holy shit," he muttered aloud. He saw three police officers spaced about fifty feet apart walking slowly, but steadily toward the trees. The middle officer was carrying a shotgun at the ready and the others had drawn handguns. He turned quickly to his right and saw three more officers standing in fixed positions along the road. The best he could tell, the officers in the field appeared to be county deputies, but the officers on the road were clearly identifiable by their gray uniforms and Stetson hats as state troopers. Bucky suddenly remembered a phrase whispered to him by Sylvia Honig in Brookwood years before when a pair of the bad asses had him cornered. She had offered to lock Bucky in his room.

"Discretion is the better part of valor," she had reassured him and led him to the safety of his room. Later, when he had a chance to ask her privately what the phrase meant, she explained that the words were from Shakespeare's *King Henry IV* and were spoken by Falstaff.

"But what does it mean?" he had asked. He felt comfortable asking Sylvia questions, because she took his questions seriously and never made him feel silly for having asked.

"I think it means that it is better to be cautious and think things through before rushing in and doing something impulsively or from anger." Her explanation made sense at the time and Bucky reasoned that the phrase surely made sense on this occasion.

He quickly surveyed his surroundings. He did not think it would be wise to approach the officer with the shotgun, so he cautiously made his way toward the deputy to the right of the one with the shotgun. Still hidden from view, he carefully approached the officer and remained concealed behind a tree.

"Don't shoot," he called out. "I don't have a gun. I'm coming out with my hands up."

The officer was momentarily taken by surprise, but quickly recovered.

"Come out with your hands over your head." The deputy squared off with his weapon pointed in the direction of the sound.

Bucky walked slowly from the trees and stopped.

"Turn around," the deputy barked, "and lay face down on the ground."

Bucky complied and before he could even turn his head, three deputies were all over him. One had a knee in the middle of his back as another twisted his arms behind him as he was handcuffed and lifted to his feet in the same motion. Bucky was taken to the county jail in Mayville. He was all too familiar with the procedures. He was fingerprinted, photographed, taken to a shower, and given jail greens. The following morning, he was led, handcuffed and in leg irons, through the tunnel that ran from the jail, under the street, and into a waiting area outside the county court room. A deputy removed his leg irons, and he was guided into the courtroom and told to sit on a bench against the wall. He noticed three men in suits standing around a table whispering. Finally the taller of the three took a folder that was offered to him. He quickly scanned the contents of the file and walked toward Bucky.

He introduced himself, but Bucky did not catch his name other than to hear him say that he was from the public defender's office. He explained to Bucky that he faced a list of charges "as long as your arm," which included grand theft auto, unlawful flight, obstruction of justice, reckless endangerment, obstruction of governmental administration, and the list went on. He even suggested that more charges were likely to be added later. He asked if Bucky had a lawyer and when he learned he did not, he suggested Bucky plead not guilty at least for the time being. He also told Bucky that if he could not make bail, he would be returned to county jail until his hearing.

Their discussion was interrupted when a bailiff announced the arrival of the judge.

"All rise. The Honorable Lee Towne Adams presiding," the bailiff's voice filled the entire courtroom and County Judge Lee Towne Adams took his place behind the bench. Judge Adams was a slender, wiry man with thinning gray hair and the faint trace of a moustache across his upper lip. He dispatched several cases in rapid succession, had the court clerk assign trial dates, and signed a handful of documents given to him by the clerk before Bucky's name was called.

"Good morning, Mr. Phillips," Judge Adams smiled politely and tipped his head slightly toward Bucky to acknowledge his presence. The DA rattled off several things to the judge, and before he knew what was happening Bucky was being led away.

"Wait a minute, Judge Adams," Bucky called out. "I want to say something."

Judge Adams, who always maintained a gentlemanly appearance and remained courteous even toward the most callous offenders, lifted a robed arm to expose a white-sleeved wrist with his palm raised in a cautionary gesture.

"Mr. Phillips," he smiled, "I suggest you remain silent at least until you've had a chance to confer with your lawyer. And, even then," he added, "it probably would be in your best interests to remain silent."

"No, Judge Adams," Bucky protested, "you know me. You know I am a thief. You know that, but you also know that I don't lie. I've never lied to the police, and I've never lied to you." Bucky turned to face the judge and lifted his handcuffed hands under his chin. "Judge, I've never hurt anyone, and you know that. But," he insisted, "you've got to investigate what went on here. I was running, there's no doubt about that, but when I came over that hill and saw a school bus with its lights on, I stopped. I don't know, they must have had a half-day of school or something. I almost hit the bus head on, but I stopped." Bucky paused to catch his breath and threw a glance toward the DA and the half-filled courtroom that was listening with rapt attention.

"Judge Adams, the cop that was chasing me was absolutely nuts. He was crazy. I was stopped right in front of that bus and all of a sudden, he shot out my back glass and windshield. He shot four or five times. He could have killed me, but even worse he could have killed the bus driver or some kids. You've got to look into that Judge."

Judge Adams sat expressionless as the deputy led Bucky toward the exit. Bucky turned on his way out and called out to the Judge.

"Judge Adams. Check it out. If you don't find bullet holes in the front of that bus then I'm lying, but if you do, then he's lying. Check it out."

Bucky never learned whether his story was ever followed up on, but on March 17, 1983, when Ralph James Phillips appeared in Chautauqua County Court, there was no mention of unlawful flight to avoid arrest, no grand theft auto, and no reckless endangerment or obstruction of justice charges. Instead, Bucky pled guilty to a single charge of third-degree burglary, a class D felony. Judge Lee Towne Adams sentenced him to serve a minimum of two years and six months with a maximum sentence of five years. Bucky stayed in county jail for forty-three days before he was transported to Fishkill Correctional Facility, a medium-security prison downstate in Dutchess County to begin serving his sentence only eleven days after he had turned twenty-one.

From the time he left Brookwood Correctional Facility as a young boy of fifteen, Bucky was in and out of county jail so many times that he lost count. After that, Bucky became acquainted with prison guards from Attica to Elmira to Auburn to Fishkill and twice at Dannemora. Including his time in reform school and with hard prison time, Bucky has been incarcerated longer than he has ever lived free. The longest stretch of freedom Bucky ever had was the first thirteen years of his life, and those were years of unrelenting poverty.

Bucky was paroled on May 29, 1986, from Fishkill after having served two years, eleven months, and one day of a five-year sentence, but in less than nine months he would be doing hard time in Auburn, a full-maximum-security prison. Auburn was the first "full-max" prison experience for Bucky, and although he found it harsh and unyielding, he adapted quickly and learned to cope with its extremes.

The prison at Auburn was established in 1816 and is historically significant for being the state's oldest state prison facility, but it was also the first prison in the world to house prisoners in one-man, or single, cells. Prisoners were dressed in striped clothing, forced to march in lockstep, and remain silent for the entire day. Unruly prisoners were subjected to harsh punishments, brutal beatings, and flogging. Regardless, the Auburn System was a model for worldwide prison reform and was instrumental in establishing procedures still practiced throughout the penal system.

The prison at Auburn was such a revolutionary departure in how crime was studied and punished that it attracted visitors from across the United States and throughout Europe. Government officials, foreign dignitaries, scholars, and the notably curious arrived at the prison in such numbers that officials began to charge admission for tours. The facility attracted so many visitors that the twelve-and-a-half-cents admission was doubled in 1822 in a blatant effort to discourage visits. Despite the increase, the annual income from visitors averaged more than fifteen hundred dollars and paid the salaries of several prison officials, including the chaplain and a prison doctor.

Prison conditions would dramatically change again at Auburn and around the world in 1913 when a man named Thomas Mott Osborne headed a commission to study prison reform and entered Auburn disguised as a convict. His findings resulted in the creation of the Mutual Welfare League, which for the first time allowed prisoners a voice in how the prison was run and how prisoners were treated. The Mutual Welfare League was actually a governing body of prisoners and represented one of the earliest attempts at rehabilitation rather than punishment.

Subsequently, the prison at Auburn became the location for innovative and effective changes that had a worldwide impact on crime and criminals. In another first, shortly before 7:00 a.m. on August 6, 1890, an Auburn prisoner named William Kemmler became the first person in the world to be legally electrocuted. A Buffalo dentist named Alfred P. Southwick invented the electric chair, and prisoners in Auburn's carpentry shop used oak to build the final version. The Auburn electric chair was ultimately destroyed in the 1929 Auburn prison riots.

In 1902 an Auburn prison guard named James Parke and his son Edward were credited with creating and implementing a fingerprint identification storage and retrieval system, which was heralded throughout the world. Fingerprints had already been established in England as a unique means of individual identification, but Parke's method replaced a cumbersome and time-consuming task of cataloging individual body measurements that were commonly used for identification. But the story of an Auburn inmate named Robert Buffum demonstrates how incarceration can so totally obliterate a man's past.

Lt. Robert Buffum was an officer in the Union Army during the Civil War. He was one of twenty-two members of a Union Army spy network known as Andrews' Raiders. The Raiders' mission was to sneak behind Confederate lines and disrupt rail service to Chattanooga, Tennessee. The team burned railroad bridges, captured a locomotive, was successful in disrupting communications, and delayed confederate troop movements. For gallantry against the enemy, Lieutenant Buffum became the third person in the entire country to receive the Congressional Medal of Honor, which was personally awarded to him by President Abraham Lincoln.

Sadly, after the war Robert Buffum suffered psychological damage from time spent as a Confederate prisoner of war and was confined to a mental hospital for three years after he left the army. He became a chronic alcoholic and shortly after his release from the hospital, he killed a man after the man vilified President Lincoln during a drunken argument. Buffum was convicted of murder and sentenced to the State Asylum at Auburn for the criminally insane, another nineteenth-century innovation. On July 21, 1872, Buffum barricaded himself in his single cell at Auburn and slashed his throat. His Civil War heroics remained unknown to prison staff, and he was buried on the prison grounds when no one claimed his corpse.

One hundred and twenty-three years later, in 1994, and after years of research the Congressional Medal of Honor Society of the United States of America ran across an account of the violent suicide of Robert Buffum recorded in a local newspaper. Their investigation revealed that Buffum's body had been moved to an unmarked, mass grave containing bodies of prisoners who died in the Auburn prison. There, on July 29, 1995, members of the Medal of Honor Society, together with many of Buffum's family members, dedicated the resting place of Lt. Robert Buffum with a marker in tribute to his gallantry during the Civil War.

Chapter Twelve

HARD TIME

Bucky would spend nearly four years doing hard time at Auburn before being paroled in October 1991 at the age of twenty-nine. But freedom in Bucky's mind was only an abstract concept derived from his individual experience. He expected to be in jail; confinement was as much a part of his life as attending school or holding down a steady job. Sure enough it was not long before he was back in county jail. During our interview, Bucky must have sensed my bewilderment over his propensity to be so easily rearrested.

"You don't understand the criminal justice system, do you?" he asked while flashing a broad smile and rising from his chair. He laced his fingers behind his head and stretched slowly sideways several times. "You believe in truth, justice, and the American way."

Before I could respond, Bucky continued in a nonmocking way. "That's okay," he said and leaned forward at his waist and grimaced slightly as if to rid his body of some invisible muscle contraction. "Have you ever been in jail? I mean behind bars." Bucky turned the interview around.

"No. I never have." I answered truthfully.

"Good," he beamed. "Believe me, you haven't missed a hell of a lot." Bucky returned to his chair, threw his leg across his knee, and assumed a comfortable pose. "You believe in due process, but due process only works for a favored few." Bucky abruptly shifted the conversation.

"How many inmates did you see on your way in here?" he asked.

"I don't know," I shrugged and shifted my weight in the chair.

"Seriously," Bucky continued, "how many? Twenty-five, maybe thirty?"

"Seems about right."

"Conventional wisdom holds they're all guilty, otherwise they wouldn't be here. Right?" Bucky pressed on.

"Sure," I acknowledged the obvious.

"Would it surprise you to learn that out of the thirty or so inmates you saw on your way in, there are five, maybe six, who are not guilty of any crime? Or," Bucky paused to give his words greater impact, "that probably a third pled to an even greater crime than the crime they initially committed?"

"Why would they do that?" I asked incredulously.

"They believe the cops are cutting them a break." Bucky raised his leg toward his chest and grasped his knee with both hands. He gently rocked back and forth. "Suppose a couple of street kids hit a convenience store. They claim they have a gun. The clerk doesn't see one, but hands over the money. They flee on foot, make it a couple of blocks, and run across Friend Freddy who has a car. They tell Friend Freddy they'll buy him a tank of gas if he'll drive them across town. He agrees. Cops pull them over before they've driven a block." Bucky paused, shifted his weight forward, and pushed his face close to the plexiglass barrier. "Guess how many are going to jail on the convenience store robbery?"

I had to agree that I would not have wanted to be in Friend Freddy's shoes.

"Yes, but here is where the cops work their magic." Bucky sat back, folded his arms across his chest, and introduced another intriguing element into the story. He asked me to assume that Friend Freddy had a couple of priors, petty stuff, but probation. He then escalated the circumstances by saying Friend Freddy had an outstanding warrant, perhaps unpaid parking tickets, maybe a speeding ticket, but outstanding warrants. "Now," Bucky said and poked the air with his thumb and forefinger to illustrate a pistol. "What if the cops find a pistol in Friend Freddy's glove box?"

Bucky was rolling out so much information so fast that I wished I'd been able to keep my tape recorder. To compensate I created a mental mind map in comic book form complete with text balloons. "What happens next?" I asked and inserted a mental text balloon over my imagined caricature of Friend Freddy.

"Here's where the cops work their magic." Bucky explained that the cops would tell the two perps about the warrants, about the gun. "Cops are very sophisticated. They're really smooth." Bucky shook his head in resigned acceptance. He said the cops would leave the impression that the gun may be connected to other crimes. He said they would implant the thought that the gun might have been used to kill somebody, maybe even a cop. "By now," Bucky emphasized, "the two perps are willing, even eager to plead to armed robbery. Who knows, they may even be willing to implicate Friend Freddy, say it was all his idea. Without Freddy and the gun, they aren't charged with armed robbery. They pled to a greater crime than they actually committed."

Bucky must have sensed a certain amount of skepticism on my side of the partition. "Look Ray," Bucky was emphatic. "Let's say I've exaggerated by half. Say that half of what I've said is bullshit." Bucky threw out a challenge. "Tell me what half you want to throw out. Do you really believe that some version of what I just laid out doesn't go on every day in police departments across the state, across the country?" Bucky suddenly slid from his chair and squatted to the floor. He pumped his knees rapidly up and down in a series of quick knee bends accompanied by a corresponding number of deep breaths and mumbled something about staying in shape.

"Hands down," he said as he spread his legs slightly and twisted his torso several times at his waist. "I'm probably the best car thief here. I can get inside a locked car and drive away in less than a minute; if I can't, I just walk away." Bucky slumped into his chair and declared without vanity or empty boasts, "I don't leave prints either; maybe a stray hair, but a hair is useless unless it has DNA." Bucky paused momentarily to allow me to catch up with his narrative. "But," he then continued, "bottom line is I've probably stolen more cars than anyone in this prison, maybe twice as many. But," Bucky's voice took on a serious tone, "I've never spent one day in jail for car theft, not a single day."

I was surprised at Bucky's statement, because by the time he was ten he was reputed to be Chautauqua County's most notorious car thief. But it was true, as I would later find out. I retrieved as much of Bucky's adult record as I could find and failed to find a single instance of him ever being convicted of stealing a car.

"There are even more innocent people doing time in county jails. Poor kids mostly." Bucky's countenance suddenly changed, his voice trailed off, the smile vanished from his face, and heaviness filled the room. "The poor have one justice system, the middle class another, and the well off another." A faint, but despondent grin tugged at the corners of his mouth and the words slipped from his lips in a near whisper. "Guess which system sends the most people to jail?" Bucky convincingly expanded his narrative.

"A kid gets arrested for a minor fracas on Friday night. Doesn't actually threaten the cops but argues a little." Bucky clasped his hands and vigorously rubbed his fingers together. "Before he knows what's happening, he's thrown on the ground, cuffed with his hands behind his back, and is carried off to jail. Now, here are his options." Next, Bucky methodically laid out a chain of circumstances so compelling that it left little doubt he was speaking from personal experience. He explained that if the kid had the cash, two hundred fifty to five hundred dollars, he could post bail almost immediately. "That's usually not an option," Bucky pointed out. "Chances are the kid has never even seen two hundred dollars in a single pile at one time."

Bucky explained that the kid's next option was a telephone call. "Call a friend?" Bucky quickly answered his own question. "Maybe, but his friends are just as broke as he is. That leaves him with a call home." Bucky paused momentarily, shuffled his prison-issued canvas shoes back and forth, and reached down to straighten his white socks. "More often than not the kid comes from a single-parent home, a mom with one or two younger children." The picture Bucky was painting was clear; even if the mother had the bail money, she would have to wake the sleeping kids, pack them in a car, and drive to a police station in the middle of the night to post bail.

Bucky continued with his hypothetical tale that acquired more authenticity as he carried me deeper into the details. He explained that the kid might get before a local justice of the peace the next day for a bail hearing, but it was more likely he would not appear before a judge until Monday at the earliest. Bucky quickly pointed out that even if the kid went before a judge on Saturday, his bail would likely be set at five hundred dollars. "As far as the kid is concerned," Bucky shrugged, "his bail might as well have been ten thousand dollars. He can't make it anyway."

"What happens next?" I rose from my chair and rubbed my rear end that had become numb from sitting in a chair that a more skeptical person might have concluded was purposely designed to be uncomfortable.

Bucky stressed that if the kid failed bail, he would be transported to the county jail. "Worse yet," Bucky said. "The kid could sit in county for an entire month and never even see a public defender." He said when the prosecutor finally gets around to the case and looks at the charges, all he wants to do is get rid of the case. "The kid has a whole shit load of charges—public disturbance, resisting arrest, maybe public drunkenness, and the most chicken shit charge anywhere in the state is something they call obstruction of governmental administration." Bucky shook his head from side to side and threw up his hands. "They always tack that one on. But ask any judge anywhere in the state about it. They can't even tell you what it means. But it is serious," he said, "you can get up to a year in jail for it and nobody knows what the fuck it is."

Bucky related that at some point the district attorney would propose a deal to the public defender and explained the sequence of events. The public defender walks over to the jail and meets with the accused, probably for the very first time, and tells him that he's cut a deal for him, a split. Tells him to plead guilty to one of the charges with a sentence for time served, accept six month's probation, and he could go home that day.

"Now Ray," Bucky continued in a serious tone. "This kid may not even be guilty of anything more serious than a violation, like a traffic infraction. He can turn the deal down and go to trial, but do you really believe he's going to stand on principle?"

Bucky's understanding of the criminal justice process proved to be credible. Four years earlier I had spent nearly six months digging out a similar story in Chautauqua County. Several inmates in county jail filed more than thirty complaints or grievances with the state bar association regarding split sentences and the lack of legal representation. The outcome of the complaints were placed "under seal," covered up somewhere inside New York State's Eighth Judicial District.

"They didn't do the kid any favors," Bucky quipped, "but everyone is happy." Bucky allowed that the judge was happy because he got to clear a case from his calendar, the district attorney was happy because his office was credited with a conviction, the public defender was happy because he had successfully settled a criminal case, the county sheriff was happy because he got a bed freed up to rent to another prisoner. The police officer and his police department were also happy because although only one insignificant young man was incarcerated, the arresting officer's personnel records reflected as many individual arrests as the charges that were filed. The police department could justify their annual budget increase by showing a corresponding increase in crime and an inflated number of arrests. Even the young man whose punishment exceeded his crime was relieved. "The only losers," Bucky mused, "are those who cling to the fanciful notion that justice and due process are an integral part of our justice system."

The only time Bucky displayed any sign of anger was when I asked about his attempted escape from the Chautauqua County jail in 1991 and the charges that were brought against his girlfriend for her involvement in that effort.

"That's horseshit." Bucky exclaimed and pounded his fist against the palm of his hand. "That's total horseshit."

I was momentarily startled by the intensity of Bucky's response, and he just as quickly sensed my apprehension.

"Ray," he said, "they were fucking with me. Look," he resumed in a more controlled and direct manner. "I was already stacked up to twenty as a habitual offender. I mean, I was going down for the count and they knew it." Bucky dropped his head slightly to one side and pulled the fingers on his left hand gently across his brow. "They were fucking with me," he repeated. His voice trailed off and his entire body seemed to be occupied with the pain of a deep, distant memory. "They didn't give a shit about Lisa." His voice was uneven. "They used her just to fuck with me."

Lisa Shongo was a young woman Bucky met shortly after he was paroled from Auburn in October 1991, but what began as a casual friendship rapidly turned into a budding romance. Lisa had been involved with a police officer and was having a hard time severing that relationship when her attraction to Bucky became apparent. During their time together, Bucky was arrested on two burglary counts and two counts of grand theft. Lisa continued to visit him at county jail while he was awaiting sentencing. It was during one of her visits that deputies found a handcuff key in her purse and arrested her on the spot. Both she and Bucky were charged with conspiracy and attempted escape. Bucky pled guilty to conspiracy in the fifth degree and was sentenced to a year in county jail. Lisa was given a conditional release.

"It was a set up," Bucky snapped, and his eyes flashed angrily.

"Why do you believe you were set up?" I asked, trying hard to understand Bucky's reasoning.

Bucky stood, stretched his arms above his head, and rapidly snapped his fingers back and forth into tight fists several times before twisting his shoulders sharply backward. "I know I was. I know it and the cops know it." Bucky grasped the back of his chair with both hands and slowly stretched first one leg then the other backwards several times. Then, he moved his chair closer to the partition and sat slightly sideways. "Ray," he said. "Do you remember those twenty-five or thirty inmates you saw on your way in?"

"Yes."

"Every one of those inmates, everyone to a man knows how to find a handcuff key in this maximum-security penitentiary in less than fifteen minutes. If I had wanted a handcuff key in county jail, I sure didn't need someone to smuggle one in from the outside." Bucky had regained his composure and arranged his arguments with precision. "The key was a plant."

Bucky explained that during Lisa's previous visits she had always and without exception handed over her purse to a guard who placed it on a shelf behind the counter. On that particular day Lisa handed her purse to the guard before going through screening. The guard opened the purse, gave it a cursory peek, and instead of placing it on the shelf promptly returned it to Lisa.

The small room used to accommodate jailhouse visits was bare except for a heavy, wooden table that occupied the center of the room and was outfitted with benches on either side. The table was divided down the middle by a short, wooden barrier designed to establish a boundary between inmate and visitor and discourage intimate contact. Inmates and visitors were allowed to exchange a kiss over the barrier, but a guard seated against the wall at the furthest end of the table watched to make sure nothing was passed between them. Lisa was allowed inside the visitors' area and leaned over the short barrier and greeted Bucky with a brief kiss.

As soon as Lisa was seated, a male and a female deputy took positions behind Lisa, and two male deputies stood on either side of Bucky. The female deputy picked up Lisa's purse and immediately emptied its contents on the table. She shifted through the items spilled across the table and found a handcuff key. Both Lisa and Bucky were immediately restrained, handcuffed with hands behind their backs, and placed under arrest.

"It was a set up," Bucky said. "It was prearranged. The purse, the deputies, they had everything in place." The faint glimmer of a bitter smile tugged at Bucky's lips. "On that particular day," Bucky lowered his head and pushed his hands through his hair. "On that particular day there were entirely too many coincidences."

Bucky recited the sequence of events: He questioned why the guard had allowed Lisa to carry her purse into the visiting area. He questioned why four sworn deputies were there to make an arrest. "A jail guard can only hold a suspect." Bucky likened jail guards to security guards in a department store. "They can hold a shoplifter, but it takes a sworn cop to make an arrest."

"How did Ms. Shongo get the handcuff key?" I asked, interrupting Bucky's narrative.

Bucky insisted the answer was obvious. "It came from a cop. Her former boyfriend."

"Did he give it to her?" I pressed the issue.

"I don't think so. I think the prick planted the key to get back at me."

"Did you ever ask Ms. Shongo?"

"No. I didn't want to embarrass her. She had enough grief because of me. I never asked." Bucky speculated that the cop might have met Lisa shortly before her visit, planted the key, and alerted the sheriff. He reasoned they might have met over lunch or dinner and in an unguarded moment he planted the key in her purse. "Who knows," Bucky conceded, "Maybe he slept overnight. It doesn't matter. They used Lisa to get to me."

"Why would the deputies go along with something like that?" I remained curious if not actually skeptical.

"Simple. They were fucking with my time." Bucky must have noticed my puzzled look and was quick to respond. "You don't understand how local cops work," he said. "They were sending me a message. They were reminding me that regardless of any judge in any court, or any prison, or any sentence I might serve, they could fuck me up and there was nothing I could do about it. They were showing me that they could add time to my sentence, even years. They added three years to my sentence."

It must be noted that local authorities who were still around and had a recollection of the handcuff key incident, dispute Bucky's account. People from the Chautauqua County District Attorney's Office and employees and former employees from the sheriff's department claim the handcuff key in question was "removed from the officer's belt." Although no one will elaborate, the clear implication is that the officer was either lured into a compromising situation or was voluntarily placed in that circumstance. Joseph Gerace, who served as Chautauqua County Sheriff from 1995 to 2018, had little recollection of the specific incident but totally rejects Bucky's account. Sheriff Gerace said he seemed to recall that the officer in question lost his job over the incident. "In any case, if he didn't, he should have."

Despite our propensity to disregard the mutterings of a career criminal and a man tagged as a cop killer, Ralph James Phillips presents a powerful and persuasive condemnation of our criminal justice system. His arguments are so precise and his logic so compelling that his words cannot be easily ignored. Whether Bucky's specific allegations are true or not, there remains little doubt about his understanding of the complications inherent in the everyday operation of our splintered criminal justice system.

"Ray," Bucky flashed a broad smile that spread across his entire face. "I'm going to educate you about jail days and about local documents that accompany the convicted to prison." Bucky pushed off the partition wall with his legs and slid his chair backward. He assumed a more comfortable position, crossed his arms atop his chest, and laid out a compelling argument.

Bucky began his lesson by defining who goes to state prison. A person must be convicted in county court of a felony and must be sentenced to at least one year. He indicated that a person convicted of a felony could be given a determinate, or indeterminate sentence. He explained that he was given a determinate sentence of ten to twenty years for his 1992 felony convictions. "That meant," he said, "that I had to be incarcerated for a minimum of ten years before I was eligible for parole. If I never make parole, I serve the full twenty. On the other hand," Bucky added, "as a practical matter indeterminate means a sentence with no minimums. Theoretically, if I was given twenty max on an indeterminate, I would become immediately eligible for parole." Bucky hesitated. "I believe Pataki [referring to then-New York Governor George Pataki], might have changed that to something like requiring an inmate to do eighty-five percent of the max. I'm not sure."

Bucky slid his chair toward the partition and pushed his face closer to the plexiglass. "Ray," he said. "This is where my story becomes more interesting." Bucky backed away from the partition and continued his professorial lecture. He explained that a sentence to state prison only begins when a county judge has the convicted standing before the court and actually speaks the words "you are hereby sentenced." He told me that people unfamiliar with the process often think that once a convicted felon is sentenced, he is carted off to state prison immediately.

"That's not the case," Bucky explained. "The county must make the prisoner state ready." Bucky raised his hands in mock protest. "Their words not mine." He went on to explain that the county is required to assemble any number of relevant records and documents that must accompany the inmate to his destination. Among those documents is the presentencing report: history of criminal activity, any medical records or psychiatric reports, including any legally prescribed medications. The report gives detailed accounts of any violent acts or assaults and attempts at escape or suicide that occurred while the inmate was in custody. When all the records are assembled, the county notifies the state that they have a "state-ready" prisoner. After that, the Department of Corrections designates a reception center where the prisoner can be delivered, processed, and evaluated.

Bucky paused momentarily and began to slowly pace back and forth as if to reassemble his thoughts. He stopped suddenly and without looking in my direction poked at the empty air with his forefinger. "The '91 handcuff key episode is still biting me in the ass. It stays on my records as an attempted escape forever. Do you know," he said and turned suddenly in my direction. "That that 1991 incident is part of the reason I've been in solitary confinement ever since I came to Clinton? They knew what they were doing. They knew I'd plead to protect Lisa. They fucked me really good, didn't they?" There seemed to be a lack of bitterness in Bucky's voice as he recounted the handcuff key incident. Although he remained obviously angry over the event, one could detect a slight trace of begrudging admiration for the ultimate success of his detractors.

Bucky positioned his palms together and waved his forefingers in my direction. "This is where the County Mounties screwed my time with all that handcuff key bullshit." Bucky picked his words carefully and was deliberate in his presentation. "There is something the state calls "jail days," Bucky smiled proudly. The state, he explained, wants to ensure that a prisoner is given credit for all time served on his offence. "That includes county jail time," he said with an obvious bit of ridicule.

He said Chautauqua County sent another piece of paper that certified the number of days he had served in county jail on the specific offense that landed him in state prison. "Follow me on this," Bucky cautioned, "this gets a little tricky." He was arrested and placed in county jail in October 1991 for parole violation and two counts of burglary and two counts of non-auto grand theft. Bucky made plain that he had been in county jail hardly a month before the handcuff key occurrence. He said he pled guilty in October to conspiracy in the fifth and was sentenced around the second week of November 1991 to one year in county jail. "I wasn't sentenced for the burglary charges until nearly a year later." Bucky stated that he was transferred from Chautauqua County to Great Meadow in November 1992 for classification and processing.

"The handcuff key is the gift that keeps on giving to the cops," Bucky said jokingly. "Although I spent more than a year in county jail, less than two months of that was applied toward my felony offence. The handcuff key was a different offense and didn't count against my state time." He said the handcuff key was listed as an attempted escape and automatically moved his parole date from ten years of eligibility to longer than thirteen years before he was finally paroled.

"Chautauqua County pulled the same shit this last time." Bucky sighed and shook his head. He recalled that after he pleaded guilty to murder in Chautauqua County, one of the deputies who accompanied him to Elmira for processing submitted a four-page, single-spaced, typewritten report that accused Bucky of making threats toward law enforcement personnel and making boastful remarks about escaping from a maximum-security prison. Court records show where that four-page deposition was relied upon to place and keep Bucky in solitary confinement at Clinton Correctional Facility. "Here I am, going away from Chautauqua County, doing double life," Bucky shook his head in obvious bewilderment. "But, that wasn't enough. That deputy wanted to fuck with me. He did, but what if he made the whole thing up? What can I do about it? I'll never have an opportunity to challenge his lies. He knows that."

Chapter Thirteen

NEW YORK'S DEPARTMENT OF STATE POLICE—
THE BEGINNING

The New York State Police was created at the beginning of the twentieth century to exclusively protect rural New Yorkers. Ever since, the state police have jealously guarded that mandate and resisted and resented efforts by rural counties to assume more responsibility for local law enforcement. Despite events with narratives all but lost to modern memory, nowhere was that jurisdictional clash more apparent than in Chautauqua County. Although Chautauqua County was not the first rural county to break with tradition, the New York State Police saw such efforts as deliberately offensive acts and an assault on their proud heritage. In a peculiar twist of history, Bucky Phillips benefited from a dispute that took root sixty years earlier when the local sheriff in Chautauqua County assumed part-time road patrol duties.

As the nineteenth century ended, New York State had been settled and divided into counties, villages, and towns for at least fifty years. The so-called Eighth Wonder of the World, the Erie Canal, had been in operation for seventy-five years, providing a waterway passage from the Hudson River to Lake Erie. Although the canal helped with expansion and trade, most of the state's rural counties and villages remained remote and isolated. Unlike neighboring Pennsylvania, New York's industries were located near its cities and its rural areas were given over to farming. But advancing railroads and the advent of the automobile breached that once splendid isolation.

City dwellers now had the ability to reach rural hamlets and communities in only an hour or two by car when that same travel previously required a full day's journey. But it was that accessibility that allowed rural areas to become easy prey for crime and for criminals who had previously concentrated their nefarious pursuits in the cities. A common feeling among New York's rural inhabitants was that if the train had brought the tramp to their door, the automobile brought the crook.

The most common form of law enforcement for New York's rural counties, towns, villages, and hamlets was left to the constable or deputy who served warrants and investigated crimes when he wasn't busy with his own farm work. Established prior to the Revolutionary War, the constable or deputy, adequate for its time, was no match for the modern criminal who could drive from Manhattan to Albany, commit a robbery, then quickly hightail it out of town. As crime spread throughout New York's rural areas so did the call for the state to provide some form of statewide police protection. Efforts to create a force patterned after Pennsylvania's State Police, which had responsibility for that state's rural areas, met such fierce resistance that legislation never made it to the floor of either house of the state legislature.

Opposition to a state-directed police force seems strange in today's law and order environment, but at that time nearly all of the Democratic Party and a brash political upstart named Al Smith were universally opposed to the idea. The Democrats and a fledgling labor union movement had seen what had happened in Pennsylvania to striking coal miners during bloody and brutal confrontations with the Coal and Iron Police. The Coal and Iron Police were in reality created by the mill and mine owners, and they became more lawless and more reckless than the striking workers. Those so-called "Cossacks of Capitalism" were touted as defenders of the peace and were actually commissioned as police officers by the State of Pennsylvania.

Opponents of the measure in New York were horrified at the prospect that New York would go the way of Pennsylvania and deputize a group of outlaws paid for by business owners and industrialists to crush union workers. Opposition to a state police organization remained strong, but that all began to change with the 1913 murder of a man during a payroll robbery in Westchester County. Murder was nothing new to rural New York, but this crime captured the public's attention because of the inaction of the local sheriff and village constable who were fearful of the culprits and allowed them to escape.

Sam Howell was employed as a construction foreman for a woman named Moyca Newell, who was the unmarried, orphaned heir to a vast family fortune. In 1910 Ms. Newell met a young writer named Katherine Mayo, who was a published author and had become something of a social reformer. The two women would become lifelong friends, with Newell providing the money for Mayo's writing projects. In 1913 Newell began building an estate for the two of them in Bedford Hills located in Northern Westchester County. Today, the historic hamlet is only a forty-five-minute drive north from New York City.

In her book *Justice for All* that was published in 1917, Mayo described in vivid details the killing of Sam Howell and of the events that followed:

"Howell was riding a motorcycle, bringing the payroll to the house where the carpenters were at work. Four Italians, all armed, stepped from cover at the roadside and attempted to hold him up. Faithful to his trust, he bent low over his machine and rode into them. They shot but they could not bring him down. With seven bullets in his body, Howell rode his motorcycle to the house and pitched off. He turned over the payroll to his employers, and by name identified two of the four men who had shot him. They had been hired by him. Then he fainted and three days later died."

Newell and Mayor were horrified at the wanton killing of Sam Howell, but it was what happened next that so outraged the women and launched them on a crusade that would eventually lead to the creation of "The Department of State Police." Mayo picks up the story in her book:

"A clearer case of identification, an easier case to handle will never occur in the history of crime. Both the identified men were Italians. One, a character well known in the region, as well as to every man on the construction, had red hair, a conspicuous scar on his cheek, and a [sic] pockmarked skin. All four spent some hours, and in all likelihood, the entire day, lying in a small islet of woods, surrounded by open fields, practically on the scene of their crime. But no attempt was made to arrest them throughout the day. No bar was put in the way of their escape.

"This statement I make without qualification for the reason that I spent the entire day of the murder on the spot and was personally cognizant of all that was done and left undone.

"I saw the complete breakdown of the sheriff-constable system. Both county sheriff and village constable present on the scene proved utterly unrelated to the emergency and for reasons perfectly clear. I saw a group of twenty or more union workmen, encircled by twice their number of unskilled helpers, standing with hands down. And I heard these union men refuse to even surround the islet of woods, a thousand yards distant, in which the murderers of their comrade were hiding.

"'We earn our living on country jobs, among men like these,' said the carpenter boss, nodding toward the listening foreigners, 'knives and guns are their playthings and when they want me, they'll get me, just as they got poor Howell. We have to think of our families. We can't afford to earn gunmen's ill will. There is no protection in the county districts. Sheriffs and constables don't help us at all. *Howell was only a workingman. You'll have forgotten him in a month.*'

"But it is impossible to forget. The truth is too hideous—the truth that in the great rural State of New York protection of life and property is a private luxury to be obtained only by those rich enough to pay for it—the truth that every man carrying a dinner-pail, the farmer driving home from the store at dusk, the woman alone in an isolated homestead, are as safe and easy prey to criminal attack as if they moved in the wilds of Mexico."

President Theodore Roosevelt wrote an introduction to Katherine Mayo's book, and it became an immediate best seller. The book and the persistence of Newell and Mayo are credited with helping to lay the foundation for the creation of the New York State Police. By 1917 Alfred Smith, one of the most the respected opponents of a state police force, was effectively removed from the opposition when he became the sheriff of New York County. With Smith out of the way, the Wells-Mills Bill, which appropriated $500,000 to establish a Department of State Police, was passed by one vote in the senate on March 20, 1917, and by a more comfortable margin in the state assembly. On April 11, 1917, Governor Whitman signed the bill into a law that mandated the New York State Police provide police protection for the rural areas. The basic role of the state police as established in the original law is essentially unchanged to the present day.

From the very beginning, New York state troopers assumed the aura of an elite force. Today the force of more than four thousand sworn officers proudly proclaims on their historical webpage that "since the first 237 men rode out of their training camp on horseback to begin patrolling rural areas, troopers have been there to fulfill the law enforcement needs of the people of New York State with the highest degree of fairness, professionalism and integrity." The department's first superintendent was George Fletcher Chandler, and he is credited with the militaristic nature of the organization and for establishing *esprit de corps* within the unit. Chandler was a physician without experience in law enforcement, but he had a clear vision of what the force should become. He was a brilliant organizer who was involved in everything from giving physicals to the new recruits to buying horses and McClellan saddles.

Chandler also made good use of symbols and symbolism to bolster morale and to emphasize even-handed justice. Even early uniforms were manufactured in a particular way to reinforce that symbolism. Uniforms were made of wool with equal parts of white and black fibers interspersed to symbolize the impartiality of justice. It was Chandler who called for troopers to wear their weapons exposed on a belt, which was not a common practice of the time. Wearing weapons exposed on a belt was such a drastic departure from convention that Chandler was booed for suggesting the same at a meeting of police chiefs in Detroit. Chandler insisted that a trooper needed quick and easy access to his weapon as a matter of personal safety. In a short span of time all law enforcement agencies would adopt the practice. Even trooper uniforms were treated with honor, and—like

American flags—when discarded they were collected and ceremoniously burned.

As the years passed, the New York State Police blended into the ho-hum activities of law enforcement and became an accepted part of the framework of state government. But that all changed in November 1957 when a New York state trooper named Edgar Croswell and his partner Vincent Vasisko became suspicious when the son of suspected crime figure Joseph Barbara began reserving motel rooms around the Binghamton, New York, area. Sergeant Croswell and Vasisko staked out Barbara's house in the small Southern Tier town of Apalachin, New York. They were surprised to find expensive automobiles parked around the house and in the street.

After they ran the license plates, they learned the vehicles belonged to who's who of organized crime. The Apalachin Conference, as it later became known, was attended by nearly all of the mafia crime bosses from the United States and Canada. On November 14 the New York State Police raided the meeting and created widespread panic among those in attendance. Mafia bosses were captured fleeing through the woods or stopped at a roadblock as they tried to escape. The arrests at Apalachin were the beginning of the end of a powerful, criminal cabal that had previously operated in near total secrecy. The work of Croswell and Vasisko had such a profound impact nationally that FBI Director J. Edgar Hoover was forced to restructure the FBI. That was a bitter pill for Hoover, who had for years denied the existence of crime families and ridiculed the idea of organized criminal activity. But, to his credit, he acknowledged his error and praised the work of the New York State Police.

New York state troopers were riding a wave of worldwide recognition, appreciation, and admiration. The next year they even scrapped their wool uniforms for a lighter, grey fabric with a black stripe extending down both pant legs. The black stripe was incorporated in remembrance of those troopers who gave their lives in the line of duty. From the beginning troopers were arrayed in purple ties with a band of purple ribbon stretched around the crown on their Stetson hats emblematic of the elite Praetorian Guard that once protected the Emperor Octavian.

Whether it was pride or arrogance, or both, or perhaps New York State's most elite police force had lived for too long on past accomplishments—whatever the reason, the unimaginable happened. Trooper David Harding, a seven-year veteran of the state police easily got an interview with the Central Intelligence Agency in Washington, DC. At some point in the interview, he was asked if he would violate the law to protect his country. He said he would and went on to explain in detail how he had falsified fingerprint evidence in cases where he knew the suspects were guilty. The CIA concluded the interview, thanked Trooper Harding, and politely showed him the door.

Trooper Harding returned to Troop C Sydney and for the next fourteen months went about his business as usual. The CIA had notified the Justice Department in March 1991 about Trooper Harding's admissions, but it was not until May 1992 that federal authorities passed that information to the New York State Police. No reason was given for the lapse, but court records would subsequently reveal that during that fourteen-month lapse two state troopers admitted to faking evidence in fifteen cases.

In the fall of 1992 Governor Mario M. Cuomo appointed Nelson E. Roth, a forty-three-year-old lawyer from Ithaca, New York, as a special prosecutor in the first evidence-planting case. Harding pleaded guilty to fabricating evidence in four cases and implicated others, including Trooper Robert M. Lishansky, who was sentenced to six to eighteen years in prison for fabricating evidence in twenty-one cases. After Troopers Harding and Lishansky, Lt. Craig D. Harvey, a sixteen-year veteran, pled guilty to fabricating evidence in three cases.

Special Prosecutor Roth initially thought he would only be on the case for a couple of months, but after two years Roth ran headfirst into a "purple and grey" wall of silence. In a February 14, 1995, newspaper article Prosecutor Roth said that he "continues to be surprised by the extent of the corruption," because some of their colleagues "have done everything they possibly can to frustrate the investigation."

In that same article Roth expressed frustration with the rank and file for failing to cooperate with the investigation. "We have experienced a tremendous amount of hostility, a refusal to cooperate and apparently an intentional undermining of the investigation," he said. "When we're done with the investigation, there may still be people working for the New York State Police who were involved with the tampering." Roth said that some troopers failed lie-detector tests and that others had taken the Fifth for fear of incriminating themselves. He also concluded that others, including troopers and supervisors, knew about, or even participated in, the faking of evidence and that corrupt troopers could escape prosecution.

James W. McMahon, the State Police Superintendent, said he would leave "no stone unturned" in the investigation, but at the same time conceded that he had not disciplined troopers for failing to cooperate. He said the reason he had not taken disciplinary action was because Prosecutor Roth had not asked him to. This once venerated law enforcement body reeled from charges of corruption and convictions and closed ranks to all outsiders.

Roth and his investigators examined thousands of cases across the state and concluded that from 1984 to 1992 state police investigators in Troop C Sydney had routinely faked fingerprint evidence. Mr. Roth said the guilty troopers would usually take a suspect's fingerprint from a police station booking card, or from an object the suspect touched, in one case a soft drink bottle, and swear they found the print at the crime scene.

On February 4, 1997, the *New York Times* reported the following: "Concluding a four-year investigation into the worst scandal in state police history, a special prosecutor said today that troopers were able to plant evidence routinely in criminal cases across a broad swath of rural New York because they had no fear of detection by supervisors."

Throughout this sorry episode there is one terrifying and perplexing truth: It remains troubling that Trooper Harding would not have been discovered had it not been for the high regard other government agencies held for the New York State Police. That included the CIA, who granted him an interview on the basis of a telephone call. Legal experts claim the New York state trooper scandal is one of the largest cases of evidence tampering in the United States. No longer could the elite of New York State law enforcement claim the highest degree of fairness, professionalism, and integrity, as their history so proudly boasted.

Chapter Fourteen

CALM BEFORE THE STORM

On November 5, 1992, Bucky Phillips returned to the sights, sounds, and smells of a piece of familiar geography. Every jail and every prison where Bucky had spent time had its own peculiar sounds and smells. Bucky was convinced he could be delivered blindfolded and under cover of darkness to any jail or prison in New York where he had spent time and immediately be able to identify the location just by its sounds and smells. He knew, for example, that Clinton's predominant sound was a heavy but dull thumping noise that permeated the entire facility whenever metal doors were opened and closed.

Auburn made a sharp, rattling sound and smelled of antiseptic and citrus, while Clinton smelled of subdued detergent. The smells common throughout New York's prison system were those odors that emanate from confined human beings. The malodorous result of an overflowing toilet was the same everywhere, and the scent of human odors was ever present. Bucky was processed at Elmira, spent time at Great Meadow, and two years at Clinton, but the majority of his sentence was spent at Auburn. It was at Auburn where Bucky spent some of his best time with the worst results.

Bucky was a model prisoner. He cooperated with prison officials and avoided confrontations with inmates. He occupied his time by working at various prison jobs and adopted a personal philosophy that required him to do his very best regardless of the assignment. He was mechanically inclined and possessed an insatiable curiosity about how things worked. He developed an uncanny ability to isolate the most complex problems into a simple series of easily understood operations, a trait inherited from his father.

The elder Phillips had taught Bucky about the internal combustion engine and about timing and the firing order of six- and eight-cylinder engines. Bucky picked up a lot from observation, but his father used simple, everyday illustrations to which a preschool-aged child could easily relate. Bucky understood electrical circuits based upon a simple illustration used by his father. For example, his father had told him to consider a car battery as a barn filled with cows. "The cows are electricity," his father once told him, and all that he needed to do to create electrical circuits was to move the cows around.

Bucky understood that if he wanted to move the cows from the barn to the hay meadow, he had to move the herd down a narrow, fenced lane and through a gate to the meadow. He easily understood the fenced lane represented a two-wire circuit and the gate to the meadow was an "on-off" switch. If he wanted the cows to go to the pond side of the meadow, he had to close one gate and open another. Later in life he would learn about transistors, resistors, capacitors, and diodes and understood how they functioned like a barbed wire fence that controlled cattle. He learned the language of their color-coded bands. He created prototype electronic circuits on a "breadboard" and became familiar with the terms and components necessary for "and," "or," or "nor" gates common in more complex electronic circuits.

As fate would decree, it would be his knowledge of electronics that would become an albatross forever tied to his prison record. It all began when Auburn replaced handheld radios with newer models and discarded the old units. The old units were smashed, but Bucky asked for and was granted permission to field strip a couple of the units for parts. He became immersed in a project that would occupy his every waking moment. He created electronic circuits on an imaginary "breadboard" during the day and would transfer them to paper in his cell at night. He divided the project into a series of simple circuits that he hoped would achieve the desired results. He discarded circuit after circuit and would go days at a time before he developed a circuit he thought would work.

Then, one Sunday morning nearly two months later and with a few minor on-the-spot adjustments, Bucky tuned in a frequency and heard a familiar but static-filled phrase: "Breaker, breaker one-nine," a voice crackled, "this is the Bread Man, anybody got their ears on?"

Bucky was absolutely elated. He had created by mental trial and error a citizen's band radio, a CB receiver capable of picking up six different channels. At the end of the day, Bucky would return to his cell and listen to truckers trying to find a route that bypassed the tolls on Interstate 90 between Rochester and Syracuse.

Two weeks later Bucky had added a transmitter to his radio and could actually communicate with the truckers. He seldom transmitted because most of the truckers were asking for directions around Auburn, or for the locations of any of the several wineries scattered throughout the region toward Ithaca. Bucky was unfamiliar with the immediate area and had only a brief glimpse of Auburn proper once when he was delivered to the prison from Elmira. Then, one day while he was working in the main reception area, he happened to pick up a Cayuga County visitors guide published by the Chamber of Commerce. Bucky leafed through the booklet and saw that it contained a map of Cayuga County and an inset for Auburn. He handed the book to one of the guards and asked if he could keep it. The guard flipped quickly through the book to check it for contraband and returned it to Bucky.

Bucky was proud of his creation. He had scavenged all the parts from discarded prison equipment, including the frequency crystals salvaged from obsolete hand-held radios. Prison officials knew what he was doing from the beginning, had given him every component for the radio, and allowed him to keep the Cayuga County tourist guide. Guards were aware of the CB, and several were impressed with Bucky's ingenuity and said as much. Then, one day while Bucky was on work assignment, ranking prison officials performed a routine inspection of the cellblock. In cell A-9-13 they confiscated a homemade radio capable of transmitting and a map of Cayuga County and the city of Auburn.

Prison employees on Bucky's cellblock realized after the fact that the CB radio was contraband, but had not considered Bucky's activities nefarious or any way improper. But prison officials declared the radio contraband and argued that Bucky's possession of a local map was evidence he was planning an escape. Bucky was brought up on charges. The Department of Corrections has a three-tiered disciplinary system. Depending upon the circumstances, even what appears to be a minor infraction can bring more serious charges against an inmate. DOC literature declares that there is no "one size fits all" approach and tossing a paper cup at a guard could be more severe depending upon the situation and circumstances. If the paper cup incident occurred in isolation the offense would be viewed differently from the cup being tossed in front of other inmates that could provoke a general disturbance.

The disciplinary system begins with Tier-I and deals with the most minor infractions. A sergeant who can impose a maximum penalty of loss of privileges for no more than thirteen days conducts Tier-I hearings. Tier-II and Tier-III hearings are reserved for the most serious offenses and are conducted by a lieutenant and a captain, respectively. Almost any charge that includes the words "escape," or "attempted escape" is considered serious, but Bucky pled guilty to a Tier-I offense and lost privileges for three days. Although he never knew for sure, Bucky suspected that some of the cellblock employees came to his defense and may have even been more harshly disciplined.

Although Bucky received minimum punishment for the contraband radio, the words "escape" and "attempted escape" remained on his record. That incident, paired with the 1991 handcuff key escape conviction from Chautauqua County, automatically added years to his incarceration. Bucky never had the opportunity to challenge the circumstances of either charge.

Not everything that happened to Bucky while he was locked behind the walls at Auburn was awful. Even before his last arrest, his future appeared tragically predictable to family and friends alike, but in 1995 Ralph Phillips and long-time friend Terry were married at Auburn barely three years into his sentence. From an early age both held a steadfast, friendly fondness for the other. They did the things of children; they held hands and skipped through the meadows, they climbed trees and played tag and hide-and-go-seek and played house together using bales of hay for furniture.

Terry thought Bucky was the bravest person she knew. He was not afraid of the dark. He did not whine and carry on about sleeping alone in the barn or coming home from the woods after sundown. She even liked that he could shoot a .22 and skin a rabbit. It was Terry who always had an encouraging word for Bucky Phillips. It was Terry who never criticized or complained about Bucky's boisterous pranks, but who unselfishly shared her sandwich, candy, or cookies with him. Those without professional license might have rightly speculated that Terry Gloss and Bucky Phillips loved each other from the very first time they played together. With that precious innocence available only in childhood Terry was just about the only person who accepted Bucky Phillips for what he was. She ached for him when others made fun of his heritage or his worn clothing. She consoled him when children ridiculed him for backing down from a school-yard fight. She smiled and clapped her youthful hands on those occasions when Bucky exceeded the expectations of others and listened intently when the youthful explorer told her about finding a bee tree in the wilderness. And she was convinced no one, not even grown-ups, knew more about cars than her young playmate. Time and circumstance separated the pair before Bucky was hauled off to reform school, but Terry Gloss cried secret tears when she first learned of her friend's plight.

Bucky saw Terry several times when he returned from Brookwood for the last time, and they kept in touch after he left school, but while they enjoyed the other's company, their relationship remained platonic. In the summer of 1991, however, their relationship turned romantic.

The couple would never live together as husband and wife and Bucky ultimately discouraged the prison marriage as being brutally unfair to Terry. Even though the marriage ended in 2003, the couple never divorced. Terry Phillips admitted that she spent a day with Bucky during his escape.

"He just called up," she said. "He wanted to know if he could come over." The couple went to the Laundromat, ran some errands, and went shopping at a supermarket. That was June 9, 2006. The next day, Bucky would shoot Trooper Sean Brown.

Chapter Fifteen

DREAMS AND THINGS

Bucky had at first been furious when he realized that the Chautauqua County handcuff key episode had not only cost him nearly a year in county jail but had also interfered with his early parole. He was not angry for serving time for his crimes; "do the crime, do the time" meant something to him. But he was angry for doing time that rightly should not have been his to do. The cops screwed him, and they knew it. Police, he believed, had a license to do the unconscionable, and prosecutors and judges turned a blind eye. He was seething, but he had observed during his very first year in max that inmates who took their anger out on prison property or prison officials were always big losers. Bucky kept his anger in check when around officials, but he was less inclined to spare his fellow inmates from his outbursts.

Not long after he had learned his parole had been extended, and at a time during which he was struggling with his anger over the injustice, Bucky was paired on a work assignment with an aging inmate to open a new flowerbed in the prison's main courtyard. The old man, who was a jailhouse philosopher of sorts, convinced Bucky that he could not change a corrupt policeman by hating him. "Your hate will never be a heavy load for the police officer. Your hate is only a heavy load that you alone drag around."

Bucky bristled at the thought and mumbled something about respect.

The grizzled old man listened attentively to Bucky's carping for nearly a week but shook him to the core during a morning break from the work detail. He told Bucky that respect should not be expected from those to whom it is not given. "Every time you steal from someone you disrespect a human being." The old man spoke softly, but his words carried a sharp sting. "You're both thieves," he added. "You stole property; the cop stole part of your life." The old man wiped his brow with his shirtsleeve and continued to break up clods of earth in the new flowerbed with pain-filled hands gnarled and stiff from arthritics. "A thief should not ask his victim for respect, only for forgiveness after you have made him whole."

The next day Bucky was given a new work assignment in the kitchen, considered a prime job in a maximum-security prison, a position that Bucky's good behavior around police officials had earned him. He never saw the old man again, but the old man's words jarred him into the reality of his situation and made his life less contentious. Several months later one of the general population inmates said he'd heard the old man had been released to a nursing home somewhere down state.

In November 2005 Ralph James Phillips walked for first time into the twenty-first century as a free and very happy man. He was assigned a parole officer and given a bus ticket to a halfway house in Western New York. He was forty-three years old, mentally alert, and physically fit, but he was also acutely aware of his societal deficits for having spent twenty of the last twenty-three years behind bars. He only had bits and pieces of life experiences. As a result, Bucky became a man without an anchor in his own generation, a man lacking generational identity. Although most of Bucky's life had so far been one of captivity, interrupted by brief spurts of freedom, he was confident he would adjust.

Bucky found himself living at the Buffalo Halfway House on Glenwood Avenue. The halfway house was actually more than a three-story building with "three hots and a cot," as some former residents describe the facility. Located two blocks from a Buffalo Rapid Transit Station and three miles from downtown, the Buffalo Halfway House is a nonprofit organization that contracts to provide housing and meals as well as counseling services and around-the-clock supervision and accountability for parolees, parole violators, and court-ordered referrals. The house offers laundry and kitchen facilities that can accommodate fifty-one residents.

Life at the halfway house was awkward for Bucky, but he managed the best he could without a car. Living in Buffalo without a car was more than a little inconvenient. If he had an 8:00 a.m. appointment, he could call a cab if he had discretionary money, or he could leave an hour early and walk two blocks to the Utica Street metro station. Bucky was so unfamiliar with transfers and bus routes that he hardly ever arrived for an appointment at the proper time. That became a source of frustration for Bucky and a concern for his counselors, but such incidents should have been expected. Bucky suspected that it was the personal hostility of one particular counselor that resulted in the parole violation and his return to jail after hardly two months of freedom.

Bucky's parole violation baffled nearly everyone, but no one was more perplexed than Bucky himself. He readily admits that he was angry about being sent back to jail simply on the word of his counselor. He did not feel there was a single good reason for being violated by this counselor, a young woman in her twenties, and for his return to jail. At first, he thought it was a joke, and then he thought she would be overruled. She told Bucky she had received numerous complaints and feared he presented a physical threat to some of his family members. He and the young counselor had a heated exchange over that very subject. "Look," he once told her, "if I wanted to harm my family I could have done that at Christmas. I was standing at the table carving a turkey with a big knife. I didn't scare anyone."

The counselor told Bucky that it had also been reported that he had boasted about hating Black people. He was flabbergasted. Bucky did not live in a color-conscious world in a strictly racial sense. Even though his antagonists in reform school were mostly urban Black kids, he never once considered their assaults racial. Bucky had observed that the bad asses at Industry and Brookwood would have beat up a Black kid as quickly as any other detainee. They were punks, not because of color, but because they were punks. Despite that observation, Bucky acknowledged there was more segregation in a maximum-security prison than in the outside world. Nearly every inmate recognized that prison authorities used segregation as an unofficial, but effective means of control.

"Even if I were a sheet-draped racist," he argued in an effort to persuade his counselor to logically consider that he knew his parole officer was Black. "Why would I risk insulting my PO? Think about it. Why would I do that?" He pleaded, but his pleas fell on deaf ears. As had happened so many times in the past, in January 2006 Bucky was confined to the Erie County Correctional Facility.

"I've paid time for my crime." He shook his head slightly sideways during our interview and lowered his voice. "But my violation just on the word of my halfway house counselor was wrong. It was unjust." He raised his head and stared intently at me through the plexiglass partition and recounted in rapid succession his list of grievances—his lingering resentment over the handcuff key incident, his failed stay at the Buffalo Halfway House, his confrontation with a young counselor. "After twenty years, seventeen in full-max. After that, they sent me to a halfway house, a fake jail. What for? To teach me how act in civilian life?" He called the halfway house program a joke and declared it a total waste of time.

"I needed help alright," Bucky conceded. "I could find a job on my own, but without a car, how am I going to get to work? I could find a place to live, but how can I pay rent? I can't even get my gas and electricity turned on. I didn't come out of DOCs with a severance package, and I sure wasn't in the state retirement system." Instead of practical help from the halfway house, he argued, he got group sessions with drug addicts who talked about staying clean and sober. Bucky claimed to have never used drugs. He participated in counseling sessions about adjusting to the outside that were run by people who did not have any idea what it was like to have been on the inside. "Instead of the state spending money on halfway houses, they could spend a little up front on necessities. Give a guy responsibility up front and help him financially until he gets on his feet."

"There was absolutely no reason for me to be violated," Bucky insisted. "I was in jail for a disagreement, an argument?" He paced back and forth but never raised his voice. After all, he explained, he'd just finished thirteen years in a maximum-security prison and that was right behind three years of hard max time. "Twenty of the last twenty-three years in jail should account for something." At the very least, he concluded, those twenty years should have outweighed an argument with a twenty-five-year-old counselor.

There could be little doubt that Bucky was angry at being returned to jail. He had not committed a crime, he had not stolen a car, or even pilfered a single cigarette. Once again Bucky encountered the capricious authority of strangers and was returned to jail at the personal whim of another person. While he was sitting in the Erie County Correctional Facility, he tried to think of why anyone would want him back in jail. They either viewed him, Bucky thought, as an irredeemable criminal incapable of reform, or his counselor might have personally disliked him or even feared him. Try as he might, he could not come up with a reasonable explanation, but there was one recurring scenario so farfetched that even he thought it outrageous.

The youthful female counselor reminded him of a woman he once dated. The woman he dated had a daughter that in 1990 was around eleven years old. The age math worked, and his young female counselor shared the same given name. But there were other mannerisms and coincidences that triggered distant memories. Her smile was a template of the smile of the woman he had dated years before. She twirled stray strands of hair above her right ear with her thumb and forefinger like the woman he knew. She even had that funny way of cocking her head slightly sideways and smiling coyly whenever she twisted her hair. But it was her melodious laughter that reached a certain lilt and lingered in the air that so fascinated Bucky. He never once thought of confronting the young woman. Some deep-seated, chivalrous restraint convinced Bucky that to bring up the subject would have been a betrayal of the woman he once dated. And, he thought, all of the similarities could be a string of coincidences.

"I could've served my twenty and walked out with no halfway house, no counselors, no parole officers, and no parole." Despite his obvious disappointment Bucky's voice was free from malice. "I could've told them all to screw off. I should have stayed for twenty." Finding himself sitting in an Erie County jail on the flimsiest of reasons for parole violation must have been a blow for Bucky, but that wasn't the motivation for what he did next.

If Bucky's parole violation was baffling to his friends and family, even total strangers were mystified at his escape from the Erie County Correctional Facility on April 2, 2006, with four days remaining on his violation. Fox News reported that he escaped because he feared going back to jail. Other accounts held that Bucky was unaware of the calendar, and still others claimed he had been deliberately misled.

The reality was that Bucky did not fear returning to jail; he'd actually had second thoughts about being released on parole. Although he leaned heavily against the partition and slumped wearily into his chair, he managed a genuinely warm smile. "No. As far as I know, I wasn't misled. I knew I only had four days left."

"What?" I wanted to leap from my chair. For the first time during our lengthy interview Bucky's answer was totally unexpected.

"I wasn't four days away from going home." Bucky explained. "I was four days from appearing before Judge Cummings for disposition." Bucky lowered his head and vigorously rubbed his face with both hands. "Besides automatic revocation, she was going to send me to shock incarceration for ninety days." Shock incarceration was a program that first appeared in the early eighties. Similar to military boot camps, the program was strict, physical, and demanding.

"How did you know that?" I asked.

Bucky would not tell me how he had learned of the judge's decision other than to say he had received the message from someone he trusted. "All of a sudden, it just hit me," Bucky shrugged. "People will believe what they want." Bucky felt humiliated, and the thought of spending ninety days in shock incarceration was the ultimate degradation. Regardless, Bucky understood the math. Chances are, he reasoned, he would be tried again as a habitual offender. "If it were a simple revocation, seven years; I could handle that and walk away."

But Bucky was convinced the shock incarceration sentence was a deliberate trap. "They were setting me up to fail." He explained that after the ninety days he would have still had automatic revocation. Bucky said he could have done the seven, but even the most trivial violation during shock would add years to his sentence. "I would have gone back with a new parole date, plus they would have hit me again as a predicate felon with a fresh ten. I'm not doing seven. I'm doing minimum seventeen, but more likely twenty-five." Bucky fidgeted nervously in his chair and shuffled his feet back and forth. "If I live to be eighty. What's that? Ten to twelve years short of a life sentence?"

Bucky had been emotionally torn after he'd learned of Judge Cumming's pending decision. It became obvious that he could not continue on his present course. And it was equally obvious that he was limited to a choice between dreadful options. The thought kept turning over in his mind. Could he trust the system? He said he really wanted to believe that he would do the shock plus seven. But, in the end he knew that would not happen. Later that night as he laid on his bunk in the solitude and sounds of an overcrowded human warehouse, his world was suddenly still. In that most unlikely setting, Ralph James Phillips experienced a brilliant moment of clarity that might not have been a meeting with God, but was a glimpse of eternity.

His entire life played through his mind in sharply focused, three-dimensional imagery. He saw his father and mother in the smallest detail; the way they walked, talked, and smiled. He saw his brother and sisters and saw his younger self and the barn and the wilderness all in a colorful panorama. He recognized all his crimes and every arrest and felt the unbearable summer heat and the unrelenting winter chill of solitary confinement. In that moment of clarity, the unambiguous doctrine of the wilderness returned as the standard measurement for all the events of Bucky's life.

Suddenly his heart beat faster and he could feel blood rush through his weary frame. He looked for the first time at his past and saw his future in gruesome detail. His existence had become nothing more than a slow and agonizing wearing away of flesh and bone, a piece of slowly rotting refuse discarded without hope for a better world.

Flawed humanity seeks perfection, and dreams of a mountaintop experience where peace and justice and goodness and immortality exist. For the Greeks it was Mount Olympus, for the Hebrews Mount Sinai, and Mount Fuji for the Japanese. For Ernest Hemingway it was a leopard frozen for eternity in the snows of Kilimanjaro. For Ralph James Phillips it was a fleeting glimpse of a better life, something between his troubled juvenile years and his adult incarcerations. Ralph Phillips wanted to return to that time and that familiar geography of his youth where all creatures of the wilderness were guided by the simple doctrine of survival, and dreams were always fresh and new.

Wilderness survival was harsh, free from entanglements peculiar to the human race, and mercifully precise. In that indescribable instant, Ralph James Phillips experienced total peace and remarkable clarity. Even though he saw only a faint, flickering light at the end of a very long tunnel, he made a life-altering decision. He was absolutely certain; there was no turning back. He wanted to make it to that mountaintop whether it was in Canada or Alaska or Brazil or Timbuktu.

As much as he would like to be near his family in Chautauqua County, he knew he could never pull it off. The next best option was to run far away. That would mean he would have to surrender all physical contact with his family, but that was going to happen regardless. Canada might be an option, he thought, maybe even Alaska. He could go south, Mexico was out, but once during yard talk, he'd heard that if an escaped con married a Brazilian woman he could not be extradited. Alaska seemed a likely getaway. He imagined that in Alaska a person might get a fresh start with no questions asked, and in the age of the automobile even a mediocre mechanic could find work. Bucky could think of a lot of places to go, but the problem was getting there.

Chapter Sixteen

APRIL 2, 2006—ESCAPE

scaping from the Erie County Correctional Facility in Alden, New York, had been much easier than Bucky had imagined. On Sunday, April 2, 2006, at 5:00 a.m., Ralph Phillips was one of sixteen inmates who reported to work in the kitchen. Bucky went directly into a storage room, climbed on top of a walk-in cooler that extended nearly to the ceiling, and squeezed through a two-foot-square hole to the roof. He scampered across the roof, tripped an alarm, jumped to the ground, passed a security post. and was later seen on surveillance tape crossing a visitors' parking lot before disappearing down Walden Avenue. For the next 161 days, Ralph Phillips embarked upon a rambling journey of crime and survival. He ultimately became the subject of a bizarre manhunt fueled by a bitter, personal rivalry between a state police commander and a fleeing felon.

Bucky was a skilled wilderness survivalist, an expert car thief, and wily in the ways of jailhouse life. But his greatest asset was the ability to recognize when the convergence of chance and circumstance created opportunities to alter the course of events. In that regard, Bucky had a profound appreciation of how institutional lore drove prison life on both sides of the bars. Bucky embraced prison lore and was amused how excited prison officials were when an inmate conformed and how eager they became over the prospects of a new remedial program. That was all good, he believed, the con acquired new skills, but from the con's standpoint his greatest achievement was the acquisition of good days that reduced his time served.

Although many cons did not have much in the way of education, some did. There were even those who had college degrees. But the real classroom work for a con took place in the cellblock or prison yard. Teachers were as tenured as the length of their sentences, some were old men, some could barely read or write, convicts all, but they were all repositories of knowledge, and each individual possessed unique abilities.

There was an old man at Auburn, a medical doctor who, not surprisingly, was called "Doc." While cons seldom spoke of their own crimes, Bucky once heard that Doc had killed his own wife. But that didn't really matter inside. Doc could tell you how to sniff salt water up your nostrils to relieve sinus infections and how to treat and stitch wounds and gashes. He could even tell you how to remove a bullet, provided the wound was superficial. He could also explain the distinction between the simple and more serious of wounds. He suggested a variety of over-the-counter drugs that would fight infections, relieve pain, and emphasized that washing wounds with clean water was equally beneficial. "Remember," he would smile, "it's more important to wash your hands before you take a piss."

Another con was a certified public accountant who was serving time for money laundering for big hitters in the drug trade. Although he didn't know an "airhead" from an "all-American" when it came to drugs, if he liked you, he would tell you nearly everything about the business of the drug business. There was an older prisoner from Pennsylvania who Bucky remembered used to work in the Pennsylvania woods splitting firewood before the days of portable, hydraulic splitters. He instructed Bucky on how to use black powder, explosive cords, and dynamite to blow things up.

He explained how he would drive a cone-shaped, hollow wedge with small holes down its side into a stubborn stump or a block of hardwood, then fill it with just the right amount of powder. He would string a fuse from one of the holes in the wedge, light it, and step back out of the way. "Nine times out of ten," he said, "the chunk would split smack down the middle. Hardly make a sound."

Bucky spent the better part of one summer walking around the yard with the man, learning how to use powder and dynamite to blow up everything from trees to concrete walls to metal doors. He told Bucky that all matter has a weak spot; manmade concrete has cavities and seams, even stainless steel is flawed under a microscope. "That's what you have to know. Look for the flaws, and it's always easier to go with the grain."

There was another con, a counterfeiter who copied everything from driver's licenses to passports to currency. While the hard-core cons were treacherous and could not be relied on for anything, there was a fraternity of sorts among the "honest" cons. Counted among the honest cons were those imprisoned for crimes of passion, or the "paper" cons who were caught up in nonviolent transgressions. Bucky discovered that cons like that could be relied upon even when they were out of prison.

They wouldn't pull a job with you, but they wouldn't ask questions either; they didn't want to know what you were up to. But most of them could be counted on to give you a few bucks or tell you where to get a new ID, Social Security card, or a passport. They knew where you could be put up for a day or two, and they would not turn you in. Bucky would have naturally gravitated to those teachers if for nothing but pure entertainment. Over the years Bucky had developed a remarkable facility to keep track of their whereabouts when they left prison. He was grateful for their association and realized now more than ever that if he was going to flee to Alaska or Timbuktu that sooner or later he would need the services of such men.

Bucky understood that the sociology of every prison changed with the levels of incarceration. A minimum-security facility tended to turn over its population every three years, medium security turned over in less than ten, and except for lifers, a full-max turned over in ten to twenty. Although the Erie County Correctional Facility is a state-owned prison, it operates as a county jail. The population consists of those awaiting trial, inmates serving one year or less, parole violators, and revenue-producing federal prisoners from the US Marshal's Service.

Unlike prisons with longer-serving populations, prisons with quick turnovers of inmates retain very little in the way of knowledge passed to succeeding populations by tradition or anecdote. But an unintentional and rare bit of folklore was the reason Bucky was working in the kitchen in the first place. His presence there was the result of a casual conversation he chanced to overhear between two prisoners. It happened during a break on a work detail when a repeat offender spoke of two cons who had been busted for having a whiskey still on top of a cooler inside a storage room in the kitchen.

"This one dude was gored every day," the repeat offender said, delighted in the fact that nearly all inmates knew about this guy's drunkenness, but the staff was too busy to notice. He said it wasn't until four or five guys kept getting "really shit-faced" that it caught the attention of the brass. "The brass put on a full-court press," he chortled. He said the place was turned upside down and the still was discovered after some boxes were shoved aside on top of the cooler in a kitchen storage room. "What really pissed them off," the storyteller shook his head in amusement. "They found a working bar outfitted with paper cups and plastic chairs on top of that cooler. Even found a fucking ice bucket. The keepers were so mad," he laughed aloud, "that they locked the place down for a week."

This tiny fragment of prison lore that seemed no more than a humorous exchange between inmates tantalized Bucky's ear. To a seasoned inmate even the tiniest bit of information was revealing. The story confirmed what he suspected, the facility was overcrowded and understaffed. He also recognized that the natural consequences of such conditions resulted in lax discipline, low morale, and compromised security throughout the facility. Although Bucky had yet to devise a method of escape, all he needed was a convenient opportunity. That seemingly casual conversation drove Bucky to get a job in the kitchen.

Bucky also knew the most sought-after job in any prison was in the kitchen and that he needed to get in front of a long waiting line. Several days later he filed a grievance complaining about the quality and content of his food. He claimed his scrambled eggs were ice cold and stuck fast to the bottom of his serving tray. He said his toast was overdone and that he was deliberately shorted on cheese. He knew his grievance was bullshit, his jailers knew the grievance was bullshit, but he also knew that his harried keepers would rather settle the issue than have it move forward. Bucky reluctantly suggested that he might be willing to take a kitchen job in exchange for tearing up his grievance. "At least the food will be warm," he grumbled and grudgingly accepted the offer that he almost certainly knew would be forthcoming.

On his second day at work in the kitchen, Bucky was sent to the storage room to retrieve some food from the cooler. He was surprised to find that the top of the cooler had not been enclosed to block access, especially after the still and open bar had been discovered. He hurriedly climbed atop the appliance and found that he had enough room to sit upright. Aside from the dust, the first thing he noticed was a small separation, about six inches long, at the seam in the metal ceiling.

The ceiling drooped slightly at the middle point of the separation almost enough for Bucky to stick the tip of his little finger through the opening. Later, he would lie flat on his back and pry at the seam with an eight-inch-long, straight-edge screwdriver that was stored in the kitchen. He was careful not to arouse suspicion. There were days when he didn't work on the seam, but when he did, he made sure he spent no more than five minutes atop the cooler. And he always remembered to replace the screwdriver in the same drawer near the dishwasher.

Bucky proved to be a hard worker in a kitchen environment that was constantly under pressure to provide nearly three thousand meals a day. The Commissioner's investigation concluded that Bucky was a quiet inmate who used his mechanical skills to keep a variety of appliances and assorted pieces of kitchen gadgets operating smoothly during hours of peak demand. The investigation found that he was so competent in completing his assigned tasks that food service personnel assigned him to a wide range of kitchen duties. He gained the trust of the kitchen staff, and it was not uncommon to see him wandering unsupervised throughout the kitchen area brandishing an assortment of hand tools.

Bucky kept working the ceiling separation until he had a nearly two-inch gap. On the morning of his escape, he used a commercial can opener that was a one-inch square metal bar nearly twenty inches long for a pry bar. Although it took a lot of physical strength to exploit the metal ceiling, breaching the roof with a screwdriver was daunting. Bucky frantically gouged at the gypsum board roof and had to pause several times to catch his breath. At one point he thought he might have to abort the effort, but he discovered that as he made the hole larger it became easier to chip away larger chucks of the heavy gypsum slab. He nearly panicked when he tried to penetrate the rubber membrane with the screwdriver. The slack in the membrane limited the puncture to the exact size of the screwdriver blade. Bucky had to use the top of his head to push the exposed membrane tightly upward and used the screwdriver and a folded can lid like a knife blade to rip and tear open the roof. Bucky left the can opener, and several can lids atop the cooler, but he kept the screwdriver.

On the morning of the escape, and after fifteen minutes, a civilian cook noticed that Bucky was not performing his assigned task and began a search of the kitchen. A more extensive search by kitchen workers failed to locate inmate Phillips, and he was reported missing to prison officials. Records show that at 5:40 a.m. the facility went into a full emergency lockdown for a head count that was immediately followed by interior and exterior searches. At 6:12 a.m. the sheriff's patrol and Troop A of the state police were notified of the escape, and it was an hour later, at 7:12 a.m., before search teams arrived and extended the outer search perimeter five miles from the prison.

Early the next morning, a 1997 Ford Taurus was reported stolen on Lapp Road in Wyoming County ten miles from the Erie County Correctional Facility. On that same morning the commissioner of the New York State Department of Corrections launched an investigation into the escape of Ralph Phillips. Six days later the Ford Taurus was found abandoned on Burnham Road near Bucky's boyhood home in Chautauqua County. The investigation would last four more months.

In August 2007 the commissioner released the results of his investigation titled *In The Matter of the Escape of Ralph Phillips an Inmate of the Erie County Correctional Facility.* The fifty-four-page report was scathing in its condemnations and cited a serious failure of managerial and operational policy so severe that it rose to the level of "willful negligence and professional incompetence." The report concluded that the facility was egregiously overcrowded and dangerously understaffed, which resulted in the intentional abandonment of mandated security posts.

The convergence of circumstance and chance played a powerful role in Bucky's escape and continued flight from the Erie County Correctional Facility as evidenced by the commissioner's report. Citing directly from the report, "While traversing the facility roof, Phillips triggered a valid, (later verified), roof mounted motion detector alarm. Based on an independent review of the facility's digital alarm records, this alarm was acknowledged and deactivated by facility control room staff without notifying appropriate personnel. The rooftop microwave motion detection system was in poor repair and the subject of multiple malfunction complaints by staff that were confirmed by the private electrical contractor following Phillip's escape but were never addressed by the facility administration or the Sheriff's Department. At the time of the escape, it did, however, detect Phillips on the roof of the facility. . . ."

The commissioner's report cited another serious deficiency, a security measure Bucky could not have known that would have thwarted his escape if the facility had been properly staffed. After Bucky jumped from the roof, "video surveillance cameras indicate that Phillips then crossed the visitor's parking lot and proceeded toward Walden Avenue, bypassing an outdoor security post while the post officer was on a break but not relieved." The guard was on a bathroom break inside the prison. The investigation cites specific breakdowns in procedural policy, but failures to respond during the first minutes to the roof alarm and being chronically understaffed effectively gave Bucky a two-hour head start. During that time, Bucky had trekked far beyond the five-mile extended search area.

After he cleared the prison grounds, Bucky ran east on Walden Avenue for nearly a mile before he ducked into a wooded area and followed the railroad tracks for a short distance. Bucky was lightly dressed; the air was cold, but he was sweating. He had to keep moving. If he slowed down, he would chill to the bone. As the morning kept pushing back the night, Bucky was keenly aware that he had to avoid being spotted. He continued south and east and remained secluded in a narrow band of woods but had to abruptly change his course sometime later when he accidentally blundered into the Town of Alden Memorial Park.

He made his way through a patchwork of houses that quickly turned into overgrown building lots surrounded by scraggly undergrowth, stunted pine trees, and rough terrain. He managed to stay out of sight in the thin woods, but he was hungry and cold. "You can't imagine what it's like to be on the run. Looking back," he said, "that first day was really bad." He even tried to scratch out a nest of leaves and pine needles to curl up in for an hour, but the ground was too damp and cold.

"I bet I walked fifteen miles," he said. "My feet had blisters on blisters." By late afternoon on that first day, a tired, cold, and thoroughly miserable escaped convict had unsuccessfully scavenged garbage cans and overturned rocks in a streambed looking for crawfish. It was Bucky's nose that led him to an upscale neighborhood that stretched along the shores of a small lake. "Lucky for me," Bucky smiled. "Some dude had cabin fever and was rushing the back yard grilling season." Bucky pilfered two partially cooked hamburger patties and a hot dog from a momentarily unattended backyard grill. The food gave him a temporary boost, but of more importance to Bucky was approaching nightfall and automobiles available for the taking.

As dawn approached on the third morning a cold shiver spread through his body and his heart pounded, but his current condition brought a smile to his face. He was free. He had made it home. It was that time of year in Chautauqua County when fragile rays from an infant springtime sun challenged winter's grip. Gradual warming temperatures struggled against dreary, gray skies and left patches of dirty snow scattered across the landscape. There was an uncomfortable bite in the air.

Ralph "Bucky" Phillips sat astride the decaying remains of a hemlock tree felled by the wind, and the faint echo of a dog barking in the distance pulled his head toward the sound. He watched as retreating shadows uncovered sights and shapes and sounds of a familiar, but at once strange, geography. Landscapes and landmarks that had been so familiar in his youth appeared smaller through the eyes of an adult. Objects that had once seemed separated by great, sweeping expanses had remarkably closed the distance. The vast wetlands that he knew so well as a youth were now little more than a debris-filled, weed-choked patch of rotting vegetation.

The cast-off remains from higher animal forms replaced tree branches and small saplings that once had been meticulously arranged to create a beaver dam. Instead, a refrigerator lay tilted on its side and was partially submerged in the middle of what had been living quarters for a family of beavers. Several abandoned automobile tires accompanied by an assortment of plastic and Styrofoam containers bracketed the faded, avocado-colored kitchen appliance where clear, clean water once created a pleasant melody of trickles. And the plastic-cased remains of a television set stared grotesquely through its shattered, glass picture tube in stark defiance of time and the elements.

Bucky straightened his upper body, squeezed his shoulders together tightly, and slid slightly sideways on the moss-covered log. His sharp, dark eyes instinctively followed a solitary crow that flew silently above the treetops until it dissolved into the morning light. His ears detected the faint sounds of a tree leaf, dried and wrinkled from the ravages of winter as it bounced lightly against barren tree branches on its way to the ground.

Bucky clinched the filtered end of a cigarette between his teeth and drew warm smoke deep into his lungs. He allowed the smoke to escape slowly from his nostrils and focused his attention on a small trickle of water that sought its way around a small, mud dam in a drainage ditch. The dam had been created after he had fallen backwards and landed hard on his ass when he had tried to jump to the high side of the ditch.

He remembered when, as a boy, he had hunted these same woods for small game. He recalled his father had slapped him hard with the back of his hand for "gut shooting" and killing a black squirrel in this same stand of trees with a single shot from a .22-caliber rifle. The shot ruined most of the meat, and his father tossed the remains to the dogs. But Bucky learned his lesson well enough to know never to bring home a gut-shot squirrel again. He would simply clean the animal as best he could and roast it over a slow fire rather than carry it home.

With time and practice, and before his tenth birthday, Bucky Phillips could kill even the smallest red squirrel in the highest of hemlocks with a single headshot. He even remembered when the remains of the ancient hemlock tree he was sitting on once provided support for one end of a snow laden lean-to and stood in bold defiance of man and nature. And he knew the dog barking in the distance was nearly a mile away at a local dairy farm.

Bucky denied that he had had any direct, outside assistance in the escape, but he also refused to disclose his exact whereabouts for the first few days. "I'd like to tell you that I stayed in motels and ate in fancy restaurants when I first got out, but I didn't." He acknowledged he had help during the first day or two of his escape. A smile tugged at the corners of Bucky's mouth and evolved into a hearty chuckle. "I was so tired. I ached all over. I was so dirty and felt so scruffy." He admitted to emptying the hot water tank in a long, luxurious shower and sleeping the entire night and late into morning in a real bed. He adamantly refused to reveal his benefactors, insisting, however, that his family never once provided assistance.

"That asshole Manning," he said referring to Major Michael Manning, the local state police commander, "brutalized my family, my daughter, from the get-go. He knew damn well I would never involve my family. He knew it, but did it anyway." A frown covered Bucky's face, and he twisted uncomfortably in his chair. "There are child molesters serving life that didn't harm their victims as bad as Manning hurt my daughter and my grandkids. The rotten son of a bitch had CPS snatch her kids and put them in foster care. She didn't do anything to deserve that, and her kids sure as hell didn't. What did those kids ever do to that prick?"

Although he repeatedly denied having a network of friends and family willing to help him at a moment's notice, he did admit to having "three or four" friends he could count on. "Sometimes," he said, "a friend can be closer than family."

Bucky seemed to still be astonished as he recalled how events unfolded. He told me there were several instances when he was only seconds away from being apprehended, or even shot. "I had a lot more luck than skill."

Regardless of luck or skill, the first few days of his escape were his best days. After that, time became a relentless blur of fast-paced movement and events. Perhaps it was self-preservation, or a deeply embedded personal code acquired as a consequence of nearly a lifetime of confinement that compelled Ralph Phillips to remain noncommittal regarding crimes for which he was accused but never convicted.

When confronted, he usually smiled, shrugged, chuckled, or laughed aloud and left it to the listener to draw their own conclusions. During his 161 days on the run, the state police associated him with, or suspected him of, committing nearly seventy crimes exclusive of wounding two state troopers and killing another. He was directly associated with or suspected of stealing more than thirty vehicles with an equal number of burglaries and may have stolen more than a hundred firearms.

There is no question that Bucky used the 1997 Ford Taurus stolen on the day of his escape from Erie County for at least five or six days. The car was found April 9, 2006, undamaged and abandoned on a heavily traveled road near his boyhood home. Two days later on April 11, police suspect Bucky stole a white utility van in the town of Little Valley in Cattaraugus County, New York. The vehicle was found a week later abandoned nearly thirty miles away in a parking lot in Bradford, Pennsylvania. The state police suspect that the very next day, April 12, Bucky stole a 1991 Ford Ranger extended-cab pickup truck on Limestone Run in the town of Carrollton. The pickup was never recovered. On that same day there was a report of a Dan Wesson .357 magnum stolen from a residence between 9:00 and 11:00 a.m. when the owner was away. At this point Bucky injected a bit of skepticism into the record.

"Look at the geography," he said gesturing with his hands palms up. He explained that it is less than thirty miles from Little Valley in New York to Bradford, Pennsylvania. "From Bradford back to Limestone, fifteen miles." Bucky's face takes on a confused look. "Why would I drive to Bradford just to abandon a car and double back to Limestone to steal another one? What's the difference if I abandon a car in Limestone or a few miles away in Bradford?"

The next day of his escape would have been a Thursday, and Bucky had waited until after nightfall to steal a 1983 Suzuki motorcycle from a residence on South Nine Mile Road near St. Bonaventure University. Bucky preferred to travel the roads less traveled and had followed the river road south and east from the village of Allegany to Portville. The trip had been uneventful, and he had covered the ten miles in less than twenty minutes. The next morning, Friday, April 14, 2006, police had investigated a break-in at J & R Auto in Portville. The front door had been pried open and $400 in cash taken. The auto store may have been a crime of convenience, because immediately next door to J & R Auto was Southern Tier Polaris, a snowmobile dealer. The door had been pried open, but the only thing taken was a black motorcycle helmet.

"Hey, man. What can I say?" Bucky smiled and shrugged his shoulders. "New York has a helmet law." Although the crime appeared to be a whimsical misadventure, Bucky had realized that riding a motorcycle without a helmet would attract the attention of even the most inattentive lawman. But what happened next was at once unusual and grotesquely strange.

"The problem with being on the run," Bucky stressed without amusement or malicious satisfaction, "is being on the run." He said there was hardly an hour he could call his own. "Even when you sleep, you don't relax." He said during the entire episode he experienced either severe bouts of stress or rushes of adrenalin. "Either one is exhausting." The feverish pace of his days on the run had left Bucky exhausted and desperately in need of a few hours of seclusion and uninterrupted sleep.

Ancient trails and campsites created by the rugged conditions of Native American life remain part of the wilderness charm and appeal of Cattaraugus County. Everything from ramshackle hunting camps to elaborate camping trailers to luxurious seasonal residences are deeply submerged in the region's vast and uncompromising topography. Hungry Hollow Road meanders across a narrow valley between Oyer Mountain and Smith Mountain and presents some of the area's most challenging terrain. Bucky was in and out of both stores in Portville in less than ten minutes. It took him almost that long to get the helmet properly adjusted on his head as he sped away on the Suzuki with Hungry Hollow Road his destination.

Even though Bucky knew exactly where he was going, the twenty-mile trip took nearly forty-five minutes. It was nearly four in the morning when he arrived at a deserted seasonal residence. The structure was sequestered behind a circuitous driveway and would have been completely hidden from the road when trees were in foliage. The door had a good lock, and Bucky had to remove part of the frame, which damaged the door around the deadbolt. Once inside, he was surprised to find the house was in working order. Bucky toured the house and, satisfied its owners would not show up before the weekend, stretched out fully clothed on a sofa in the front room. He covered his body with a knitted afghan that was spread over the back of the couch and fell asleep.

Bucky slept soundly and it was past noon before he awoke. He hadn't eaten since a late breakfast the day before and he was hungry. Bucky let the hot water run in the bathroom, but it never warmed up. He splashed his face with cold water and brushed his teeth. He was preoccupied with searching for food and didn't hear the approaching car until it was too late. Bucky ran to the door and saw a man standing by his open car door staring with a puzzled look on his face at the Suzuki parked by the side of the house.

Both men stared at each other in stunned silence. Bucky was first to speak. "Are you the owner?"

The man nodded and walked slowly toward Bucky.

"My name is Ralph Phillips. Bucky Phillips. You may have heard. I escaped from Erie County. I'm not here to hurt anybody or steal anything. I just needed a place to crash for a few hours." Bucky felt foolish and more than a little sheepish and all he could do was blurt out the truth. "The cops are looking for me."

The man walked closer and pointed to the busted door. "You broke my door."

Bucky was relieved that the man remained calm and unthreatening.

"I did. I broke it and I'll pay you for it." Bucky retrieved the wads of bills he had shoved in his pants pocket. He quickly counted out several bills and shoved them toward the man. "Here's two hundred. Will that be enough?"

The owner took the money and nodded.

"There's nothing else wrong. I didn't trash your house. Look around. I'll make everything right." Bucky felt he should be more convincing. "Look," he said, "I'll give you my guns. You can keep them, sell them, or give them to the cops. I don't care." Bucky pulled two pistols from his backpack and laid them on the kitchen table.

The man looked around and finally spoke. "Did you find anything to eat?

"No."

"We don't usually keep much food around. It draws squirrels and mice."

Bucky nodded. "Look," he said. "I'm going to leave. I know you'll do what you have to do. You'll call the cops. But, man, I'd sure appreciate it if you could give me a little time before you make that call." Bucky shoved his arms through the straps on his backpack, adjusted the helmet snugly on his head, and fired up the Suzuki. Once he hit the main road, he twisted the accelerator hard and sped away. "Jeez," he muttered, "I didn't even ask him his name."

Bucky had not eaten, and he was hungry, but hunger was not his priority. He had been made with the Suzuki. He hoped the guy would give him some time, but he knew he could not count on it. He had to ditch the bike. Instead of continuing south toward Interstate 86, which was routinely patrolled by state troopers, Bucky took a meandering route across back roads and finally turned south on North Nine Mile Road. Although Bucky had avoided meeting any cars over the twisting trails, the trip had consumed the clock. He knew he had to ditch the bike and ditch it now. He was in luck. He sped past a chained driveway that was most likely the entrance to a secluded camp. He turned the bike around and parked it upright nudging the chain that stretched across the entrance.

Bucky walked at a leisurely pace for about two miles. With St.

Bonaventure University nearby, hiking students and professors with backpacks were not uncommon sights. He made it to South Nine Mile Road that was a favored walking route of students and graduate students who lived off campus. Unbeknownst to Bucky, chance was about to intervene again to his advantage. From a distance Bucky observed a man backing a white pickup truck inside a large, metal-framed building. As Bucky approached, the man closed the overhead door and got in a car parked next to the building with a woman behind the wheel. As the car sped from sight, Bucky nonchalantly walked around the building.

Two minutes later Bucky drove a 2003 White Dodge quad cab from the building, leisurely stepped from the truck, and closed the overhead door behind him. He refused to reveal how he entered the building so quickly, but the keys were left in the ignition and the seat was still warm from its previous occupant. The Dodge had been a crime of convenience, but what Bucky did not know was that the truck would not be reported missing until the following Monday morning. By that time, Bucky would be as far away as Toledo, Ohio, or Detroit, Michigan.

During that same weekend the Cattaraugus County Sheriff's Department investigated several reports of break-ins at seasonal residences with only firearms and ammunition taken. The firearms ranged from collectible pistols to shotguns and technically advanced handguns with a wide assortment of ammunition. Although one of the handguns was later tied to Bucky, he remained faithful to his self-imposed creed and steadfastly denied complicity. He did acknowledge that firearms and ammunition was a favored currency among the lawless class. He explained that "hot" or stolen merchandise, even car parts, typically sell on the underground market for fractions on the dollar. "Guns," he said, "always hold value and some even sell at a premium." He mentioned that ammunition is almost always sold at a premium. "Hollow points, especially jacketed hollow points, and armor piercing rounds are always tops. Even lower velocity wad cutters bring top money, but a full charge wad cutter is premium plus."

Despite reports of local burglaries and car thefts Bucky sensed that his escape was not a top priority among local law enforcement agencies and the state police in particular. Although he escaped from a state-owned facility, local law enforcement and other state agencies universally placed responsibility for the escape on the beleaguered Erie County Sheriff Timothy Howard, who operated the facility. That did not mean, however, that Bucky could let his guard down.

He understood all too well that the convergence of chance and circumstance could also work to his disadvantage. He had heard the stories since he was in reform school; most felons were never apprehended by brilliant police work, but by careless or accidental encounters. A busted taillight, crossing a double yellow line, one too many beers in a notorious local bar; hundreds of felons, some really smart crooks, were apprehended by a "Mayberry" cop for "failure to yield."

Chapter Seventeen

POINTS WEST

Despite reports that Bucky was spotted on Tuesday, April 18, 2006, near his hometown in Stockton, New York, he was actually having breakfast at a diner in Defiance, Ohio. Three hours to Chicago, two hours to Detroit, and less than an hour's drive to Fort Wayne, Indiana, made the geography of Northwestern Ohio ideally suited for Bucky's purposes. Bucky consistently refused to acknowledge those with whom he was in contact with unless he is specifically linked to an individual in an official police report or court document. But there is absolutely no presumption that he was in Ohio in a stolen Dodge truck from New York on a casual sightseeing trip. Bucky Phillip's trip west was purely business. Indeed, his every act from the day he first arrived in Ohio until that desperate morning in June in Chemung County, was purely business.

In Ohio, as in New York, Bucky reasoned his greatest exposure would be incidental traffic patrols. He was careful to drive within the speed limit and forced himself to smile politely at a Toledo cop that pulled alongside him at a traffic light. It was always the unexpected, the accidental encounter that Bucky most feared. Bucky had hardly been in Ohio for a week and was happy with what he had achieved, but he had one final business transaction to conclude before he returned to New York. He had done business with the person before and believed him to be as reliable as anyone in the criminal industry.

Bucky had developed the habit of always knowing exactly where he was going and the best route to take to get there. If he had a meeting at an unfamiliar place or address, he would arrive at least two hours early, often the day before, to determine the best route and observe the surroundings before charging in. On this particular morning Bucky knew exactly where he was going; he had driven past the house several times the previous Sunday without stopping for a visit and was an hour early on this, his second trip. Nothing seemed amiss or out of the ordinary throughout the neighborhood when Bucky parked on a parallel street behind his house. He casually strolled through an alley to the back of his friend's house and had just started to knock on the back door when it suddenly swang open with such force that Bucky jumped backward.

"You gotta get out of here." His friend said excitedly. "The cops are watching the house. A state cop car has driven by at least twice this morning." The man's face was flushed and he was obviously alarmed. The friend pulled the door closed, and Bucky quickly retraced his steps without having said a word. He was driving away when he saw a state police cruiser turn onto the street for another drive-by and seconds later it was joined by two unmarked cars and a S.W.A.T. team vehicle.

His acquaintance had been alerted, but Bucky was shaking so hard that he could barely drive. His stomach twisted into a knot; a bitter gall erupted in his mouth and stung his nostrils. He had a strong, inner sense of doom; a feeling that was not modified by his realization that he had narrowly averted disaster. A four-way stop sign gave him just enough time to regain a measure of composure.

He had lost all sense of direction and drove around aimlessly for nearly an hour on country roads adorned with well-kept farmhouses and neatly painted red barns. The more he thought about it, the more he realized that he had pushed his luck. On April 26, 2006, deputies from the Lucas County Sheriff's Department recovered a 2003 white Dodge pickup with New York plates abandoned on a service road in Swanton near Toledo, Ohio. The next day the Fulton County Sheriff's Department reported the theft of a 1996 Ford Ranger pickup nearby in Wauseon, Ohio.

After Ohio, reports and sightings of Bucky Phillips dried up for nearly a month. Bucky would not elaborate on his exact whereabouts during that period, but he did acknowledge that he spent time in Chautauqua County. He said that although he did not want to be completely inconspicuous, his intentions were to lie low and wait. His "quiet time," he called it.

"Wait for what?" I remembered asking.

"Who knows?" Bucky shrugged. "Maybe something would fall out of the sky."

Bucky returned to Chautauqua County with money in his pocket.

"How much?" I asked.

"Enough." That was all he said about money.

Bucky stashed the stolen Ohio pickup in an accessibl but secure location and returned to the woods with a Thermos of coffee, two prepaid cell phones, and three plastic bottles of water. He had a large gym bag slung over his shoulder crammed tight with several items of clothing, including a pair of camouflage fatigues of the kind worn by state troopers. He wore a pair of lightweight combat boots vintage Vietnam and packed another pair similar to those worn by police S.W.A.T. teams. On his back was a smaller backpack filled with toiletries, three pocketknives with blades of varying length and design, a carton of cigarettes, and a tube of Copenhagen. His hair was closely cropped Marine style and he was clean-shaven. He had a .38-caliber handgun in his backpack and 9-millimeter Glock outfitted with a clip for inside-the-waistband concealment without a holster.

Bucky refused to reveal the origins of his extraordinary treasures but admitted he went on a grand shopping spree. He said he ate real food and never realized how wonderful it was to eat at Denny's and Bob Evan's Restaurants whenever he wanted. Cracker Barrel Restaurants had become a favorite of Bucky's, but they catered to families and eating alone in a Cracker Barrel store was a sure-fire way to attract unwanted attention. But, in the wilderness none of that mattered.

Once in the woods, Bucky attempted to follow familiar pathways of his youth, but he was frequently forced to detour to avoid tangled growths of vines, briars, and brush and search for a more accommodating passage.

Bucky found the steep, narrow trails that he had easily traversed as a youth more challenging as an adult. Although he moved at a brisk pace, he had to constantly maneuver the gym bag around. Finally, between trees, saplings, and ground pine that had overgrown the trails, he was relieved to find a resting place. He stopped in a small clearing, dropped the gym bag at his feet, and plopped down on a moss-covered stump. Bucky lit a cigarette, inhaled deeply, and slowly forced the smoke through pursed lips in a tight stream toward the ground. He watched the smoke scatter around the toe of his boot and force two ants to hastily recover and resume their journey across a tiny leaf lodged against the tender fronds of an emerging fern.

Bucky field stripped his cigarette in military fashion, separating the filter fibers into tiny strands and throwing them to the wind. He repositioned his backpack, grasped the gym bag by its handles, and threaded his way through nearly a mile of tangled undergrowth to the base of the adjoining mountain. He skirted the edge of the mountain in favor of more accessible terrain and had been on the trail barely fifteen minutes when he caught a glimpse of a dull-colored piece of aluminum protruding from the underbrush.

A closer examination revealed a small, aluminum camping trailer that had outlived its useful highway life. The trailer had been converted into a hunting shelter before it was finally forsaken and left to the mercy of the elements. The front part of the roof had collapsed from the top and swung awkwardly sideways. The door swung precariously from a single hinge and the rear of the trailer had slipped off a pair of concrete blocks that once provided a level foundation. The frame was twisted sharply at the corner.

Inside, the trailer floor slanted toward the rear where a collection of leaves and pinecone husks accumulated around a five-gallon bucket that, judging from appearances, once held the tar that was spread in clumps across the roof. Despite its obvious deficits, the interior was dry and noticeably warmer than the outside air. Almost entirely concealed by rapidly growing hardwood saplings and a thick growth of ground pine, the abandoned camper suited Bucky's purposes.

He tossed his gym bag inside, removed his backpack, and scattered the pile of leaves and pinecone husks to make sure it was not home to any number of small critters. He leaned his back against the high side of the trailer, stretched his legs straight out and savored the peace and quiet. The only distractions that penetrated Bucky's hiding place were the occasional call of a crow intermingled with the sounds of seasonal birds and the incessant chatter of a red squirrel. Life for Bucky since the escape had been at such a stress-filled, grueling pace that there had been little time for relaxation. For the first time since his escape, he was embraced by the soothing stillness of the wilderness and was at peace with the world.

Bucky had forgotten what it meant to be so completely removed from the everyday sounds of human activity. Noise, he thought, had penetrated nearly every moment of human existence. Traffic noise, construction noise, the background noise of a radio, even the ticking of a clock is difficult to escape, but there are remote stretches of solitude in the most unlikely settings. Comfortably encased inside a discarded relic from the Common Era in a stretch of wilderness marred and scarred by human contact, Bucky surrendered to his surroundings and fell fast asleep.

However, Bucky did not remain cloistered and over time made several trips to the cities of Jamestown and Dunkirk. He did not flaunt his freedom, but never hesitated to go wherever he wanted. He openly traveled back and forth between his camper hideout and the Cattaraugus Reservation. He even caught a couple of movies in Erie, Pennsylvania's Tinsel Town Theaters. He made a trip to Olean, New York, to meet a friend for lunch at a popular steak house restaurant. "Believe it or not," he shook his head in mock disbelief. "There were people who had not heard that I escaped and was on the run. My friend hadn't heard."

"Did you tell him?" I asked.

"Sure." He suggested his friend just laughed and said he wasn't surprised. "After lunch, he gave me his mother's telephone number if I needed to get in touch again."

Bucky spent the last days of April and the month of May in his wilderness hideout. "There were some interesting things that happened," Bucky recalled, "especially during spring turkey season." He said he had equipped his makeshift camper with a Styrofoam cooler; a canister-fueled, two-burner camp stove; and had acquired a nice sleeping bag from Walmart. "Can you believe Walmart? They sell stuff really cheap, and," he stretched his hands sideways for added emphasis, "they have nearly everything." Bucky even had a small television set jury-rigged to operate from a twelve-volt marine battery.

One of the most frightening incidents for Bucky occurred on a Saturday morning in May. Bucky was curled up nicely in his sleeping bag inside his makeshift quarters. Although the sun was shining brightly, there was an unusual chill in the air and Bucky chose to sleep late. Suddenly and without warning a loud explosion jarred Bucky awake and jerked his body upright. The explosion was quickly followed by two more blasts accompanied by the sound of metal hitting metal. Immediately after the first blast Bucky heard the chilling but unmistakable sound of a shell being racked into the magazine of a pump shotgun. He flipped flat on his stomach and slithered along the floor to peek through a tiny split in the camper siding.

He saw two teenage turkey hunters arrayed in expensive hunting camos. Obviously frustrated by their lack of success, they seemingly choose to kill the tar bucket Bucky had carelessly left setting outside a few feet from the camper. Bucky instantly feared for his life and pressed his outstretched body flat against the slanted floor. What if they decided to use the camper for target practice? What would he do? He chose to lie perfectly still and watched as one of the boys kicked the buckshot bucket toward his companion like a soccer ball. He said something Bucky could not make out and both boys laughed. Fortunately for Bucky, they walked away with their shotguns slung over their shoulders. Bucky rolled over and lay flat on his back for a long time.

Chapter Eighteen

FINAL PREPARATIONS

Ernest Hemmingway begins the *Snows of Kilimanjaro* with a story about finding the frozen carcass of a leopard near the western summit of Africa's highest mountain, snow-covered Kilimanjaro. There was no reasonable explanation for the leopard to have been in that place. What brought the leopard to such a strange and exotic place, a place so uncharacteristically removed from its normal existence? The same can be asked of Bucky's presence in New York's Finger Lakes region. And what pulled Ralph Phillips to places as far away as Kentucky and Detroit and back to Ontario and Chemung Counties in New York, places uncharacteristically separated from his past? Was it chance? Was it fate? Whatever the reason, like the leopard frozen in the snow, Bucky was a stranger in a strange land, and like Hemingway's leopard, that strange land would determine his future.

The police believed Bucky was in New York's Ontario County in late May. Reports indicate that on May 23, 2006, an Ohio-registered 1996 Ford Ranger pickup was recovered in a service area on the New York State Thruway at Clifton Springs. On that same day a green 1996 Ford Taurus was reported stolen on County Route 13 in the same vicinity where the Ford Ranger pickup was abandoned. Using the wilderness of his youth as a convenient base of operations, Bucky Phillips, driving stolen vehicles, traveled nearly five thousand miles in less than a month. In the normal course of events, Bucky Phillips would not have had a convenient reason to even be in the Clifton Springs area.

Bucky does not reemerge in the public record until the following Saturday, May 27, 2006, when he was reported to have been involved in two altercations on the Tuscarora Indian Reservation in Niagara County. It was also reported that Bucky was driving a 1996 green Ford Taurus and brandished a handgun during the second altercation. A week later, June 3, 2006, Bucky is listed as the prime suspect in an attempted arson complaint at the Arnold Rickard residence in Lewiston. Police reports indicate a search of the area uncovered fresh tracks and an empty gas can. Bucky steadfastly refused to even acknowledge he was in Niagara County during that time, and when asked about Arnold Rickard, he shrugged off the acquaintance. "I know who he is. That's all." Actually, Bucky had served time with a younger Rickard and remained friends with Peggy Rickard, the young man's mother.

I was convinced that Ralph James Phillips, born in the month of the Berry Moon in 1962, dreamed of a mountaintop experience. I suspect he examined his options and saw a faint glimmer of light at the end of a very long tunnel. I do not know what conclusions he reached concerning how he had lived his life, but believe he realized that despite the odds, he had a glimpse of a life better lived. "They call me a career criminal," he told me. "Boy," he exhaled the words softly through his teeth and shook his head slightly sideways. "They've missed the boat on that one. I haven't had an impressive career as a criminal. I'm really a career convict."

Bucky's presence in the Finger Lakes and the Lake Ontario shoreline may have been legs of a marathon run toward a new life. A new life for Bucky had immediate demands, a new identity, safe passage to a destination, and cash. But the essential ingredient for a life on the run remains money, lots of money. He had to recognize that small-time burglaries and petty crimes that made up so much of his criminal activity and tagged him as an "habitual offender" would provide little more than a meager existence. Bucky needed to accumulate cash, a $30,000 cushion perhaps, at least enough to transport him to some version of a new life.

In an earlier time, notorious outlaws like John Dillinger, "Pretty Boy" Floyd, and Bonnie and Clyde relied upon a network of pals, an empathetic public, and a suitcase full of cash for a safety net. And Willie Sutton robbed banks because that was where the money was. Today there is little reluctance to "rat" people out as evidenced by an Emergency 911 system frequently overloaded with cell phone calls from a mobile citizenry fearful of everything from trans fats to terrorists. Bucky may have had three or four friends closer than family, but it was not much of a network, and none of them were in a position to ever give him more than a few dollars. And with a typical bank heist averaging less than a thousand dollars, Willie Sutton would have had to resort to food stamps today. Since the local bank is no longer a convenient source of cash, and in the absence of spontaneous assistance from a sympathetic public, the options available to a felon in flight are limited. But those who are willing to take risks associated with illegal drugs can acquire enormous amounts of cash in a relatively short time.

The cash returns in illicit drugs are proportionally off the charts, but there is probably no other enterprise riskier than illicit drugs. Conversely, eighty percent of legitimate business start-ups fail, but legitimate entrepreneurs just lose money—those that fail in the illicit drug trade can lose their life; the luckier go to jail. So powerful is the allure for quick, undocumented cash that more than a few prominent businessmen have fallen under the seductive spell of illegal drug deals to rescue a failed dream.

Economists describe the "competitive" economic model as one that has an easy entrance and an equally easy exit with a high turnover or failure rate. The illicit drug trade does not require a professional license or a college degree, and at the entry level where arrests account for the highest turnover, the lack of a high school diploma is not a hindrance. Almost any law enforcement officer, from patrolman to chief, will privately admit that news accounts of drug arrests amount to a perpetual "jobs posting" for applicants in the illicit drug trade.

The governments of the United States and Canada acknowledge that South American cocaine enters the United States through Mexico and mixes with illegal firearms and bundles of ill-gotten drug money that ultimately finds its way to Canada. Once in Canada, cocaine is linked to a cross-border exchange for Canadian-grown marijuana, Canadian Ecstasy, and other manufactured chemical products that are smuggled back into the United States. Successful drug interdictions along the Pacific Canadian coastline during the closing years of the last century forced drug smuggling activities to inland ports and eastwardly along major highways that intersect the US–Canadian border. New York State shares a long, unguarded border with Canada that includes Great Lakes ports, rugged wilderness routes, common hiking trails, and highways.

From the Thousand Island Region of New York westerward to Niagara Falls, smugglers have developed a labyrinth of illegal cross-border trade routes along the shores of Lake Ontario. Commonly available technologies like GPS have created more efficient ways to deliver products. Drug smugglers use private planes, helicopters, boats, cars, trucks, all-terrain vehicles, snowmobiles, and hikers to transport drugs. Small boats and planes cross the waters of Lake Ontario and hikers, bikers, and ATVers drop backpacks and packages along New York's rugged border for others to pick up. The operation is simple. Paid in advance, the driver, biker, or hiker drops the backpack anywhere in a secluded area then activates the silently operating GPS and walks away.

During the winter months the street profit from an ounce of cocaine can be enormous. But cocaine is more often sold on the streets in "twists." A twist is a half-gram of cocaine placed in the snipped off corner of a plastic bag and tied with a wire twist tie. One ounce of cocaine will produce fifty-six twists. If that same ounce is turned into crack or rocks, each rock can be sold separately. Three rocks can be created from a single twist.

A seventy-pound backpack of high-grade marijuana can have a street value in the hundreds of thousands for an anonymous drop; this has a magnetic attraction to people already given to an out-of-doors lifestyle. That midstate strip of New York, the Finger Lakes, is ideally situated for drug smuggling. The region is easily accessible by air, bracketed by interstate highways, and has a four-season tourism appeal that attracts thousands of visitors every year. Location, geography, and topography make the region ideally suited for access points to various corridors for cross-border drug smuggling.

The notion that Bucky Phillips might have negotiated a contract with shadowy figures as a drop courier was never investigated. In many ways, Bucky would have made an ideal drug courier for an importer. A man as elusive as Bucky could have littered the Finger Lakes Region with hundreds of illegal backpacks for others to retrieve. If he got caught, he was going to jail for a long time regardless, and except for his life, he had little to lose. Bucky may never have achieved his financial goals, but during the height of his flight he had enough discretionary cash to spend a thousand dollars for a motorcycle. His money had come from someplace, and it was not from pilfering hunting camps or from financially well-off friends and family.

Chapter Nineteen

THE BEST LAID PLANS

The circumstances that placed Bucky Phillips on a road less traveled in the early morning hours of June 10, 2005, remained sequestered behind the cloistered walls of Clinton Correctional Facility. But around 1:00 a.m. in Chemung County in the town of Veteran near the city of Elmira, Ralph James Phillips shot New York state trooper Sean Brown twice. The first shot hit the officer in the chest and was deflected by the officer's protective vest. The shot hit the trooper with such force that as he was falling backward, his vest hiked up just enough for the second bullet to rip through his lower abdomen. Trooper Brown was hospitalized in critical condition, and after several weeks of convalescing returned to work. In that split second Bucky knew, whether the trooper lived or died, the hounds of hell would be turned loose and render what was left of his life a wretched existence.

I remember asking Bucky why he was in Chemung County in the middle of the night in the first place. He twisted uncomfortably and slightly sideways in his chair and lifted his hands in a shrug. "Business," he said, and then proceeded to tell me as much as he would about that night and the event surrounding the shooting. Bucky said the green Mustang was hot on both ends, it was stolen, and it was hot under the hood.

"The car drove like a dream." He said he had spotted the car parked in a used car lot on Routes 5 and 20 near the village of Silver Creek in

Chautauqua County. "If you like cars, you don't forget the one that catches your eye," Bucky explained. He claimed that the first time he saw the car he liked it right away Bucky said he was driving at a reasonable speed and did not immediately recognize the car behind him as a cop car. "I thought someone was screwing with me." He explained that the car would speed up and hug his back bumper then drop back. "That happened three or four times." He said he finally goosed the Mustang and sped away from his pursuer. But when he glanced in his rearview mirror, he saw the car's headlights rapidly approaching through the darkness.

Bucky said he was frightened and as soon as he found a wide spot in the road, he swerved to one side and suddenly braked to a stop. Even before the Mustang came to a stop Bucky had already reached under the driver's seat and retrieved a breaker bar wrapped in a T-shirt. He slipped a .38-caliber pistol from his backpack and slid it his jacket pocket. Bucky had told me earlier in our interview that he had acquired two handguns after his escape, but he remained deliberately vague. He said he left one in his gym bag inside his wilderness hideout and carried the other in his backpack. He wouldn't tell me how, or when, he came into possession of the weapons. I pressed him several times on that issue, but as far as I know he could have picked them up that very day. Bucky simply refused to implicate anyone who might have helped him.

He told me he had hardly braked to a stop before the car was on his back bumper with red lights flashing. He said it was at that precise moment when he recognized his pursuers were troopers, but there was no turning back. Bucky's world slowed to quarter time. He was already out of the car when he saw a slender trooper walking toward him. Bucky related the incident with remarkable clarity. The trooper's head and shoulder tilted slightly downward and to his left, and his right arm was frozen in midair with his elbow bent awkwardly outward. Bucky could see the trooper's fingers closing around the grips of his holstered sidearm, and at the same time he could feel his finger press the trigger backward on his .38. He watched a bright yellow flash erupt without sound from the end of the barrel, expand then stretch outward in a thin red line of dying embers before it disappeared.

Bucky heard the second explosion and watched the trooper's face twist into a grotesque mask. He watched the upper half of the man's body tilt sharply backward, his wide-brimmed Stetson fell slowly in front of his face, and his left knee jerked upward in an automatic reflex. Bucky saw the entire episode unfold at the same time he was moving backward toward the driver's side door of the Mustang. He said when he got under the wheel and sped away, he glanced in his rearview mirror and saw a second trooper emerging from the rear of the cruiser. He was suddenly very sick to his stomach.

"I was soaking wet with sweat." He said he stopped the car, got out, and threw up. He said he hoped the guy was okay. "I figured he had a vest. But," he added, "at the time I didn't know if I had killed him or not." Bucky said he didn't learn of the trooper's condition until he heard the story on the morning news. As circumstantial as the evidence may be, I did not believe it coincidental that the shooting of Trooper Brown occurred near State Route 14, which runs directly north to Sodus Point on the shores of Lake Ontario. Bucky had been in that region in May and abandoned an Ohio vehicle near the on-ramp of Interstate 90 near Clifton Springs. Clifton Springs is less than thirty miles from Sodus Point. Despite his denials, I believed Bucky Phillips may have been involved in a drug drop on that fateful morning.

Regardless of purpose or plan, Bucky was in a real predicament. He knew the shooting was instantly reported and the getaway car was repeatedly broadcast to every law enforcement agency throughout the area. His first priority was to abandon the Mustang as quickly as possible. He said he continued south and found himself on the outer edge of a residential neighborhood. Bucky said his heart was almost pounding though his shirt and that he got a temple-throbbing headache when he suddenly realized he was driving toward a state police barracks in Horseheads.

He said he turned on the first road he came to and immediately spied a house that looked unoccupied. He turned off the headlights and parked the Mustang in plain sight in the back yard. Bucky Phillips was a practiced car thief. Over time he developed a meticulous technique of wiping a car clean. In more favorable circumstances he would have used wet wipes on the rearview mirror, door handles, and radio buttons. He would have made sure the shift lever was wiped clean and given the dashboard and visors a good once over. And Bucky never used an ashtray in a stolen car. He might leave hair and fibers, but he had learned a long time ago never to leave fingerprints. Although he didn't have wet wipes, he made an effort to wipe the car. He would have been more precise if this were a customary act of thievery, but shooting a state trooper, probably killing him, was of such magnitude that even he could not comprehend the mess he was in.

He said thoughts flashed rapidly through his head, but one remained constant. "They can't tie me to the car, they can't tie me to the shooting." Bucky said he heard the phrase over and over in his mind. Instead of smoking inside a stolen car, Bucky substituted Copenhagen snuff, smokeless tobacco, for cigarettes, and had thought to bring a metal spit can aboard the Mustang. He used a pull top soup can that he stuffed with facial tissues as a portable spittoon. Bucky said he was shaking like a leaf. All he could do, he said, was to put on his backpack, shove the spit can in his jacket pocket, and grab the T-shirt-wrapped breaker bar and toss the keys on the front seat.

He said he walked in the shadows along the backside of the houses and hoped he didn't stumble over a dog tied up in someone's back yard. He said he had not gone very far when he saw a yard shed, the kind used to store lawn mowers and yard implements situated on the backside of a large lawn. There was an older two-story house at the farthest corner, and there were no outside lights. He said he laid flat on his stomach and shoved the T-shirt-wrapped breaker bar as far under the backside of the shed as possible. About three houses removed from the shed were three plastic garbage cans neatly arranged at the rear of a house that sat at the end of a long driveway. Only one container had a garbage bag, the other two were empty. He fumbled with the yellow plastic ties before he realized they were tied in a slipknot. He opened the bag and shoved his portable spittoon deep into it, retied it, and replaced the cover.

"Who would have thought they would have ever found them?" Bucky appeared surprised. "Someone had to see me." He said the cops would later claim they found both items inside the Mustang. "They tie me to the car; they tie me to the shooting."

Bucky said he could not remember how far he walked, or even the direction he was headed when he saw a white pickup truck backed into a driveway. "Looking back," he said, "it couldn't have been very far." He said he hunkered down and crept behind the pickup when he found the door on the driver's side locked. Still crouching, he reached for the passenger door and pulled it open. He was startled momentarily when the interior light came on bright like a spotlight and lit up the entire area. He immediately slid inside and gently pulled the door closed. Stretched flat across the seat with his head nearly under the steering wheel Bucky was in for another surprise. Dangling from the driver's side visor was a set of car keys.

He realized the driveway was gently sloped toward the street, so he cautiously slipped the gearshift into neutral, released the hand brake, and silently glided into the street. He rolled down the street and was several houses removed before he started the engine and drove away. Bucky said he drove north from Horseheads on Route 13 toward Ithaca and southeast on Route 79 toward a remote destination nearly a hundred miles from where he shot the trooper. He said he had used his cell phone to call a "guy" he knew and was hoping to hook up with him to get a little breathing space. Despite the fact that the state police had identified Bucky's "guy" before the end of the first day, Bucky remained true to form and refused to mention the person's name. He would only acknowledge that he had done time with him.

While a cumbersome command structure of the New York State Police fumbled the ball so frequently in the search for Bucky Phillips, the ground troops performed absolutely brilliantly. In less than ten hours after the shooting of Trooper Brown, and by 10:30 on the same morning, state troopers found the Mustang abandoned on Wygant Road in a residential area in Horseheads. Law enforcement descended upon the neighborhood in force. Not only had they determined the automobile had been stolen, but they had the name of a suspect, Ralph J. Phillips. An immediate ground search of the area by uniformed officers revealed that a white Chevrolet pickup was reported stolen overnight.

Bucky claimed that before dawn on the morning of the shooting he was asleep in the rear bedroom of a camping trailer secluded in the wilds southeast of Binghamton near the New York–Pennsylvania border. The owner of the camper was a man named Paul Gross who had served time in prison with Bucky. The manner in which the name of Paul Gross emerged on the very same day Trooper Sean Brown was shot remains a stunning accomplishment of those state troopers who doggedly pursued an obscure lead. An unidentified state investigator must have undertaken the mundane review of Bucky's prison records and discovered he had once called a telephone number in Binghamton from the prison.

The Horseheads command post immediately requested Troop C officers investigate the lead. When troopers arrived at the residence, they learned that the former occupant was deceased, but that the current occupant was a relative who did not know Ralph "Bucky" Phillips. She did tell investigators that her brother, Paul Gross, who lived in Binghamton, had been a cellmate of Bucky's and that he and his wife owned a wilderness camp where they often spent weekends. Before 8:00 p.m. the two investigators and one state trooper had located the camp and saw a white Chevrolet pickup parked in the drive.

Bucky's skills as an outdoorsman cannot be underestimated, but the bungling of the bureaucracy of the New York State Police cannot be overstated. What follows is an excerpt from the Phillips Manhunt Operational Review published by the New York State Police of what happened after officers called for assistance and were ordered to hold their positions and wait for support.

Troop C deployed a contingent of uniformed and BCI members, requested the response of an MRT team, and the Troop Commander responded with additional command staff. Roadblocks were established on State Route 79 to the North and South ends of the Gross property. At about 11:30 p.m. a vehicle left the property, and a traffic stop was conducted a distance from the property. The vehicle occupants were Paul and Sandra Gross, both of whom denied being with Ralph Phillips. However, they subsequently admitted that Phillips had been at the property when they left, but he was packed and ready to leave the area. Paul Gross informed investigators that at about 9:00 p.m. he had heard vehicles on the road and walked down his driveway where he spotted a black Impala police vehicle. He returned to the residence to advise Phillips. It was later determined that he and his wife would drive down the road to see what was there.

Initial arriving members of the Mobile Response Team (MRT) were briefed and equipped with night vision equipment. Two MRT members were deployed to conduct surveillance on the Gross's trailer while awaiting the arrival of additional MRT personnel. The "inner" perimeter was supplemented with uniform force members, including one Troop C Rifle Team member. With the arrival of additional patrols, a roving "outer" perimeter was created to travel between fixed posts on the surrounding roads. Shortly after midnight, a command post was established at the Colesville Volunteer Ambulance building on State Route 79 in Harpursville, and additional uniform and Bureau of Criminal Investigation (BCI) personnel were recalled to duty. The New York State Police Aviation Unit was dispatched to respond to the scene, as were Troop C canine handlers. As additional patrols arrived, the roving posts were reduced in size. Sometime after 3:00 a.m., once sufficient MRT personnel had arrived, the trailer and immediate area were searched. The surveillance team had observed no inside movement and the trailer was found to be unoccupied. The stolen truck was still there, suggesting Ralph Phillips had fled on foot into the surrounding, heavily wooded area.

That splendid police work, occurring only hours after one of their own had been shot, identified the stolen Mustang, developed a suspect, and located the perpetrator's whereabouts before twilight of the same day is nothing short of brilliant. But what followed is a vivid account of a bloated bureaucracy actually aiding in the escape of a suspect. Despite the fact that Mr. and Mrs. Gross admitted that Bucky was inside the trailer, perhaps out of a sense of loyalty or fearing a defect in his possible appeal, Bucky would not admit the same.

"But," he said dryly, "if it had been me, I think I might have left when the black Impala was first spotted."

With a six-hour head start, even on foot, Bucky could have easily been thirty to forty miles away. By the time the state police command had established a command post, deployed an MRT, positioned sharpshooters with automatic rifles, and secured the scene, the suspect could have as easily been more than two hundred miles away. The scene was reminiscent of one ninety-three years earlier, when Moyca Newell and Katherine Mayor watched in anger and frustration as Sam Howell's killers were allowed to escape.

In less than twenty-four hours, the dogged persistence of uniformed state troopers and BCI investigators had located the man who shot their comrade. Despite that brilliant police work, a bloated bureaucracy and an ego-obsessed command structure intervened and allowed the perpetrator to escape. If the state police command will not accept responsibility for bungling, they should at the very least give medals to those officers and investigators who so quickly found Bucky Phillips.

Chapter Twenty

MAN HUNT

Bucky Phillips had been shaken to his core when he had discovered the car behind him was a state police cruiser. Actually he had been horrified, because he had expected to be robbed or even killed for the cargo he denied having on board. If Bucky were involved in drug drops, an allegation he denied, he would have faced a more serious threat from those who wanted his cargo than from law enforcement. When the car behind the Mustang repeatedly charged his rear bumper, he expected the worst. Before the Mustang ever stopped, Bucky was prepared for a life-or-death struggle and the outcome would have been the same whether the occupant was a hijacker, a state trooper, or Santa Claus. He realized from the moment he shot the state trooper that he had lost the war and killed his dream.

From that moment forward Bucky resisted the impulse to have his life become a series of continuous, chaotic movements. After the initial shock, Bucky was able to effectively compartmentalize his overall objective of eluding his pursuers and returning to Chautauqua County into a series of simple, attainable goals based on the immediacy of the moment. He recognized that the police and public focus would shift from a perfunctory if not casual inquiry about an escaped parolee to a declaration of war against a fleeing felon.

Bucky had little choice but to return to Chautauqua County. He acknowledged he had friends on and off the Seneca Nation and the Tuscarora Reservation. But he remained uncertain about how willing his friends would be to assist someone on the run for shooting a state trooper. He also knew that he would be cut off from friends closest to him and all of his family members. He accepted that under the best of circumstances even old friends would be reluctant to provide little more than a few dollars, and not one would jeopardize the safety or security of their families to assist him. Besides, he would never place them in that position. The timing of events was now completely out of Bucky's control. He needed time to figure out some way to regain a slight advantage and achieve a sliver of separation from his pursuers. But, by any measurement, Bucky Phillips was in a desperate situation.

Bucky had the advantage of time to adequately prepare for his departure before being forced to leave the Gross camp on foot and under cover of darkness. He had enough packaged food and snacks for several days, but he was suddenly plunged into unfamiliar surroundings. His initial instincts were to head south toward Pennsylvania as quickly as possible. He really needed an automobile, but he found there were not that many cars for the taking. There were too few cars and too many cops. Bucky estimated that for the remainder of the first night he probably walked less than five miles from the Gross trailer. Even though he could navigate by the stars, he had absolutely no idea of the lay of the land. He followed the railroad tracks for nearly two miles before detouring through a heavily forested area and reemerging on the tracks a mile or two farther down the line. He employed that tactic to delay the dogs just in case the K-9 units were in pursuit.

In the ensuing days the state police suspected Bucky of committing several burglaries north and east of the Gross camp in the Afton area and unsuccessfully planted a "bait" car on State Route 7. Bucky claims he was never anywhere near Afton and carefully avoided human contact. He was apparently successful, because there was not a single "Bucky" sighting recorded during that week when he was alone in the wilds. He insisted that for the next few days he continued to push south-by-southeast at a leisurely pace and that his path often paralleled the state police as they checked residences and campsites. One day, from his vantage point on a rocky overhang high above the Susquehanna River, Bucky watched uniformed officers patrol in a boat and check vacant hunting and fishing camps along the riverbank.

A week after the shooting of Trooper Brown, the state police investigated the attempted theft of an automobile near Hancock, New York. The perpetrator was thumped by a security system, but police claimed a latent fingerprint was later matched to Bucky Phillips. Regardless, another vehicle, a Dodge Caravan, was stolen nearby.

"No way in hell," Bucky said with an air of confidence. "If they found my print on a car in Hancock, they put it there." Bucky pumped his arms over his shoulders like he was lifting weights. "I would avoid a car with a security system like the plague. But," he grinned sheepishly, "do you know what I might do?" Bucky stretched his arms upward and outward.

"No." I replied and shook my head slightly sideways.

"I might set off a car alarm, especially if I wanted a distraction." Bucky flashed a broad smile and allowed our conversation to shift in another direction. He emphasized that that week alone in the woods gave him an opportunity to collect his thoughts. "There wasn't a day that I didn't see cops. They were all over the place." He explained that their presence forced him to slow down and move with the flow instead of becoming unnecessarily careless. Bucky actually took his time returning to Chautauqua County. He felt safer with hometown lawmen than the state police. He also had a sense of the tension between the state police and the sheriff's department. The intensity of the dispute was clearly visible when Sheriff John Bentley was alive. Although Bucky had never seen Bentley openly defiant toward state troopers, he had observed his coolness toward those who had business in the county jail. Once, while doing a stretch in county and on mop detail, Bucky became a spectator to one of Bentley's finely crafted snubs. Bentley sent his undersheriff, his second in command, on a trivial errand and had his jailer, a sergeant, escort a high-ranking state police officer, a colonel, on a tour of the jail while he deliberately sat in his office. "Make sure you walk him past my office, but don't come in," Bentley instructed his sergeant.

Bucky understood that tensions existed between the agencies, but he was uncertain how it would play out. He suspected the state police would limit the sheriff's involvement in his pursuit and that might be to his advantage.

Chapter Twenty-One

THE CHAUTAUQUA COUNTY SHERIFF'S DEPARTMENT

On Saturday morning, June 10, 2006, Chautauqua County Sheriff Joseph Gerace was home shaving when he first heard about the shooting of a state trooper near Elmira on the local news. When word had first reached the sheriff's department in April that a Chautauqua County local, Ralph Phillips, had escaped from Erie County on a parole violation Sheriff Gerace automatically recalled the "spatter pig meat" threat.

"Damn," he muttered, and a cold shiver swept through his body. His thoughts immediately turned to Bucky Phillips. Although it was Saturday morning and he had promised to spend the morning with his wife and children, he felt compelled to drive to his office in Mayville. His suspicions were confirmed a half hour later when he arrived at his office and was briefed on a state police alert for a green Ford Mustang convertible sought in connection with the shooting. He remembered a green 1995 Ford Mustang convertible without plates had been stolen from a car lot near the village of Silver Creek three days earlier. Sheriff Gerace knew the search for Bucky Phillips would return to Chautauqua County—it was inevitable.

The sheriff was respectful of the protocols between his department and the state police and clearly understood the limits of his jurisdiction. It was their guy who took a bullet, and he agreed that now was the time to act quickly with a massive show of force. Gerace was careful to follow established protocols. His department had already notified the state police about the stolen Mustang, and he personally passed his suspicions about Ralph Phillips to the Troop E command post in Horseheads. Mindful of the historical sensitivities, the sheriff pledged full cooperation with the local state police command. They listened without comment and politely thanked him for his offer of assistance.

That was about all he could do at the time, but his gut instincts kept telling him that if Bucky were the perpetrator, he would be returning to Chautauqua County as quickly as he could move. Since his deputies routinely patrolled in single-man cars around the clock in some of the county's most remote areas, he alerted his road patrols. As an added precaution he personally briefed the commander of his tactical response team and placed unit commanders on alert. He would make his deputies available to assist in the operation, but he knew that it would not be easy. For years the relationship between the Chautauqua County Sheriff's department and the New York State Police had been fraught with mutual distrust and suspicions. Gerace was acutely aware of the historical antipathy that existed, and he desperately wanted to change the atmosphere. He committed his department to a new generation of leadership more interested in professionalism and cooperation than feuding over grievances from the past. But he knew that would be easier said than done.

Geographically, Chautauqua County covers nearly a thousand square miles along the extreme southwestern edge of New York State. The county picks up the Lake Erie shoreline south of Buffalo and stretches westward to the state line twenty-two miles removed from Pennsylvania's port city of Erie. Demographically the county, at the time, supported approximately 137,000 citizens disbursed throughout twenty-seven towns, fifteen villages, and two cities. Public safety and law enforcement duties fell to a handful of municipalities, such as Jamestown, which had nearly 30,000 citizens and a state-certified police department with approximately seventy sworn officers. Dunkirk, about half the size of Jamestown, had a full-time police department and, except for a few other villages and towns with much smaller departments, most communities looked first to the Chautauqua County Sheriff's Department and then to the New York State Police for protection.

Chautauqua County had a well-trained force of sworn deputies who routinely patrolled in one-man cars day and night in some of the most remote regions of the county. The sheriff's department had sworn officers who flew helicopters in search and rescue missions and provided emergency air ambulance transport to local hospitals and medical centers outside the county. Deputies patrolled the waterways and lakes, including Lake Erie and its shoreline along the border of the county. In collaboration with other police departments, the sheriff oversaw a first-rate team of forensic investigators who preserved crime scenes and employed sophisticated methods to gather evidence that might otherwise go undetected. Sheriff Gerace's S.W.A.T. team trained routinely with local police and had joined forces with neighboring counties to form the Southern Tier Drug Task Force to stem illegal drug trafficking across county lines.

The history of strained relations between the Chautauqua County Sheriff's Department and the New York State Police can be traced as far back as 1949 when the sheriff's department first assumed road patrol duties. What miffed the state police was not only a turf loss, but the idea that the county was only going to operate road patrols on a part-time basis with continued reliance on the state police. A letter dated June 9, 1949, from Sheriff Clarence D. Bell to the Chautauqua County Board of Supervisors requests two patrol cars and four additional men for creation of a road patrol. Sheriff Bell pointed out that all counties in Western New York had road patrols except Allegany County and that he was only requesting afternoon and night patrols.

Sheriff Bell argued that automobile traffic was increasing and after July 1, 1949, sixteen-year-olds would be legal to drive all hours of the day instead of from sunup to sundown. He added in his letter that road patrols would check petty thieves and other crimes. Over the objections of the New York State Police on August 8, 1949, the Chautauqua County Board of Supervisors adopted Resolution No. 657 authorizing the sheriff to employ four patrol deputies and purchase two patrol cars effective on the first day of the New Year.

As time passed and despite initial disappointment over losing the road patrols in Chautauqua County, relations between the state police and the county sheriff's department remained professional and even cordial. But that cozy relationship turned to outright bitterness by the eighties and was steeped in suspicion ever since. John Glenzer, a retired PhD from the State University of New York and a long-time county legislator became Chautauqua County's Executive. The county executive is responsible for preparing the county budgets, even the sheriff's budget, although the state constitution mandates the office and requires election by popular vote. The perennial "big three" budget items for county taxpayers are always social services, the sheriff's department, and the department of public works.

The county had no real control over the costs of social services; those expenses are mandated by the state and only partially reimbursed. When there are pressures to cut spending, that leaves only the sheriff's department and the department of public works that are funded almost entirely with local tax dollars. Although a Republican loyalist, Glenzer was a collegial, happy man who disdained the pettiness of politics, especially within his own party. His years in academia as a professor of environmental sciences had taught him to listen respectfully to the ideas of others, but he tried to avoid confrontations and preferred to leave the details to others. Faced with political pressure to cut spending, County Executive Glenzer was willing, even eager, to listen to ways to cut the county budget and ease the property tax burden.

That was why he agreed to listen to an unsolicited but detailed proposal from a command officer of the New York State Police that would return the road patrols to the state police. If implemented, the plan would save county taxpayers millions of dollars and eliminate all but a handful of county deputies. While not enthusiastic over the idea, Glenzer felt obligated to advance the idea to the county legislature. The idea never even made it to the County Legislature's Standing Committee on Public Safety, much less to the floor of the legislature.

Glenzer knew Sheriff John Bentley would immediately recognize that the state police plan would effectively eliminate the sheriff's department and relegate the sheriff to little more than a jailer. Glenzer also knew that the plan would not fly without Bentley's support. But he thought if Bentley wanted to retire, he could take credit for saving millions of dollars for county taxpayers and might even be persuaded to run for county executive someday. John Glenzer told the state police official that the plan would not work without Bentley's support.

"Sell the sheriff, and you've sold me." Glenzer thanked the officer and told him to take his plan to the sheriff.

Nearly forty years after Sheriff Bell had put four patrol officers on the road, the sheriff's department had grown to an effective force with most of that expansion under the leadership of former Sheriff John Bentley. Bentley was an imposing figure; he was a big man, six-six, nearly three hundred pounds, but he was not fat. John Bentley came up through the ranks and although he was a Republican, he cared more for his department than he did partisan politics. He was not entirely apolitical, but he was one of the few elected county sheriffs who understood and practiced the art of local politics and was immensely popular with the electorate.

Despite his widespread popularity, Sheriff Bentley had few close friends and even fewer people knew his true feelings. Bentley loved police work. When he became county sheriff he had a single mission: He wanted to create one of the finest law enforcement agencies in the United States. He deliberately grew the department. In order to accomplish his ends, Bentley openly courted favor from county Democrats. It was a peculiar twist of irony that his best and closest friend was George Ritzer, the County Democratic Chairman. After the election Ritzer, a tried-and-true union man, answered a call from the newly elected sheriff and agreed to meet for breakfast.

A hardheaded Democrat, Ritzer was also a political pragmatist. He realized that the Democrats might never have a candidate who could wrest the sheriff's department from John Bentley and the Republicans in an election. The two men were very much alike, each had risen to the top of their respective perches through the school of hard knocks. By the end of that breakfast meeting and in a political quid pro quo, Bentley had agreed to appoint a Democrat as his undersheriff and, as a result, almost always ran for reelection unopposed. The two men became fast friends, but it was a friendship that would be tested.

Chautauqua County Democrats never bothered to search for candidates to oppose Bentley, and as far as the County Committee and George Ritzer were concerned, the matter was settled. That was the way it was until one election cycle when a candidate declared his intention to run against Bentley and asked for the Democratic endorsement. County Democratic Chairman George Ritzer had already gone on public record in favor of Sheriff Bentley. Governor Hugh Carey was up for reelection, and as the titular head of the Democratic Party in the state of New York, he demanded that David Carr, a retired state police investigator, be given the nod. The Democrats endorsed Carr, except for County Chairman George Ritzer. He placed a Bentley sign in his yard and had his picture taken shaking hands with the sheriff.

Bentley easily won reelection, but Ritzer paid a political price and fell out of favor with the governor and other state officials. John Bentley honored loyalty and never forgot Ritzer's stand. Years later when George Ritzer was diagnosed with terminal cancer and without insurance, John Bentley gave him a badge, strapped a sidearm on a man without any police training, and appointed him a court bailiff. Ritzer held the position until he died. Both men would believe for the remainder of their days that New York State Police officials at the highest level had become involved in local politics and intervened with Governor Carey on behalf on one of their own. John Bentley saw the actions as an attempt by state police officials to get rid of a county sheriff who they thought was getting too big for his britches.

In another instance, hard-line Republican political operatives were furious when they learned Sheriff Bentley had hired a young man as a deputy and crime scene photographer. The deputy's father of the same name had, years, before left a successful and expanding law practice and was the first Democrat to head the Chautauqua County Board of Supervisors. Joseph Gerace would eventually be elected as the county's very first county executive. Bentley's hiring of the county executive's son raised an immediate hue and cry from party loyalists. Accusations swirled in political circles that the sheriff was merely trying to garner favor with the deputy's father. That uproar spawned a meeting in the county jail with a handful of political operatives who were determined to set the sheriff straight.

As was his custom, Sheriff Bentley confronted his critics face-to-face. As usual, he was polite. He explained in simple terms why he hired young Joe Gerace as a deputy and had appointed him as a crime scene photographer. He told his critics that he had seldom seen anyone so young who had such a love for law enforcement. He recounted his first meeting with young Gerace. He said Joe had been only eighteen years old when he drove to Mayville and asked for a job as a deputy. Impressed by his enthusiasm Bentley told him he was too young, but advised an obviously disappointed young man to return to school and get all of the police training and education he could.

Four years later, after college and attending a private police training school in Florida at his own expense, Joseph Gerace returned to Mayville and became a deputy sheriff. Young Gerace's skills as a crime scene photographer eventually earned him his sergeant's stripes. Sheriff Bentley told those assembled that he admired the work of Deputy Gerace as a crime scene photographer. He related how the deputy's work had been instrumental in obtaining criminal convictions. He pointed to one case in particular in which Deputy Gerace's photograph of a shoe imprint left on a dusty stair thread helped convict three men of the murder of an elderly Dunkirk woman. Bentley firmly believed his deputy's investigative techniques were as good as any in the state and limited only by the lack of the latest technology.

Bentley challenged his critics to either believe that story—which he insisted was true—or believe that he hired young Gerace to gain political favor with his father—either way, he said, he didn't give a damn, and he declared the meeting over. Bentley felt certain that state police commanders were responsible for "stirring up" political trouble with county Republicans because they resented his efforts to build up the department's forensics capabilities, which included Deputy Gerace.

Sheriff Bentley was a man of foresight, at least when it came to his department. He was one of the first county sheriffs in New York State, if not in the entire country, who successfully exploited the national war on drugs. He acquired powerful speedboats seized by federal agents in drug raids for use on the waters of Lake Erie despite the jurisdictional authority of the US Coast Guard. His deputies patrolled and made arrests on county lakes that were actually the property of New York State. He even managed to acquire a couple of helicopters through sources that remain yet unclear and hired deputies to fly them. Local politicians, Republicans and Democrats, fumed about the expansion of the sheriff's department and joked derisively that Sheriff Bentley had built an empire complete with an army, navy, and air force.

Immune to political criticism, Bentley argued that with the coast guard sixty miles away at Buffalo, it made practical sense to have a local response to boaters in trouble on Lake Erie waters off the Chautauqua County shoreline. Sheriff Bentley's actions were validated after a dramatic rescue on Lake Erie and in the aftermath of an alcohol-related boating accident on Chautauqua Lake that killed several young people. His case for the helicopters was advanced when a seriously injured child was airlifted in a life-saving flight to Buffalo's Children's Hospital.

His deputies, particularly rookies, had to wonder if he ever slept. He once called from home and instructed his dispatcher to order a young deputy in a patrol car to break off a high-speed chase with a motorcycle. He said the chase was unwarranted and dangerous; it stemmed from a simple traffic violation. The sheriff had followed the action on his bedside scanner. It was 3:30 a.m. Ironically, there was one person, a prisoner, who did not seem intimidated by Sheriff Bentley—it was Bucky Phillips. He and the sheriff had a long history together; parallel careers Bentley once told Bucky. Bentley had watched Bucky grow up in crime, but on one occasion when led into county jail handcuffed, Bucky saw Sheriff Bentley standing in the cellblock.

"Hey, Big Bad John," Bucky called out and flashed a toothy smile at the sheriff. "If you take these cuffs off, I'll flip you on your long, tall ass." Bentley just shook his head and turned away.

No one knows exactly what was said that day when the state police captain laid out his plan to take over patrol duties when he met with Sheriff Bentley, but the meeting lasted less than twenty minutes. The deputy in charge of the jail claimed the state official was visibly shaken when he escorted him through the checkpoints to the door. He said the captain's lips were quivering, his hands were trembling, and his face was flecked with beet red and pale splotches. The deputy claimed he could see the movements of the trooper's throbbing neck arteries as he tramped heavily across the parking lot to his car.

Despite his political reputation and imposing stature, Sheriff Bentley was a quiet man who barely spoke above a whisper to politician or prisoner. Even after his departure, his was the dominant presence that lingered in the room. But it was neither his physical stature nor demeanor that was so intimidating—it was his eyes. His eyes were big and round; always open wide and even appeared to bulge slightly as they rapidly flickered up and down and back and forth, carefully scanning all those who stood before him. But when he locked his gaze on those in his presence there was not a single person who could not immediately detect rejection, anger, approval, or disapproval.

After the meeting with the state police captain, Sheriff John Bentley walked across the street to the Gerace Office Building. He was immediately ushered into the executive's office. John Glenzer recalls that Sheriff Bentley, always a gentleman, and always polite, extended his hand and spoke in a voice with neither anger nor angst. "Jack," he said, "I know you're under pressure with the budget, but if this thing goes any further it'll be all out war."

Jack Glenzer smiled, shook Bentley's hand, and knew that it would be half a century before the suggestion would ever be brought up again. Although the two men would remain fast friends, John Bentley felt saddened that his old friend would have even thought about removing road patrols. But Sheriff Bentley would reserve his deepest resentment for the high command of the New York State Police. He made sure that every deputy and every employee knew that the New York State Police had tried to destroy their jobs and remove bread from their table. Until the day he died in May 1994, Sheriff John Bentley cooperated with the operational command of the New York State Police, but viewed it with disdain and suspicion.

After the death of Sheriff John Bentley nearly everyone expected one of his sons, both of whom were in law enforcement—one son was a lieutenant in the sheriff's department, the other a village police chief—to succeed him as county sheriff. After several names floated to the surface and failed to generate political excitement, his son John from the Village of Lakewood Police Department was finally persuaded to become a candidate. His opponent in the November election would be Joseph Gerace, the young photo lab sergeant Sheriff Bentley had mentored.

That election saw two of the most politically prominent families in Chautauqua County politics engaged in a countywide campaign to see who would assume what had become a politically powerful county office. When the votes were counted, Joseph Gerace became Chautauqua County's elected sheriff. Like Sheriff Bentley, Sheriff Gerace remained confident in his department's ability, whether it was rural road patrols in one-man cars, combating the spread of illicit drugs, or providing lifesaving airlifts to distant medical centers. Like his predecessor, Sheriff Gerace was proud of his department's well-deserved reputation as a top-notch investigative unit comparable to, or even better than, some in much larger venues.

Chapter Twenty-Two

THE TIPPING POINT

Operational command for the Phillips manhunt fell to Troop A of the New York State Police and its commander, Major Michael T. Manning. Manning was a thirty-year veteran who after graduating from the academy was posted to Troop E in New York's Finger Lakes region. He served as an investigator from 1986 to 1988 and was promoted to the permanent rank of sergeant. Manning rose rapidly in the ranks and served as station commander before being appointed zone sergeant four years later. He was assigned to the BCI in the Internal Affairs Division at Division Headquarters and promoted to lieutenant. In June 2002 Manning was promoted to captain and made Zone 3 Commander of Troop A and subsequently became Troop A Commander with the rank of major.

By June 19, 2006, based on reports from the Chautauqua County Sheriff's Department and his own BCI intelligence, Major Manning had already deployed search operations in Niagara, Cattaraugus, and Chautauqua counties. Attention centered on the area in and around Cassadaga, a small rural village near Bucky's birthplace. Troopers arrived in numbers from across New York with SUVs, dogs, helicopters, shotguns, rifles, night vision goggles, and a host of boastful, over-confident commanders. They filled hotels and motels and restaurants in two counties, and the money spent for their accommodations provided a much needed and immediately noticeable boost in the local economy.

Sheriff Gerace anticipated that a central command post would be created where all law enforcement leaders, including the FBI, would listen and even have input in the pursuit of Bucky Phillips. He suggested the Chautauqua County Fairgrounds would be ideally suited for a central command post and staging area. Since the fairgrounds were gated and fenced, external access could be easily controlled and would provide a secure, around-the-clock base of operations unhampered by the normal flow of community activity. The fairgrounds were also strategically located on the western edge of Dunkirk, near the local state police barracks at Fredonia and with easy access to major thoroughfares and the New York State Thruway.

Major Manning made it clear from the outset that the search for Phillips was the exclusive domain of the New York State Police and that it would be they who would get their man. Instead of the fairgrounds, the state police initially located central command at the smaller state police barracks at Fredonia, and those sitting at the command table were limited primarily to state police commanders on a need-to-know basis. That refusal to involve local authorities early in the process would prove to be a glaring mistake with disastrous consequences.

Within a week more than sixty uniformed state troopers were assigned to stationary checkpoints and roving patrols. An additional forty troopers from BCI had already circulated wanted posters, obtained search warrants for the homes of two of Bucky's relatives, and had established wiretaps. BCI investigators also installed electronic surveillance equipment and assisted uniformed troopers. Specialty units, including members of the elite state police MRT had been brought in and augmented by members of Troop A Rifle Team members and canine units.

Troopers from the local barracks remained on routine patrol duties but were available for search and support. Although investigators had been unable to confirm whether Bucky had visited the home of Kasey Crowe, the mother of Bucky's daughter Patrina, they placed her residence under around-the-clock visual observation. The New York State Department of Environmental Conservation provided manpower to assist with fixed posts and search efforts. In New York State, forest rangers are trained and armed as law enforcement officers.

The Cassadaga community was accustomed to a tranquil existence fostered by Lily Dale, an internationally renowned center for spiritualists. Almost immediately the entire community was turned upside down and inside out. Residents who were leading orderly, unassuming lives free from the pressures of urban life were suddenly confronted by a cadre of armed and anxious New York state troopers. The persistent thumping of helicopter blades and the high-pitched whine of all-terrain vehicles blended with screaming sirens, creating an infuriating cacophony of noise at all hours. To make matters worse on-site spokespersons for the New York state troopers were combative and strident to the point of assuming the characteristics of comic book characters.

Manning's machismo proved to be a poor and unlikable imitation of John Wayne. He frequently appeared before microphones and cameras to scold locals for complaining of improper treatment and for allegedly assisting Bucky Phillips evade capture. When Manning was unavailable for the cameras, his replacement was a young, blond female state trooper named Rebecca Gibbons. Lieutenant Gibbons assumed a tone of bluster and cockiness more reminiscent of Nancy Grace than someone trying to persuade the public to be more cooperative in the manhunt.

That attitude, together with the arrogant, heavy-handed way people who commuted to work were harassed at roadblocks, fractured the peace and soured residents against the troopers. People were stopped, questioned, and searched as they left their homes, detained on their return, and were often detoured for blocks with their destination in plain sight. As the search intensified, it became obvious even to the most casual observer that the New York State Police were subjecting citizens to unnecessary restraints on liberty. But the situation was about to become much grimmer.

By Saturday, June 24, 2006, and in the absence of official sightings, all law enforcement agencies, even those remotely connected to the Phillips manhunt, were convinced Bucky had returned to Chautauqua County. On that Saturday morning a red Honda ATV was reported stolen from

Cotton Well Drilling Corporation in the town of Sheridan in Chautauqua County. The theft was associated with Bucky because a Dodge Caravan stolen from the town of Hancock in Delaware County was recovered at the same location.

Armed with fresh information, the state police increased patrols, intensified intelligence gathering, and dramatically altered the daily activities of a docile community. To many county residents the manhunt did not possess the aura of a law enforcement agency dedicated to protecting the public but had the look and feel of an invading army determined to get revenge. Many local residents were persuaded by the attitudes and actions of the state police that Bucky Phillips would be shot on sight. State police pressed their search for Bucky in the town of Sheridan, and in the early morning hours of Sunday, June 26, 2006, the fears of the community became a reality. A state trooper stopped Bradley Horton, twenty-five, married, and a former US marine on his ATV in Sheridan. Here, the stories from the state trooper and local residents dramatically differ.

The state police claim that Horton sped away after a routine traffic stop. The trooper insisted his belt managed to snag on a protruding part of the ATV and that he was dangerously dragged for more than a mile. The state trooper insists that Horton refused to stop and that his only option was to shoot and kill Bradley Horton. At some point, the state trooper apparently freed himself from the ATV and called over his radio. There were reports from residents who claimed hearing over police scanners the trooper call out, "I got Bucky. I shot Bucky."

At the time, Bucky Phillips was sleeping in one of several wilderness campsites he had hastily created with as many comforts of normal life as he could acquire under such Spartan conditions. He claims to have heard the same message over his police scanner. "I didn't know what the hell they were talking about," he told me. Family members claim recordings of the shooting incident have since disappeared.

Apparently Horton traveled a distance before falling from the ATV, and as he lay wounded and bleeding, he allegedly called his wife and 911 for help. Friends and family claim they were not allowed to search for

Horton and that the state troopers made no attempt to locate the former marine. It is true that the state trooper involved in the shooting made no attempt to search for Brad Horton. Once again, in a policy confined to and understandable only to an enlightened inner circle of the state police command structure, Trooper Sean Pierce was ordered to hold his position. About forty minutes after the shooting and not bound by the same code of behavior, Chautauqua County deputies were called to the scene and located Horton. He was immediately flown by helicopter to Hamot Medical Center in Erie, Pennsylvania, where he died later that evening.

The state trooper maintained that he had to shoot in self-defense. Family members claim the medical examiner's report contradicts the officer's account. They claim the autopsy revealed five gunshot wounds to the back with no upward angle present in the entry wounds. They remained convinced the evidence contradicted the trooper's claim that he shot Horton while being dragged by the ATV. The trooper was treated at a hospital and returned to work the following day.

Shocked and angry family members demanded an independent investigation. Instead, the BCI investigated the shooting. Gloria Horton, mother of the shooting victim, claimed the shooting was a case of mistaken identity. Horton's wife Kelly agreed and insisted the Chautauqua County District Attorney launch his own investigation. Regardless of the public outcry, Major Manning angrily denounced assertions that the shooting was related to Bucky Phillips and insisted Horton's death was a separate, unrelated incident, a routine traffic stop. Manning's response only added to the anger and frustration felt by family and friends of Brad Horton and was contrary to widespread public opinion. Angered residents persuaded District Attorney David Foley to present the case before a Chautauqua County grand jury for a possible indictment. It was not until after Bucky was captured in September that a Chautauqua County grand jury returned a "no-bill," no indictment of Trooper Pierce in the shooting of Bradley Horton. District Attorney Foley acknowledged that the shooting was a hard case to make on available evidence, but the truth of his statement did little to mitigate community suspicions.

On Tuesday, June 27, 2006, the state police received a break and literally came within seconds of capturing Bucky Phillips twice within a few hours. It happened after the Chautauqua County Sheriff's Department investigated two burglaries in the town of Charlotte. One was a break in at a seasonal residence where a witness observed a man dressed in dark clothing fleeing the scene riding a black ATV. Deputies immediately processed the scene and lifted a fingerprint that identified Bucky Phillips. Next, deputies followed ATV tracks for a short distance that led to the second break in at a Department of Environmental Conservation building located nearby on Bard Road.

Armed with that information, the state police flooded the area with more than a hundred officers, including local deputies, state forest rangers, canine units, uniformed state troopers, and BCI investigators. They patrolled the area using ATVs and roving patrols and established twelve "quiet and dark" listening posts for the nightshift. The New York State Police Aviation Unit brought in a plane equipped with a thermal imaging device to assist in the search.

Bucky found the ATV useful in navigating logging trails and paths through the woods and found it particularly helpful traversing low-lying wetlands. Immediately after stealing the ATV, he used a couple of cans of spray paint and painted the machine black. He intended to stash the ATV in the woods and use it on a limited basis. But, after the witness spotted him on the ATV and with the efficiency of county deputies linking him to the Charlotte break-ins, Bucky faced an entirely new set of problems.

"It took me awhile to figure out what was going on," Bucky said. "Before the sun went down there were cops all over the place." Bucky grimaced and sat forward on the edge of his chair. "There were using ATVs. I could hear them charging through the brush." Bucky explained that he waited until after dark to move and that a canine unit almost immediately spotted him on the ATV. "I crossed the road and was almost on top of them before I knew it," he said. Bucky acknowledged that he sped down the road and quickly disappeared into the brush.

The state police report claims that at 9:00 p.m. a canine unit tried to pursue a suspect dressed in camouflage and operating a black ATV. The officers reported that soon after they lost sight of the suspect, they encountered several people standing on the side of the road. The people denied seeing the ATV pass them, but further investigation confirmed they were relatives of Phillips. The state police claim that three hours later they discovered evidence that suggested family members had delivered supplies to Bucky. That became a frequent accusation by state police spokespersons as frustration mounted within their ranks as Bucky continued to elude his pursuers.

The troopers who made the sighting relocated farther down Ames Road and established a stationary post near the Hall Road intersection. At about 1:00 a.m. the officers spotted someone moving through the woods shielding a flashlight with his hand. Bucky picks up the story from there. He said that earlier that day he had stashed the ATV and set out on foot. He explained during daylight hours there were so many cops on ATVs and foot patrols that he could not walk anywhere on a trail.

"Cops were everywhere. I had to hide in the brush and hope like hell they didn't use a dog to find me." Bucky took a deep breath and vigorously rubbed his face with both hands. "I watched them set up listening posts and cameras. They had my ass cornered." He said he had to lay very still and flat on his belly in the thick undergrowth for what seemed like an eternity but was actually only a couple of hours. He said it probably helped that he wore camo, because on one occasion a trooper's boot was barely six inches from his face. "That guy almost stepped on me," Bucky said. Although Bucky could hear the officer talking to his partner, he never saw the other searcher. He explained that he was stretched flat in a slight depression under a canopy of tangled brush and held his breath until the pair walked past.

"Fifteen minutes later I thought for sure that a forest ranger saw me." Bucky smiled faintly and ran his fingertips across his brow. "There were two of them on ATVs," Bucky said. "It was surprising how quiet the machines were. They were going really slow." He said the first officer passed by without incident, but the man on the trailing machine slowed almost to a stop, flattened his chest over the handlebars, stuck his ass in the air, and cut a loud fart. "When he had his head over those bars, he was looking me right in the eyes, but nothing happened."

Bucky knew he must eventually leave his hiding place, and he waited until all was quiet before he made his move. "I knew I had to stay off the trails. They had too many listening devices and cameras. I didn't know where they were." Bucky paused and poked the air with his finger. "Those guys were really good at hiding that shit. If I hadn't seen them install a unit with my own eyes, I wouldn't have known it was there."

Bucky said it was a struggle to navigate through the thick undergrowth and brush, but he had no other choice. "I didn't want to use a flashlight," Bucky frowned, "but I couldn't see a thing, and I kept getting tangled up in the brush." Bucky said it was pitch black, and he had no idea he was so near the road. "When I was able to lift my head, I saw the dammed car." He said the scene was frozen for an eternity in his mind. He said as soon as he looked up, the car lights came on and he could hear someone yelling. "I couldn't have been more than twenty feet from the car." Bucky shuddered and tightly squeezed his shoulders behind his back.

Bucky said he heard one of the cops yell, "Freeze!" and saw a shotgun poking through the passenger side window. He said he didn't think. "I just lunged as hard as I could through the brush." He said he dropped his flashlight and fell headfirst into the tangled undergrowth. The first time he fell he was able to bounce right up. He said he fell several times running in the dark, but the last time he fell his backpack became snagged in the brush. Bucky recalled the incident with humor. "I felt like a turtle lying on its back. All I could do was kick my arms and legs." Bucky said he struggled to free one arm from the pack and was able to turn slightly sideways to free his other arm from shoulder straps. "I found out that when you're on the run you can't fall in love with anyone or anything." He said he had no choice. He had to abandon the backpack.

The *Phillips Manhunt Operational Review* ordered by State Police Superintendent Wayne E. Bennett before he retired gives the following account of that encounter with Bucky Phillips:

"The trooper in the passenger seat exited the vehicle but did not pursue Phillips based on his understanding of instructions issued at the earlier briefing. The canine handler began following Phillip's path by paralleling his movements along the road, until he could no longer identify his location. Both members then returned to the patrol vehicle and used a cell phone to call the command post to request instructions. An NYSP Captain at the command post, who happened to be a former canine handler, ordered that the canine be released immediately. However, the handler did not do so, choosing to wait for other NYSP to arrive, noting there was no visual target for the dog to pursue. Responding members established a roadway containment perimeter consisting of 38 two-person patrols. Responding MRT members commenced a search of the woods, accompanied by the canine handler and his dog. NYSP Aviation, equipped with a FLIR thermal imaging unit also assisted with the search.

The search efforts immediately located a firearm and a backpack that Phillips had dropped when he fled. Unfortunately, the head start afforded Phillips by the delay of an immediate pursuit and failure to release the Division canine, coupled with the canine following the track to the camp verses the flight trail, allowed him the time necessary to evade capture. Subsequent canine tracks revealed that Phillips had quickly left the initial search area and retreated to a much larger section of "connecting" woods.

Inquiry into the circumstances surrounding this potential apprehension opportunity reveals a couple of key factors: (1) a misunderstanding and/or a lack of clarity to briefing instructions; and (2) a personal judgment error by the canine handler. The trooper partnered with the canine handler believes he may have been able to catch Phillips, but stated he did not enter the woods because his understanding of instructions issued at the evening briefing prohibited members from pursuing Phillips in the woods. The trooper noted, that while he believed the subject he observed was Phillips, he did not shoot, even when the subject ran back into the woods, because he was not able to see his face and verify it was Phillips, and the subject made no threatening actions toward the members. This was a proper decision, as command staff reminded all members that they needed to be certain a subject was in fact Phillips before the use of deadly physical force was considered during any apprehension effort."

There are some absolutely astonishing inferences tucked away in this otherwise unremarkable 160-page official document. Inferences that arguably support Bucky's claim that the "suicide by cop" message was tacit prior approval to shoot him on sight and that the shooting of Brad Horton was a case of mistaken identity. The evidence is circumstantial, but prosecutors frequently use circumstantial evidence to convict, even in capital murder cases. In the first instance there is absolutely no evidence in the life of Ralph "Bucky" Phillips that would suggest he was ever suicidal. There was not a shred of medical evidence to support the notion that Bucky Phillips wanted to commit any kind of suicide, much less suicide by cop.

In this instance the timeline is important: The shooting of Bradley Horton occurred less than forty-eight hours from the 1:00 a.m. sighting of Phillips referred to in the report. The trooper did not give chase or open fire even though the man he believed was Bucky Phillips was less than thirty feet away. The trooper's actions were justified in the Bennett report because "instructions issued at the evening briefing prohibited members from pursuing Phillips into the woods." The trooper's actions were further supported in the Bennett report because he followed instructions at the briefing that was conducted just a few hours before when he reported for duty. From the report: "The trooper noted, that while he believed the subject, he observed was Phillips, he did not shoot, even when the subject ran back into the woods, because he was not able to see his face and verify it was Phillips."

If the shooting of Bradley Horton was indeed a case of "mistaken identity," that supports the contention raised by Bucky and others that there was a "shoot on sight" order. Although it may be true, the notion that a trooper was dragged at high speeds from the back of an ATV for nearly a mile without sustaining barely a scratch is difficult to grasp. At the time of the Horton shooting, the state police did not know that Bucky had painted the stolen ATV black. If the shooting of Bradley Horton was unrelated to the Phillips manhunt as Major Manning suggested, why was there so much emphasis by commanders at the subsequent deployment briefing not to shoot without first verifying the identity of the suspect? Did the shooting of Bradley Horton prompt that instruction?

The report is critical of the canine handler's response during the same early morning episode: "Nonetheless, there was concern over the canine handler's failure to immediately release the State Police Dog when Phillips was first challenged as the handler exited the vehicle. . . . This situation involved a subject wearing camouflage clothing, walking out of a heavily wooded and overgrown area at night, with a light that was covertly shielded, in an area where patrols were looking for a fugitive who was wanted for escape and the attempted murder of a Trooper, and who began to flee when ordered to stop. Immediate release of the canine was not only appropriate, but was imperative. When the command post officer-in-charge, who is a former canine handler, was contacted by the trooper/handler for instructions, his immediate response was 'release the dog.' The probability is very high that an immediate release of the dog, as the handler exited his vehicle, would have resulted in the apprehension of Phillips in this situation."

The report authorized by Superintendent Bennett is harshly critical of individual troopers but has little to say about the state police command structure and total lack of common-sense planning.

"I've never been to Chautauqua County before. I wouldn't know Ames Road from Broadway. If these assholes think I'm going to chase a lunatic through the woods in the middle of the night, dog or no dog, they're crazy as hell." Those were not the remarks of the canine handler cited in the report but came from a veteran state police trooper from downstate who was sent to Chautauqua County to assist in the Phillips manhunt.

The report's conclusion that a dog would have easily captured Bucky Phillips was intriguing and prompted me to ask him how he would have reacted. Bucky said he doesn't fear dogs, but has enormous respect for a well-trained dog and the damage they can generate. Bucky explained in animated detail what he would have done if attacked by a dog.

"A dog has fear and speed in its favor," Bucky said. "The first mistake is to run. A human can't outrun a dog. You've got to kill the dog. If you can shoot it before it reaches you, all the better." He explained that a person should confront a dog head on. He said that dogs are trained to react first to the arm or hand that holds a weapon, but that they will grasp the nearest limb. At this point Bucky stood with his legs spread apart and his torso twisted sideways. "If you have time," he stressed, "wrap your least valuable arm, your left arm if you're right-handed and your right arm if you're left-handed with a jacket, even use your shirt. It will hurt but offer that arm to the dog." Bucky went on to say that the dog might knock you to the ground. "You need to understand that the dog will not turn loose. Keep one hand free and shoot the dog in the head immediately. If you have a knife, cut its throat. If you don't have either, try to choke it. Either way, twenty or thirty seconds, you've got to kill it immediately." Bucky stressed the importance of offering your arm to a dog. "A dog can do serious damage to your leg or ankle. If you're fleeing on foot, it's better to have a wounded arm than a crippled leg." Bucky turned slowly and grew more serious. "A word of caution," he added. "As strange as it seems, you can kill a man. You can even kill a cop. But, if you kill a dog, people really get pissed."

Bucky could hear the canine units trailing him through the brush but managed to slip through the police lines into larger connecting woods. After a few minutes he paused to catch his breath and realized something was amiss. He leaned heavily against a tree trunk and listened. The sounds of the police search were growing faint, more distant. He squatted at the base of the tree and stretched his legs straight out. It took him a few minutes to figure out what was going on. He knew the hunt had not been called off, after all, they were using dogs and only a few minutes earlier the dogs were hot on his scent. It could only be one thing, he thought. "Geez," he muttered, "how could I be that lucky?" The dogs were following his back scent. That was lucky for him in the short run, he thought, but terribly unlucky for him that the dogs would take his pursuers to his campsite. Although he could not be a hundred percent certain that was the situation, he could not take a chance. He would not return, as he had intended, to that particular campsite.

Even though the canine had followed a back track, it was still a good track. The Bennett report called the refusal of the handler to initially release the canine a failure, but it did credit the dog for a legitimate scent even though it took them in the wrong direction. But, that back track proved to be a bonanza for the state police. They had already found the backpack Bucky abandoned with a .38-caliber pistol that would be linked to the shooting of Trooper Sean Brown. They found the red ATV that had been painted black at the campsite as well as camping gear and canned goods.

For the next several days Bucky laid low and did not move around much at all except in a small, localized area and tried to avoid all human contact. The *Phillips Manhunt Operational Review* gives an account that occurred at 3:00 p.m. on June 28, 2006, when a New York State Police captain and a zone sergeant saw someone matching Phillips description run across the road about a quarter mile in front of them and disappear into a small patch of woods surrounded by fields. Within five minutes, a FLIR-equipped plane based at the nearby airport in Dunkirk was in the air over the area, and within ten minutes uniformed troopers had effectively established perimeter containment.

While personnel awaited the arrival of an MRT, a contingent of BCI investigators arrived on the scene and immediately launched the search. Although they came up without the suspect, they learned that the house on the edge of the woods belonged to Phillips's relatives. Officers reported that the occupants tried to interfere by telling them they were on private property and asking them to leave. Although the state police believed family members had again helped Bucky elude capture, Bucky admits to being in Chautauqua County, but has no recollection of that particular episode.

"That account doesn't click with me," Bucky chuckled. "During that time, I appreciated the darkness. I didn't move around much in the daytime."

On July 1, 2006, an owner of a hunting camp in the town of Arkwright was using four field cameras as a security system and had photographs of a man walking on a trail. The man in the photograph was dressed in camouflage and bore a strong resemblance to Bucky. Undeterred, uniformed troopers continued roving patrols and maintained listening posts while BCI investigators increased intelligence activities, maintained wiretaps, and investigated leads. They even baited the area with ATVs at strategic points, but the fugitive refused to take the bait and remained elusive. By that time more than three hundred troopers, including rifle teams, MRT units, aviation crews, Department of Environmental Conservation officers, and New York State forest rangers comprised the daily workforce. Because of the approaching Fourth of July holiday, local law enforcement units had to withdraw temporarily for regularly scheduled holiday patrols.

There were no confirmed sightings of Bucky Phillips from June 28, 2006, until July 16, 2006, and for good reason. Bucky was out of town. A couple of trips to Kentucky, a couple of trips to Ohio, perhaps one trip to Michigan; Bucky drove nearly three thousand miles back and forth over a time span of sixteen days. The state police stayed busy during that same time and were joined on July 6, 2006, by fifteen agents of the FBI's Critical Incident Response Group/Hostage Rescue Team accompanied by an additional thirty-five-member technical support team.

Major Manning was growing even more frustrated as his search teams continued to uncover one after another of Bucky's presupplied campsites. On July 7, 2006, they discovered an abandoned camper in Arkwright. Inside the camper they found two long guns, personal hygiene products, camping gear complete with cooking and eating utensils, sleeping bags, canned goods, a Styrofoam ice chest, and fresh produce. Major Manning was reportedly furious when he learned that his officers also found a television set attached to a marine battery that had been stolen from a previous burglary connected to Phillips. "For all the good we're doing," Manning exploded, "we might as well provide this son of a bitch with room service." Days later a county deputy described the campsite to friends as "a bed and breakfast furnished by Walmart."

Bucky said television reception was better than he imagined. "I picked up channels 2, 4, and 7 in Buffalo and 35 in Erie. Sometimes it was fuzzy, but the audio was always good." Bucky explained that he was particular when he stocked his campsites. He explained that soups with pull top cans were preferred. "Pop the top, sit the can on hot coals. Hot soup in less time than it takes in a microwave." He explained that Spam in pull tops was always good and that Hormel Chili, with or without beans, even came in a pull top.

If the product came in a plastic container Bucky would simply drop it in a can of boiling water. "There are a lot of really good food products," Bucky said, "hermitically sealed breakfast sandwiches, pre-cooked sausage and bacon. Even macaroni and cheese." He said he liked to shop at Sam's Club, because he said, "you can buy six or eight cans in convenient packaging." He even stocked two of his campsites with battery-powered electric toothbrushes. "Big Lots isn't a bad store either." Bucky grinned. "I bought a lot of items there cheaper than I could in the prison commissary."

Major Manning and his colleagues became convinced that a vast network of local residents, family, and friends were assisting Bucky. They grew even more frustrated when "Run Bucky Run" immediately became a familiar sign and slogan. Crudely painted "Run Bucky Run" signs suddenly began to appear on vehicles and bridge abutments throughout the area. "Where's Bucky?," "Don't Shoot—I'm Not Bucky," and "Got Bucky?"—a reference to "Got Milk?"—became bumper stickers and festooned T-shirts sold by local vendors. A local restaurant even drew the wrath of Major Manning, State Police Superintendent Wayne Bennett, and lone, local critic, a local Catholic priest for selling a "Bucky Burger."

On July 10, 2006, two BCI lieutenants accompanied state police electronics "techies" into the field to download surveillance equipment on Burnham and Skinner Roads in the town of Charlotte. They almost immediately spotted an individual about fifty yards away running along the ridgeline. Minutes later they heard an ATV start up and speed away.

They decided not to give chase because the suspect had the high ground advantage and was on the move. Two hours later when the MRT team arrived they mounted a reconnaissance of the area instead of a direct search because the suspect had fled, and they had no idea of the direction he had taken. But they did uncover another of Bucky's campsites. The campsite was outfitted comparably to the previous site, but without battered-powered appliances. The officers also found a .22-caliber rifle that was reported stolen during a burglary in Binghamton, New York, a few weeks earlier.

The very next day MRT members located a burglarized camping trailer that had a recently used fire pit, a bathroom pail, and empty Pepsi bottles. There were several freshly cut small trees and one had a string tied around it that police suspected was a marker of sorts. Bucky said he knew the area from his childhood. There were more camps now, but the area was just as rugged and heavily wooded. Bucky appreciated that much of the area remained inaccessible to mechanized machines. Snowmobiles and ATVs were confined to a few very old logging trails; narrow, rocky streambeds and sharp, craggy slopes were accessible only by the most skilled hikers.

Bucky denied ever occupying that particular campsite, and he was very precise in his wilderness toilet habits. He never used a bathroom pail. He said he always erected a latrine away from the camp in a secluded area and invariably covered waste with dirt, stones, leaves, or twigs. Bucky was careful never to urinate twice in the same area and never near his campsite. Animals could always detect human odors, and if a latrine or a common area was repeatedly used for bathroom functions, even humans could recognize the odors.

Chapter Twenty-Three

A DREAM DEFERRED

Dreams of freedom faded for Bucky Phillips in the early morning hours of June 10, 2006, near Elmira, New York, when a state trooper flipped on his flashing red lights behind a green Mustang. Bucky's most recent business forays out of state had gone about as well as could be expected, but not nearly as well as he had hoped. By July 6, 2006, he held little hope for success, but if by the mercy of chance a break would come his way, it must come through the place he was most familiar. Despite obvious dangers, Bucky recognized that his uncertain future would be determined in Western New York, in that familiar geography Bucky Phillips called home.

After Bucky narrowly escaped capture twice in one day in Chautauqua County, he decided it was time for a change of scenery. That same day Bucky made his way to a secluded seasonal residence in the town of Cold Springs in Cattaraugus County near the New York–Pennsylvania line. This instance was the nearest Bucky came to divulging how friends provided assistance without ever seeing or talking to him directly. Those who knew Bucky best realized that whenever he was in the area certain behaviors automatically became routine. A vehicle might be backed last in a driveway; always with a full tank of gas and with keys hung over a visor or placed under a floor mat. There was usually cash in the glove box; anywhere from twenty to a couple of hundred dollars depending on how tight money was for the owner of the vehicle. There was a change of clothes, including shoes or boots, inside the trunk. Yes, there was often a weapon, usually a long gun, together with survival gear.

Bucky would take the vehicle and leave a sign that designated a commonly recognized location. The message was sometimes a cryptically written note on the back of a matchbook in one or two words like "Slot Center," which was immediately recognized as Charlotte Center in the town of Charlotte. Bucky once drove away in a pickup truck without being seen but left a small doggie bone inside the owner's mailbox. That small doggie bone signified to the owner that he could retrieve his vehicle along Little Bone Run Road near the Allegany Reservoir. If a problem arose, the friend could always report the vehicle stolen without betraying Bucky or his whereabouts. Such clues never had to be verbally communicated between Bucky and his friends. It was all too simple, and a continual source of aggravation for the state police command. That was how Bucky Phillips got to Hardscrabble Road in Cattaraugus County.

Bucky had been hiding out in the seasonal residence for several days and was surprised when he heard a car approaching early Sunday morning. He barely managed to get out the back door and make his way on foot into the dense woods, but he was spotted crawling across a steep path adjacent to the property. The homeowner told police that cigarette smoke hung in the air and that the coffee pot was still hot on the stove in the kitchen. Police found a red bicycle in the house that had been painted black and a grocery bag that contained fishhooks, a compass, and an Internet print out of police radio frequencies. More importantly they found latent fingerprints that identified Phillips.

The state police command post was still in Fredonia when Major Manning received a confirmed sighting of Bucky in Cattaraugus County. By 11:00 a.m. Manning had relocated search operations from Fredonia more than thirty miles away to the village of Randolph in Cattaraugus County. From all accounts that was a good strategic move, but that impetuous decision was not without consequences, and it involved the elite FBI detail that had flown in from Quantico, Virginia, at the request of the New

York State Police. Early that Sunday morning the team of FBI specialists informed the state police command and moved into the field to install and relocate highly sophisticated electronic surveillance equipment in the search for Bucky.

That elite FBI unit came about as a result of the FBI's acknowledged mistakes in the carnage at Waco and Ruby Ridge. The highly specialized unit was incorporated with the existing Hostage Rescue Team. The team can be deployed on a moment's notice around the world for rescue of US citizens held by a hostile force in terrorist- or criminal-related incidents. They assist local law enforcement agencies with enforcement activities, hostage negotiations, and high-risk arrests. They are equipped with cutting edge surveillance equipment and sophisticated weaponry. The effectiveness of the unit was first demonstrated in 1996 in Garfield County, Montana, in a standoff with a militant group known as the "Freemen." About 150 agents and local law enforcement surrounded a 960-acre property the militants named "Justus Township" in Garfield County. "Justus Township" was a self-declared independent nation of "Freemen" led by fifty-seven-year-old LeRoy Schweitzer, a right-wing separatist who denied the legitimacy of state or federal governments. The group created their own currency, refused to pay income and property tax, and declined to renew their drivers' licenses. They had their own courts and police force and posted bounties for police and judges. For nearly two years, the group of about thirty individuals resisted eviction from the property they called "Justus Township," which had been foreclosed. The eighty-one-day confrontation ended peacefully and without a shot being fired and was hailed as a success in the FBI's new approach to crisis management.

In the state of New York and by midafternoon on Sunday, this highly trained FBI team returned from the woods and discovered that the state police command post had vanished. Although the incident is not mentioned in any written reports, there were claims that the air turned "blue" when this crack FBI team of highly trained specialists discovered they had been left stranded in the woods without being notified. The *Phillips Manhunt Operational Review* states simply that on that same day the FBI/

HRT continued to provide assistance but relocated their tactical operations to the Jamestown Airport. That was a polite way of saying the elite FBI unit was "mad as bloody hell" after the entire operational command relocated without so much as a cell phone call. The state police command did not take the incident seriously, but the FBI equated it with the US Marines sending a unit on patrol and moving out and leaving them alone behind enemy lines. "They were really pissed at Manning," one trooper commented off the record. Three days later the elite FBI unit returned to Quantico.

Local law enforcement agencies were also treated on "a need to know" basis as determined by the state police command. The only thing local enforcement agencies knew for sure was that Bucky Phillips had once again avoided capture. Sheriff Joseph Gerace appreciated that whatever Bucky had been accused of, being dumb was not on the list. He knew Bucky's history. He knew the one thing that separated Bucky from the common thief was that Bucky never fell in love with his possessions. He would abandon anything, whether a car or a sack full of money, in a "New York minute" if he faced even the slightest chance of being apprehended. It became obvious that the fugitive had gained the upper hand. Bucky Phillips was calling the shots and time after time the police could only react.

The sheriff knew Bucky would keep returning to Chautauqua County. He would not have been surprised if Bucky had twenty or thirty, or even fifty "salted" campsites between Chautauqua and Cattaraugus Counties. Bucky had "salted" drops with everything from food to weaponry to tools to television sets. He also realized what others failed to grasp; Bucky Phillips would eat anything that could walk, swim, fly, or crawl and forage on nuts and berries and burdock and dandelion greens and brew tea from tree bark to survive. He also knew that a person could walk past a fallen log without so much as a hint that Bucky Phillips was stretched out on the other side covered with leaves and tree branches and sleeping like a baby.

Sheriff Gerace understood that Bucky Phillips was not making a game out of the manhunt; he was not deliberately provoking the police, he was simply trying to survive from one day to the next. The only way Bucky Phillips would be captured, Sheriff Gerace thought, was by his own wilderness tactics. Keep him moving, keep him off balance; do not allow him time to rest or think. If you let him rest, he will beat you every time. Instead of direct pursuit, use a phalanx of law enforcement to push through the woods like deer hunters driving deer toward waiting hunters. Then, and only then, they might have a chance to capture Bucky Phillips.

There were no sightings of Bucky for nearly a month, and the state police alternated between Cattaraugus and Chautauqua counties and increased their surveillance and intelligence-gathering activities. By that time they had developed on-site Quick Response Teams (QRTs) armed with .308-caliber rifles that could be deployed immediately without having to wait for an MRT to assemble and convoy to the area. Although there was not a single indication that Bucky Phillips had contacted his former girlfriend, the state police tapped her telephone and planted a listening and tracking device on the vehicle of Lisa Shongo. The taps did not provide useful information,

By July 28, 2006, Bucky's daughter Patrina Wright was ready to give birth. Sensing an opportunity, Major Manning established surveillance at Brooks Hospital in Dunkirk and developed an elaborate plan to use an ambulance to transport and conceal his sharpshooters. Patrina had her baby, but the proud grandfather remained absent from the blessed event and the sharpshooters abandoned their bivouac.

There were several unconfirmed sightings of Bucky from mid-July until early August, but Bucky had been out of state for most of that time and had driven nearly three thousand miles. "Business" contacts with which he had previously been engaged were reluctant to do business with him. Bucky understood that shooting a cop made him more conspicuous; he found that wherever he went, whatever he did, that despicable deed made even the most habitual criminal openly distrustful and unwilling to collaborate on risky business ventures. The money he had managed to accumulate was dwindling; he had little choice but to return home. Once back home Bucky was constantly on the move. On August 8, 2006, the Niagara County Sheriff's Office received a report that Bucky had been spotted on the Tuscarora Reservation two hours earlier.

The *Manhunt Review* points out that instead of immediately notifying the state police, the Niagara County Sheriff's Department contacted the US Border Patrol's Aviation Unit. When the state police were contacted, Major Manning was furious and ordered local state police patrols to respond immediately. At the same time, Manning ordered the search detail to move from Cattaraugus and Chautauqua counties to Niagara County. Manning was equally angered when he learned that the man who observed Bucky asked him to pose for a picture and Bucky obliged. The observer said Bucky was armed with a handgun, a long gun, and a police scanner. He also said Bucky was driving a black Ford Mustang that was reported stolen on August 4, 2006, in the town of Portville in Cattaraugus County.

Bucky was spotted twice in a very short time. A BCI investigator spotted him at a distance near the residence where his friend Peggy Rickard was staying. A short time later a passing motorist claimed to have seen Bucky on the north side of State Route 104. US Customs and the Border Patrol closed down international bridges into Canada, and the state police pressed their search until well after dark.

The fugitive had to abandon the Mustang, but again luck was on his side. Bucky knew the lay of the land as well on the Tuscarora as he did in Chautauqua County where he grew up. He simply slipped through the thin perimeter established by local authorities using little-known trails through more densely wooded terrain. He also knew that a 1995 Dodge Caravan was parked in a barn nearby the search area. Bucky had observed the owner park the van in the barn on earlier visits. It was the same with the black, Portville Mustang. Bucky had spied the vehicles on previous trips and filed their locations as landmarks in his memory. He waited until deep into the night and simply drove the Dodge Caravan from the barn.

Major Manning became even more vexed the very next day when the Dodge Caravan was sighted on Pierce Run Road in the town of South Valley in Cattaraugus County. The van was located at a camp that Bucky had previously burglarized. Manning immediately airlifted two QRTs to the Cattaraugus County location, but by the time they arrived the van was gone and so was Bucky Phillips. A skeleton crew was left with a QRT in

Niagara County, and once again, nearly two hundred state troopers con-voyed back to Chautauqua County and the state police headquarters at Fredonia.

Chapter Twenty-Four

ENCOUNTER WITH A BOUNTY HUNTER

B ucky's decision to leave the Cattaraugus location proved to be providential; he had no idea he had been spotted or that Manning was flying in the shock troops. Bucky decided in Niagara County that a slight
shift in scenery would be helpful. Chautauqua County was blanketed with
law enforcement, and Bucky had heard that the $25,000 reward had been
doubled. The cops were watching his daughter like a hawk and had Kasey
Crowe's residence staked out 24/7. Bucky abandoned the Dodge Caravan
in a secluded area and slipped across the state line into Warren County,
Pennsylvania.

He spent most of the day on Thursday wandering around a wooded
area in Glade Township and staked out a house that appeared to be temporarily unoccupied. Bucky was nearly exhausted, and his body ached like he
was coming down with the flu. Under the cover of darkness, Bucky made
his way to a small car dealership and had little trouble driving away in
a Chevrolet Cavalier. He returned to the house, took a shower, and slept
undisturbed in the bed. Bucky left the house before dawn the next morning, abandoned the Chevrolet, and immediately left the area. Once again,
Bucky was one step ahead of the law. By 8:00 a.m. that same morning, the
owner of the car dealership reported the stolen Chevrolet and soon afterward the homeowner reported a burglary.

The Pennsylvania State Police located the stolen car in Glade Township and immediately notified the New York State Police. BCI investigators assisted Pennsylvania State Police with interviews and assisted in processing forensic evidence in the burglarized residence. In collaboration with the Pennsylvania State Police, New York authorities devised a plan to leave the Chevrolet Cavalier as bait for several days, but Bucky was not heard from again until August 15, 2006, and this time at a motorcycle shop in Corry, Pennsylvania.

Maintaining consistency, Bucky refused to implicate those who may have assisted him elude authorities. But on Saturday Bucky drove a Dodge Durango 135 miles one way to New Castle, Pennsylvania, in response to an ad in the classifieds for the sale of a 1983 black Honda motorcycle. The parties agreed upon a price and Bucky returned the next day, Sunday, August 13, 2006, and handed over $1,000 in cash and took delivery of the machine. Bucky remained out of sight until the following Tuesday when he rode the machine to a repair shop in Corry, Pennsylvania, for a road check. Bucky picks up the story from there.

He said there were several people in the shop, and they got to him right away. Bucky sat in the waiting room and after about fifteen minutes looked in the outer bay and saw the men standing around the Honda talking in hushed tones. He said one man was sitting behind a computer monitor rapidly clicking through screens. Bucky said he knew immediately that he had been made. He stood his ground to make sure no one used a telephone or left the room. It was obvious the men were stalling. Bucky said he took a couple of steps inside the bay.

"Hey, guys," he said in a loud voice. "I don't want any trouble. Get my bike done and I'll get out of here." Bucky said the crew was caught off guard, but quickly finished the bike. He paid them and quickly sped away.

After leaving the motorcycle repair shop Bucky returned to Kane, Pennsylvania. He had friends there, and he needed to take care of another matter that if left unchecked could prove fatal. He had learned from several sources that a local man known only as Michael was intent upon capturing or killing him and collecting a reward that would ultimately grow to nearly half a million dollars. Bucky was purposely selective on details, but watched a man wearing sharply creased, khaki camos emerge from a diner shortly after noon. The man had his pant legs tucked and blossomed at the top of a rugged pair of black combat boots and wore his hair cropped close in a military cut. He had an empty holster hanging loosely from his shoulder and what appeared to be a can of pepper spray dangling from his belt loop.

He was a young man, probably no more than thirty-five with heavy jowls and a thick neck. He was about as tall as Bucky—perhaps a shade shorter but with short, thick arms and a broad chest. His abdomen spilled over the top of his belt and ended in a single roll below his belt buckle.

He appeared awkward and uncoordinated, but Bucky noticed that despite his appearance he was surprisingly agile. The man walked erect with a quick step and did not possess the gait of a man who was pushing three hundred pounds.

Bucky followed at a safe distance as the man ran several errands. He watched as he dropped an envelope into a post box then observed him chatting with a drive-through bank teller before he finally went inside a convenience store. Bucky was not concerned so much about professional bounty hunters who worked for bail bondsmen, but reckless "cowboys," especially locals, had the potential to be disastrous. This particular individual had attempted to question several of Bucky's friends about his whereabouts. He even attempted to surreptitiously follow individuals he thought knew Bucky and had gone so far as to place their residences under surveillance using concealed cameras. His efforts at surveillance were so awkward that on one occasion he followed a car that had a passenger that resembled Bucky. He followed the car back and forth through the Allegany National Forest until he ran out of gas. When he returned to Kane, he found his surveillance cameras had been stolen. Bucky had also received reports that the man had been on the Seneca Nation asking complete strangers what they knew about Bucky Phillips.

On this particular day Bucky followed the man as he parked his Ford Explorer directly in front of the local police station. Bucky learned that the man visited the police station almost daily for any odd bit of Bucky information. The man slid easily from his vehicle and walked confidentially into the local police station. He even waved as Bucky pulled a pickup truck directly behind the Explorer. Bucky casually returned the greeting and waited until the would-be bounty hunter was inside the station before he got out of the pickup and sauntered to the driver's side of the Ford. He stuck his head in the window and saw his FBI Most Wanted Poster clipped to the visor alongside his America's Most Wanted television show flyer. Bucky casually strolled to the opposite side of the street; crossed at the corner and walked toward the entrance of the police station. His timing was unintentionally perfect.

His pursuer came out of the police station and had just squeezed between the rear of the Explorer and the front of the pickup when he saw Bucky walking in his direction. The man snapped a sharp salute in Bucky's direction and pulled open the driver's side door. Both men slid simultaneously into the front seat. Bucky's movement was so sudden that the man was not immediately startled. It wasn't until he saw Bucky's arm swing hard in a sideways motion with the butt end of a pistol protruding from his left hand that he had any inkling he may be in trouble. But it was too late. The butt end of the pistol smashed hard against his face and blood immediately spurted from his nose and mouth. The man didn't cry out but wore a pained and puzzled look and immediately covered his mouth with his hand. "Are you looking for me?" Bucky shouted angrily, cocking his elbow for another swing.

The man did not answer but lowered his bloody hand from his mouth and stared in stunned silence at what appeared to be teeth or pieces of teeth in the palm of his hand. "Are you looking for me?" Bucky asked again, this time in an even more threatening tone. The man rapidly shook his head. "No. No." He stammered behind an upper lip that was beginning to puff up like a giant blood blister. "I don't know you."

"Yes, you do," Bucky said and menacingly waved the butt of the pistol under the man's nose.

"You've got my picture on your visor. You're going to kill my ass and drag me out of the woods."

"No, no, no." All of the color drained from the man's face, and he began to sob uncontrollably.

"Listen." Bucky issued a command. "You've been talking about killing my sorry ass. I don't have a lot to lose. I can blow your head off right here and right now and it won't make a fucking bit of difference."

"No, no, that was all talk. It was just bullshit. I was just trying to impress people."

The man was blubbering and raised his trembling hands in surrender. "I just want to live, please don't hurt me. You can go. I won't tell anyone."

Bucky opened the car door and placed one foot on the sidewalk. "Get the hell out of here. Never even mention my name again, not to the cops, not to your wife, not to your girlfriend, not to anyone."

"Don't worry," the victim whimpered.

"I won't worry, but you should," Bucky warned and got out of the car. Before the man drove away Bucky saw that he had pissed his camouflaged, khaki pants.

Bucky felt badly for the guy, but he already had nearly two thousand state police looking for him, and he sure as hell didn't need a guy like this making matters worse. Hell, he thought, the cops would probably shoot him if they saw him tromping through the woods. Maybe, he thought, I just saved this asshole's life. He waited several minutes before pulling away from the police station. He didn't think the bounty hunter would return but waited for several minutes before leaving the scene to be sure. He simply drove a few blocks then parked the pickup in a supermarket parking lot where he had left his bike. He placed the pickup keys over the visor and calmly straddled the bike. It was still early afternoon when Bucky left Kane, and it took him well over an hour to return to Chautauqua County. He bypassed the busiest section of downtown Warren in Pennsylvania and avoided the city of Jamestown altogether. His destination was an apartment complex on Route 60 in the town of Charlotte.

Chapter Twenty-Five

THE BEGINNING OF THE END

Despite the Pennsylvania leads and sightings, the New York State Police were no closer to capturing Bucky Phillips than before. Luck would continue to run against the state police, but life for the fleeing fugitive was about to take a more desperate twist. The following Saturday, August 19, 2006, Bucky was returning to a residential apartment unit when he was spotted on Route 60 at 6:30 p.m. by a New York state trooper on routine patrol. The officer thought he recognized the 1983 Honda and followed the motorcycle a short distance until it pulled into the driveway of a residential apartment unit. The trooper followed at a safe distance and parked on the shoulder. From his vantage point he got the license number and observed that the suspect was wearing camouflage pants and a black leather jacket.

The officer said he could see the suspect was wearing a red motorcycle helmet with a smoke-colored face shield. He immediately radioed the state police in Jamestown for a registration check. He watched the suspect walk upstairs and called Jamestown again on a cell phone for a progress check. He described the situation to the Jamestown desk trooper who immediately dispatched a trooper who was at the station and notified the command post. Back-up units arrived at the scene within minutes and established perimeter roadblocks. They stopped and searched every car, but no effort was made to enter the residence until the arrival of an MRT.

Bucky realized immediately that he had been made. He calmly got off the bike and climbed the covered outside stairs to the second-floor apartment without removing his helmet. Bucky never stopped walking; he stepped inside the apartment and immediately jumped to the ground at the rear of the unit and fled into woods. He did not stay long enough to say anything to the residents except that he had been made. He could only mumble a terse "thank you" before he leapt from the second-floor balcony and once again eluded capture.

The *Phillips Manhunt Operational Review* would reserve its harshest condemnations not for a bungling command, but for the troopers in the field. The initial sighting of Phillips by a trooper on roving patrol and his subsequent actions on that Saturday evening were severely criticized as "a failure to follow elementary training on how to conduct high risk vehicle stops." The report claimed that his "failure to immediately initiate a police radio transmission to request backup is inexplicable." He used his cell phone instead. This was at a time when troopers in the field were obviously getting mixed and confusing instructions from command, especially after the shooting of Bradley Horton.

The report is critical of the trooper for remaining in his vehicle: "In addition, not only did the trooper fail to radio for assistance, he remained seated in his vehicle, while the suspected fugitive casually got off the motorcycle and walked away."

"We were bitch slapped for not holding our positions and criticized again for not giving immediate pursuit," one search-wearied veteran observed. "We were told to use cell phones instead of radio transmissions, but when this poor bastard used his cell phone, he's cut off at the knees."

The report concludes that "the trooper's failure to properly convey the high risks aspects of this stop unnecessarily delayed notice an arrival of assistance, despite very close proximity of other patrols. Unfortunately, this was a significant reason why Phillips had ample opportunity to flee the residence and evade capture." That was the conclusion despite the fact that it took nearly two hours for commanders to move the appropriate SWAT-type forces to the location.

All that was left for the MRT to do after they finally arrived and searched the apartment was to arrest its occupants. Timothy Seekings, 49; Alice Kelly, 44; and Natasha Berg, 24, admitted that Bucky had stayed there three or four days. All three were arrested for harboring a fugitive. By this time tempers in the state police command post were unraveling, and over the next few days a plan was hatched in defiant disregard for the consequences. Not only was the plan a blatant abuse of power and a cruel and corrupt use of Child Protective Services, but also it was a gross violation of liberties.

Angry and frustrated at being unable to either capture a fugitive or convince a doubting public that Bucky Phillips presented an imminent threat to their safety, Major Manning was convinced that now was the time for drastic action. On Monday, August 21, 2006, his investigators obtained a search warrant for the residence of Kasey Crowe, the mother of Bucky's daughter.

"Search warrants are horseshit." I remember Bucky saying as he nervously paced back and forth behind the plexiglass partition.

"What do you mean?" I asked and tilted my head backward against the stiffness that was overtaking my neck.

"You don't understand search warrants either, do you?"

"I know a judge must be convinced," I offered.

"The cops had to lie like hell to get a search warrant for Kasey, or the judge simply didn't give a shit." Bucky quickly countered. "They didn't have a shred of evidence. They had to make it up." Bucky paused to catch his breath and continued. "Judges sign search warrants as easily as doctors prescribe aspirin. Do you really believe that a judge ever questions cops on warrants?" Bucky did not expect me to answer. "Judges, cops, prosecutors; they all sleep in the same bed."

"If that's a problem, how do we fix it?" I asked and that was all Bucky needed. He sensed another opportunity to exhibit his professorial demeanor.

"I've thought about that." Bucky suddenly stopped pacing and created a rhythmic cadence by swinging his arms and snapping his fingers behind his back. "And I've got the answer," he beamed. Once again, Bucky laid out a cogent argument. "It's due process. The accused never gets due process." Before I could interrupt, Bucky continued. "We've always been taught that according to our Constitution that it should be difficult to arrest a citizen. You know, protection against unreasonable search and seizure, that sort of thing, you know, without due process."

As I listened to Bucky, I remembered a defense attorney telling me that prisoners often knew more about the law surrounding their particular case than most lawyers. He said that all too often a lawyer had to scramble to get up to speed. "Convicts live with their cases every day. They have time to think about the ins and outs," he told me over lunch. It became immediately obvious that Bucky had thought a lot about the subject. He explained that prosecutors were supposed to represent the state and that a judge was supposed to ensure prosecutors and police stayed within the boundaries of the law and the Constitution.

"What we need," he said, "is due process from the very beginning. The people need to have confidence that the system is fair." Bucky immediately plunged into a dissertation that drew a distinction between the people as the "state" and the "establishment" of the state. He explained that when police suspect an individual of unlawful activity and ask for a search warrant, the accused can only challenge the warrant after the fact. Bucky argued that at the point where the police actually appear before a judge for a warrant that they are not acting for the "people" of the state—one of the "people" was being investigated—rather, he explained, they were acting in the interest of an "establishment" of the state.

"The people need a lawyer, a legal ombudsman, like a guardian ad litem. It can't be the judge; judges hardly ever challenge warrants. It can't be the prosecutor or the suspect's defense lawyer because no crime has been charged." Bucky smiled broadly and continued. "Maybe it could be a public defender, maybe a lawyer appointed for the court, but the propriety of search warrants ought to be challenged by a disinterested lawyer, an officer of the court."

"What if the police need a search warrant in the middle of the night?" I asked incredulously.

"Go ahead, grant the warrant, but hear arguments within forty-eight hours or whatever, but before the suspect is charged. Once a charge is made, the prosecutor and a defense lawyer do what they do." Bucky rubbed his hands together and added as an afterthought. "It should also be mandatory that interrogations be videotaped. And," he added with supreme confidence, "all arguments for search warrants ought to be videotaped." Bucky explained that digital technology makes it possible, economical, and practical to video tape search warrants at all hours and under extreme conditions.

Regardless of the evidence, at 4:00 a.m. on August 22, 2006, the state police arrived in force at the home of Kasey Crowe. Kasey and her family were asleep as an MRT, BCI investigators, canine handlers, and uniformed troopers took positions around the house and secured the perimeter. On a prearranged signal an entry team simultaneously announced their presence and knocked the front door off its hinges.

"It was a horrifying experience," Kasey Crowe recalled. She said the officers never gave them a chance to open the door. "They just knocked the door down and stormed in yelling and screaming." She said they were angry and even more hostile when they did not find Bucky inside. Actually, Bucky had been staying with a friend in Pennsylvania ever since the near miss on the motorcycle and had not been anywhere near Kasey Crowe or his daughter Patrina. Regardless, the police confiscated several items from the residence that they said proved Bucky had been staying there. The *Phillips Manhunt Operational Review* indicates that based upon that evidence, Kasey Crowe was arrested and subsequently charged with hindering prosecution. However, it was what happened next that angered Bucky and dismayed an already skeptical public.

Patrina Wright and Richard Catanese were arrested for endangering the welfare of a child, and Chautauqua County Child Protective Services provided an emergency removal of their children, including the newborn with little regard that Patrina was still breastfeeding the infant. Major Manning openly discussed the plan as a strategy that would force Bucky Phillips to immediately surrender after he realized his daughter was going to jail and that she would lose her children. Public reaction to Manning's actions ranged from outrage to anger to bewilderment. There was strong opposition from local officials who even suggested that the evidence was so weak against mother and daughter that neither would ever be convicted by a Chautauqua County jury. But that did not deter the state police command; the removal and arrest were cruelly executed.

It was the next day before Bucky learned of his family's arrest, and he was frantic to learn more about what happened. His first impulse was to return immediately to Chautauqua County, and he managed to steal a Dodge pickup truck from the Sheffield, Pennsylvania, area for that purpose. He had chosen the Dodge over two newer and faster vehicles because the pickup had a cell phone lying on the console. Bucky made his way to Akeley, Pennsylvania. Akeley was a very small, rural Pennsylvania community near the state line and for years had been the location of a sawmill that harvested ash and maple hardwoods for baseball bats. Bucky hid out in the woods for the better part of the day and tried three times in as many hours to call his daughter.

By late afternoon Bucky was successful in reaching someone, he refused to say whom, and was brought up to speed on the events of the preceding day. After hearing of the raid on Kasey Crowe's residence and the arrest of his daughter, Bucky was angry, and he blamed Michael Manning. As far as he was concerned Kasey, his daughter, and grandchildren were purposely victimized by an angry state police commander. Bucky wondered why innocent children, especially a newborn, could be so forcefully ripped from the arms of its mother for the crimes of an estranged father and grandfather. Bucky wanted to rip Manning apart with his bare hands, but years of living in maximum-security prisons had taught him that regardless of the circumstance, it was always better to just walk away. But Bucky had other problems too—his reward had been doubled and he had received an urgent message the day before that at least four bounty hunters were taking advantage of the hunting season in Chautauqua County to track him down. The bounty hunters were going to work twelve-hour shifts in pairs until Bucky was brought down.

The skies had been threatening all afternoon and Bucky did not relish the idea of spending the day outside during a rainstorm. By late afternoon he had holed up in a vacant bat factory building. The large steel and tin building was dry inside and provided concealment yet offered a good view of the road in both directions. The building was empty except for a skimpy pile of remnants that remained after round blanks had been sawed from tree boles cut to the proper lengths for baseball bats. Darkness and a light rain fell early under cloudy skies, and the sounds of gentle raindrops bouncing off the metal building lulled Bucky into a false sense of security. He was soon seduced by the rhythm of the rain and fell fast asleep.

Bucky slept for nearly an hour and woke with a sudden start. He regained his composure after he realized where he was and even felt comfortable enough to create a small, but hot blaze from scraps of dry shavings to heat some food. Bucky finished his soup and was watching the fire burn itself out when he saw a flash of light in the distance. He hurried to front of the building to get a better look and saw automobile lights rapidly approaching from both directions. Unbeknownst to Bucky the state police were aware that a Pennsylvania cell phone had called Patrina Wright's home three times that day without success. Using triangulation between cell phone towers in Southern Chautauqua County in New York and Northern Warren County in Pennsylvania, electronic experts in the New York State Police were able to pinpoint Bucky's location at the bat factory.

Without once looking back, Bucky fled the building and ran as fast as he could toward the woods. He was certain he had been spotted and could sense frantic movements behind him. As soon as he was concealed inside the tree line, he took a quick look back and saw a canine handler emerge from a vehicle with his dog at the same time S.W.A.T. members were scattering from heavy-duty vans. Bucky was virtually certain that he had not been spotted by a random civilian. He understood immediately that the cell phone must have been traced, and his initial instinct was to drop it at his feet.

As so often happens in the framework of one's life, the convergence of chance and circumstance changes the course of events. Bucky had once reflected that despite the best laid plans, much of what happened in his lifetime, good and bad, was accidental. Bucky had taken fewer than a dozen steps into the forest before the skies opened up without the accompaniment of lightning and thunder. It was if the bottom of a cloud dropped away and emptied its contents in a sudden, silent downpour. He immediately became soaking wet and turned his face toward the sky. Bucky laughed aloud. The intensity of the unexpected downpour sent troopers from two of the oldest state police departments in the United States scurrying for cover. Bucky knew the dogs would be useless in the downpour, and he knew that the troopers would probably not even establish a perimeter.

Bucky left the Dodge pickup on the Cable Hollow Road near Akeley and managed that same night to return to Chautauqua County. Though he was deliberately fuzzy about the details, it was obvious Bucky had arranged a midnight rendezvous with one of the few friends he had previously described as being closer than family. My best guess was that his cab driver that night was Todd Nelson from Kane, Pennsylvania, who earlier that day contacted the Pennsylvania State Police and reported the theft of his 9-millimeter handgun.

Bucky and Nelson were close, and Nelson would later be arrested and charged with harboring his felonious friend. But well before dawn on Sunday morning, Bucky Phillips had stolen a 1996 gold Dodge Intrepid from the town of Gerry. After that, he immediately burglarized Tom's Gun Shop in the town of Ellington where he walked away with thirty-five handguns, six long guns, a camouflage jacket, and as much ammunition as he could carry in a gym bag. Both thefts were reported to the Chautauqua County Sheriff's Department on Sunday morning, and a message was immediately forwarded to the state police and other law enforcement agencies. There was never any doubt about the number one suspect in both crimes.

Major Michael Manning, and even some local law enforcement officials were convinced that Bucky Phillips was preparing for an all-out war against the police. But that was the furthest thing from Bucky's mind. If he had wanted to provoke a shootout, he had plenty of opportunities. "Would you believe that I ate breakfast with four state troopers at Grandma's in

Cassadaga less than a month before Akeley?"

"You did?" I exclaimed. His comment suddenly brought me to my feet. Grandma's was the local diner in Cassadaga that introduced the "Bucky Burger" as a menu item that so infuriated Major Manning.

He looked at me and laughed. "Eight-thirty, maybe quarter of nine, I'm sitting alone on one side of the restaurant eating two eggs over easy, toast, bacon, the works. It must have been a shift change, but four troopers came in and sat at a table directly across from me."

"They didn't recognize you?" I asked with some skepticism.

"One of the guys nodded in my direction but didn't say anything. Besides," Bucky chuckled, "I was clean shaven, had a short crew cut, blue work pants with a blue work shirt. My shirt had the name Paul on a white patch over the pocket." Bucky rubbed his hands together and smiled broadly. "I looked like the Maytag Repairman."

"Were there other customers?" I pressed the issue.

"Not many. Three or four."

"Did anyone recognize you?"

Bucky mentioned there was a man standing outside lighting a cigarette when he started to go inside the restaurant. "The man spoke to me and said the coffee was hot."

"Did you recognize him?" I persisted.

"I think so, but he just got in his car and drove off."

I pressed him on the troopers. "Weren't you afraid you'd be recognized?"

"I was scared to death," he said. "I wanted to dive through the door." Bucky said it was a good thing he had eaten most of his breakfast before the troopers arrived. "I couldn't just get up and leave, but I thought I was going to choke on every bite." Bucky said he finished most of his breakfast, left a tip, nodded toward the troopers at the table, paid his bill, and departed as inconspicuously as he could.

I remember asking Bucky if he wasn't being intentionally provocative by appearing so publicly in places where ordinary citizens might recognize him and in places that were buzzing with police activity.

"Were you deliberately taunting law enforcement?" I asked.

"Only once," Bucky chuckled. "I admit I had a powerful urge to make them look like fools," he said and shifted his chair closer to the partition that separated us. "I even felt good about things like the diner, but I was only a wise ass once."

"How did that come about?" I asked.

"Two state cops spotted me crossing the road and decided to chase me down." Bucky wore a wry smile and a twinkle in his eyes as he continued the story. "They must have been desk cops," he observed with a slightly broader smile, "because they were really out of shape." Bucky said he acted like a bird with a broken wing. "You know, like a bird drawing a predator away from its nest." He said he would run just far enough ahead to stay out of pistol range. "Then," he said, "I would lean against a tree, grab my chest, and huff and puff like I was out of wind." Bucky said he repeated the stunt several times, each time drawing the officers deeper into the wilderness. He said he finally left them behind and climbed to the top of a high ridge and watched the officers as they finally realized they were hopelessly lost. "Did you know that people walk in circles when they are lost?" Bucky asked with subdued glee.

"I suppose I have heard that," I said and waited for him to continue.

"I watched them walk twice in the same wide circle. That's how they knew they were lost. They kept coming back to the same rock pile."

Bucky said he sat down and watched them use a cell phone. "I guessed they were calling for help, but," he grinned, "they seemed good natured about it. They laughed a couple of times. I guess they knew they were going to get their balls busted." Bucky said that after a couple of cigarettes, about half an hour, he heard the unmistakable sounds of a helicopter. He said he watched as each man was hoisted in a basket and pulled inside the helicopter.

Bucky explained that on that particular morning when he encountered the four troopers at Grandma's that he was forced into the diner. He said he saw two cars from the sheriff's department parked at the end of the street. "The cars were facing in the opposite direction and the deputies were having a conversation. I would have had to walk right past them. I dodged inside the diner as a last resort. Once inside the diner," Bucky shrugged, "I would have looked even more suspicious if I didn't order something."

Bucky said there was another occasion when he donned a set of cammos and actually had a conversation with a similarly clad New York state trooper outside the Fredonia barracks. "I was clean. Even looked like a cop."

"How could that have possibly happened?" I asked and even suggested that his story seemed far-fetched.

"I wanted to do some intelligence work on my own," he explained. He said it was the day Sean Brown, the trooper he had shot in June, was brought to Chautauqua County by the state police brass for a photo op and to boost sagging morale among the troopers. "I never told him I was a cop," Bucky said. "He didn't say he was one either. We just assumed. We talked for a long time."

"What did you talk about?" I wondered aloud.

"The weather, sports. I asked him where he was from. He said Troop A Rochester. Told him I was Troop C Sydney. Said he could use the overtime, just bought a house. I asked him about Manning. He said he never saw much of him, but he had a reputation for being a prick. I suggested that Manning liked being on CNN. He agreed."

I could not confirm the veracity of either of Bucky's accounts, but I did visit Grandma's restaurant in Cassadaga, and his description of the interior matched reasonably well. Although the state police vehemently deny that Bucky ever had a conversation with a trooper in front of the Fredonia command post, Manning did order surveillance cameras installed outside the facility.

If there was a turning point in the manhunt for Bucky, it was the burglary at Tom's Gun Shop in Ellington. "I always knew Bucky was dangerous," Sheriff Joseph Gerace admitted. "Anyone who can shoot a trooper like he did Sean Brown is dangerous," Gerace acknowledged with a pained expression. "I never figured Bucky would go out of his way to shoot a cop, but he demonstrated that he'd drop a cop in a minute." Sheriff Gerace explained that after the gun burglary, he was more frightened than ever at the possible outcome. "I always hoped that Bucky would eventually give up. I thought he would get tired, run out of options, and quit. But the guns, all those guns changed the equation. For the first time," the sheriff said, "I could see Bucky in a very public place making a desperate last stand, and," he grimaced, "I could imagine the carnage."

Bucky insists that a desperate last stand never occurred to him. "I was broke. I needed money." Bucky rose from his chair and spread his arms wide. "For Christ sakes. I found a gold mine in that gun shop. It was a bird's nest on the ground." Bucky twisted his body sharply sideways several times in an exercising motion habitually developed from long periods of confinement. "My God," he exclaimed. "I had nearly twenty thousand in handguns alone, not to mention the ammunition." Bucky turned slowly, hung his head in his hands and sank heavily into his chair. "You realize," he said, "if I had known about that gun shop earlier, I would have been long gone. Sean Brown would not have happened."

Despite movements in the corridor outside the visitor's area at the Dannemora prison, an eerie silence consumed the room except for the sound of a wall clock snapping off the seconds. Bucky's voice trailed off, and in that brief instant he appeared to experience genuine regret at the magnitude of his crimes. A regret, however, that was inexorably linked to what might have been. Like Hemingway's leopard that tried to find a better life in the snows of Kilimanjaro, Bucky's dreams for a better life were frozen in time with little or no promise they would ever be recovered.

He said that before dawn on Sunday, August 26, 2006, the rains had changed to a misty drizzle, and he was back in Pennsylvania. He abandoned the 1996 Dodge Intrepid and made his way directly to the home of his friend Todd Nelson where he deposited his cache of guns and ammo. The Pennsylvania state police found the Dodge abandoned near Sheffield, Pennsylvania, the next day. Bucky spent the next few days with Nelson, and that space gave him time to think things through.

Bucky realized he had stretched his available options to the breaking point. Nearly all of the people he knew and trusted were under continued and tight surveillance by the police, including his family. Even his daughter

Patrina and her mother Kasey had been arrested on some trumped up, bullshit charges, and he knew it would be impossible to contact them even if he wanted too. Although Bucky knew he was welcome in the home of Todd Nelson, he realized it would only be a matter of time before his friend would be discovered and probably arrested. Even his connections in Kentucky, Tennessee, Ohio, and Michigan avoided him. Bucky understood that shooting a cop made him radioactive to his out-of-state friends. He also knew that all but a few friends and business connections would "trade" him out for a lesser sentence if push came to shove. That, he begrudgingly accepted, was the law of the criminal class.

With his options limited and his movements restricted, Bucky knew the end was near. He wanted to return home. Although he accepted that he could be shot on sight, he speculated that the shooting of Brad Horton might give him a slight edge with the New York State Police. He remained convinced that, despite strong denials from the state police, the shooting of young Mr. Horton was a case of mistaken identity. He also realized that, given the Horton case, New York state troopers would be under orders to be absolutely sure of their target before opening fire. There was no way for Bucky to have known for sure, but that hesitation, that fraction of a second before taking a shot, had worked to his advantage and on more than one occasion. But Bucky perceived his greatest threat would come from bounty hunters, or even the intemperate citizen or hunter who would be under no such restraint.

On Wednesday, August 29, 2006, Bucky had made up his mind. He dressed in a pair of clean cammos, carried three rifles and three handguns, and asked Todd Nelson to do him one last favor. Todd Nelson drove Bucky back to Chautauqua County and dropped him at a rest stop on Route 60 near the village of Cassadaga. When the car came to a stop Bucky quickly slipped from the vehicle without a word being exchanged and disappeared into the darkness.

By the next morning, Thursday, August 30, 2006, Bucky Phillips had stashed two rifles at as many campsites and bedded down comfortably at a third site. At the same time his friend Todd Nelson went to the

Pennsylvania State Police and told them that he had located the 9-millimeter handgun he had reported stolen the previous Saturday. As the interview wore on, Nelson admitted that he had loaned the handgun to Bucky and that Phillips had returned it. He told them that Phillips had come to his place on Sunday driving a Dodge Intrepid. Nelson told police that he had driven Bucky back to Chautauqua County, and according to reports, Nelson told police that Bucky returned to Chautauqua County to protect his family.

"That's bullshit," Bucky scoffed when I told him of the account. "Todd never told them that." Bucky paused and wiped his hand down his cheek. "Manning made that shit up to cover his ass when they blew me away. And," a faint smile tugged at Bucky's lips, "that was Manning's way of giving the order to shoot my sorry ass on sight."

Chapter Twenty-Six

AUGUST 31, 2006

Despite a maturing summer, Thursday morning on the last day of August 2006 broke with a sharp chill in the air. Bucky Phillips had spent an uncomfortable night huddled in the remains of a hunting camp left abandoned to the forces of nature. Although he was not far from a well-traveled county road, Bucky opted for a small fire. Despite a brightly burning blaze, the slightly damp mixture of materials created a small amount of acrid smoke that produced a sharp bite which left a caustic taste in his mouth and stung his nostrils. His neck and shoulders ached from spending most of the night uncomfortably wedged between a tree trunk and a section of two-by-four framing that once held a window. He had two bottles of water and several pieces of beef jerky, but he craved a cup of hot coffee.

Most of Bucky's aches and pains subsided, and his stiffness disappeared as he began to move about and scout the area. He purposely avoided shortcuts through fields and meadows in favor of heavier cover provided by seasonal foliage. As the morning aged, Bucky watched from seclusion as state troopers began to occupy positions at crucial intersections of county and town roads, and he noticed an increased frequency of roving patrols. By noon Bucky had skirted the area in a wide circle. He had chosen his route carefully and ventured cautiously at road crossings. The police appeared to have strategically covered all of Bucky's known associates within a five-mile radius. He had an uneasy feeling. He had not heard any news about his daughter or her mother. He did not know if they were still in jail, or if either had made bail. He desperately wanted to talk to someone who could bring him up to speed, but he suspected even his casual acquaintances were under surveillance. His suspicions were confirmed as he gradually worked his way from one familiar place to another.

Bucky noticed that the troopers were working in pairs, and there was nothing surreptitious about their surveillance. Clearly marked vehicles were parked directly in front of residences and he had even seen one car parked in a friend's driveway. Bucky could not immediately explain the presence of the cops, but he ruled out the possibility he had been seen. He might have triggered a remote sensing device, but the troopers were not the elite response troops and he had not seen a single canine unit. He spent the day working his way to Bachelor Hill Road and the home of Kasey Crowe.

He knew direct contact with anyone inside the residence would be impossible because police would have her residence covered with state troopers and backed up with electronic surveillance. He hoped to only catch a glimpse of Kasey. If he saw her, he thought, he would at least know she was out of jail and that would be a good sign that Patrina was free. Bucky followed a circuitous trail to the edge of Kasey's property that was so remote that few knew of its existence and so rugged that not even an ATV or snowmobile could traverse the rocky and steep terrain. He approached the house from the opposite side of the road and stopped in his tracks.

Something was wrong; there was not a single trooper or police vehicle in sight. Bucky quickly doubled back for nearly a quarter mile on either side of the property without seeing anything that would indicate a police presence. As he neared Kasey Crowe's residence, the situation was so obviously wrong that Bucky was suddenly gripped with fear. His heart was beating faster, and he broke out in an exceedingly sudden and unexpected sweat. His mind was racing wildly, but he knew he had stumbled into a trap.

Bucky stated categorically that he saw the men at the same time they saw him. He said his first thoughts were that the men were bounty hunters that Manning had set up around Kasey's residence. "That son of a bitch," Bucky's face flushed with anger when he recalled the incident, "he wanted to murder my ass and blame it on someone else." Bucky said he walked toward the men with his rifle pointing from his waist. "I had duct tape. I wanted to embarrass them. I wanted to strip them buck naked and leave them tied up with duct tape."

It will always be argued who fired the first shot; police officials insist that two state troopers were fired upon from an ambush postition. Bucky describes the circumstances differently; he claims one of the men opened fire. He said he could hear bullets ricocheting off tree branches and ripping through the underbrush and that he laid down a line of fire and began a hasty retreat. Bucky describes a scene that sticks in his mind of two men: one down on one knee and the other bending low in a crouching position with one hand pushing toward the back of his partner's head. Bucky said he saw the man grasping a pistol in his other hand with the barrel pointed downward. He insists the two men never identified themselves as cops and were wearing unmarked, camouflage fatigues. He admits he traded gunfire with the two men thinking they were bounty hunters.

The police version holds that Bucky approached from the side and shot Trooper Baker with a round that pierced his vest from the front and exited through his back. Trooper Longobardo was struck in the leg and the bullet lodged there. Police say they recovered eleven shell casings that were fired by Bucky as he fled from the scene. They also reported that Trooper Longobardo fired nine shots and that Trooper Baker never returned fire. The entire episode could have lasted no more than a few seconds, thirty at the most, but Bucky said it seemed like an eternity. Bucky alleges that it wasn't until the next day when he talked to a friend that he learned that the men were state troopers. "They didn't look like cops. They wore unmarked camos," Bucky reiterated.

Although seriously wounded, Trooper Donald Baker managed to call for help and was airlifted to Hamot Medical Center in Erie, Pennsylvania, where he remained hospitalized in critical condition. Trooper Joseph Longobardo was transported to Brooks Hospital in nearby Dunkirk, New

York, where he was stabilized and subsequently flown to Erie County Medical Center in Buffalo, New York. Sadly, the thirty-two-year-old husband and father of a thirteen-month-old son died three days later, after his leg was amputated in a valiant effort to save his life. After an extensive hospital stay, Trooper Baker would recover and return home.

As odd as it may seem, Bucky's argument against an ambush is that both men were not killed. Bucky makes the case that if he had wanted to kill two men from ambush that they both would have died with only two shots fired. "They wouldn't have known what hit them. But," he maintains, "killing someone was never my intention." But the most controversial of Bucky's assertions is that Trooper Longobardo may have accidentally shot himself when he tried to push his comrade to the ground in a heroic effort to save his life.

"It's the angle; that's the problem," Bucky contends. "They say his femoral artery was severed. He was on the ground. I wasn't shooting low." Bucky insisted. "When you consider the angle, the accidental shooting makes sense." For the first time during our interview Bucky Phillips seemed laden with guilt. "No husband. A son without a father." His voice trailed off into a mumble, and he looked tired and suddenly seemed older than his forty-five years.

Bucky's account of the shooting is vehemently rejected by all of law enforcement and the New York State Police in particular. Chautauqua County District Attorney David Foley was confident of the evidence against Phillips, including a forensic match of the gun used in the shooting of Trooper Longobardo.

"I didn't know they were cops," Bucky insisted, "I thought they were bounty hunters." Bucky also questioned the forensic evidence. "How do they know the bullet that sliced the trooper's femoral artery came from the .308?" Regardless of the circumstances surrounding the shootings of Troopers Longobardo and Baker, it was that single incident that brought an end to New York State's longest and most expensive manhunt.

Almost immediately after the shooting, one of the largest collections of law enforcement personnel ever assembled was deployed in Chautauqua

County for a common purpose. The New York State Police drew heavily from within their ranks. Staffing was increased to 150 for each shift from the uniformed division. More than one hundred investigators were pulled from the BCI and were joined by all members of the MRT. Nearly all of the sixty-five state police canine handlers were ordered to the front.

The New York State Park Police were pressed into service along with New York State's uniformed forest rangers. More than four hundred deputies and police officers from Chautauqua, Cattaraugus, and Erie counties stood united with members of the Pennsylvania State Police, and the US Border Patrol provided infrared search technology. A team of lawyers and investigators from the Chautauqua County District Attorney's Office was dispatched to the scene for legal assistance and advice to expedite warrants and searches. Wayne E. Bennett, Superintendent of the New York State Police, arrived on the scene from his Albany office and assumed command of the combined forces.

The shooting of the two troopers and the arrival of Superintendent Bennett had an immediate and obvious impact on the attitude and perception of local residents. The superintendent's delayed, but welcomed, arrival improved the situation. It proved an unfortunate coincidence that Superintendent Bennett bore a slight resemblance to Buford T. Justice, the inept sheriff played by Jackie Gleason in the movie *Smokey and the Bandit*, and he quickly became the butt of local jokes. Although solidly embedded in the command culture of the New York State Police, Bennett was much better in dealing with the press. He was firm in his public denunciations of Ralph Phillips but remained calm and assumed an apologetic tone in asking for the public's help to bring the manhunt to a peaceful conclusion. There remained little doubt in anyone's mind that the search for Bucky Phillips was all but over, a conclusion that had not escaped the fugitive.

For the first time, Bucky began to think about how his long wandering and eventful journey might end. Even though Kasey Crowe had, unknown to Bucky, been out on bail, immediately after the shooting of Longobardo and Baker, her bail was revoked and she was rearrested. Anyone in the entire Western New York region with even a remote connection to Bucky

Phillips had a uniformed trooper practically on their doorstep. All of Bucky's known campsites were covered and he was finding it increasingly difficult to maneuver through the wilderness without risking an encounter with a search team. Even crossing a remote country road became a venturesome exercise. Police were constantly moving back and forth in roving patrols and were posted at nearly every intersection.

Following Trooper Longobardo's death on Sunday, September 3, 2006, the state police increased intelligence efforts. BCI investigators obtained warrants, tapped phones, and planted electronic devices on vehicles of Bucky's known acquaintances. Investigators even planted cameras on utility poles across from the apartment of Lisa Shongo. All of Bucky's known associates, in and out of prison, were contacted and questioned about his possible hiding places.

Based on intelligence and experience, the state police developed a pattern of Bucky's movements and concentrated their efforts in Chautauqua and Cattaraugus counties along the Pennsylvania line. With his escape routes covered and his travel lanes blocked, Bucky found it increasingly difficult to move freely. While Bucky discussed things in general, he neglected the particulars. He did acknowledge that despite intense police coverage, complete strangers still came to his aid. "It might have been a sandwich left in a rural mailbox," he said. "Or, a newspaper deliberately left overnight in a rural delivery tube." Regardless how meager and in whatever form, Bucky remained grateful for the assistance. "There was this one place where a total stranger," Bucky recalled, "left a dozen cooked hot dogs on a grill overnight." But Bucky's luck was running out, and his situation was becoming more desperate by the hour.

Chapter Twenty-Seven

SEPTEMBER 8, 2006—FINAL HOURS OF FREEDOM

Despite the police presence, Bucky managed to make his way to the Seneca Nation at Salamanca. Bucky described the going as rough and the pickings slim. His safest transport was mostly by foot or bicycle. "I could have easily stolen a car," Bucky said wistfully, "but cops were everywhere." He dared to hang around in the village of Allegany near the St. Bonaventure campus. He said he avoided hangouts that naturally came under police scrutiny in any college town, but regularly ate pizza and frequented convenience stores. He spent one night sleeping inside a culvert but relied on hunting and fishing camps and even spent one night sleeping comfortably inside the cabin of a boat.

On Thursday, September 5, 2006, the Cattaraugus County Sheriff's Department received reports of an attempted break-in at 4:45 a.m. of a pharmacy in Portville, New York. A witness described the suspect as a white man wearing dark clothing, had a duffle bag slung over his shoulder, and fled the scene on a bicycle. About three hours later at Eldred, Pennsylvania, about twenty miles from Portville, police received reports of another attempted break-in at a local pharmacy. The state police reacted immediately, and for the first time in the five-month manhunt, police were controlling the events on the ground.

Instead of waiting for the MRT, two details en route from across the state were diverted to a staging area at Olean, New York. The National

Guard took to the skies in a C-26, a high-altitude reconnaissance aircraft, equipped with nighttime surveillance radar, and the Pennsylvania State Police committed a major deployment to the area. Todd Nelson was arrested and charged with criminal possession of stolen property and the ATF indicted him on a federal weapons charge.

Bucky recognized that his only chance to escape the unpleasant realities of his circumstances was to leave the area. He decided to take a chance and make a run for it. His only chance at freedom was to steal a car and sneak through the outer perimeter of the police lines. Stealing a car was easy, but Bucky had to decide whether it would be more prudent to travel during daylight hours or in the dark of night. Bucky decided to travel at night. He intended to connect with US Route 6 on the west side of Warren, Pennsylvania, and make his way into Ohio. Bucky had been driving less than twenty minutes on Scandia Road in a remote section of Glade Township when a Warren County deputy fell in behind him.

The deputy followed Bucky for nearly a mile before flipping on his flashing red lights. Bucky appropriately reduced his speed and guided the car to a stop on the shoulder of the road. He waited until the deputy was out of the car before he floored the accelerator. He could not see the expression on the deputy's face, but he knew he had taken him by surprise, because it took him a minute or two to recover and give chase. But Bucky had misjudged the deputy. The deputy knew the terrain much better than Bucky and wasn't worried about losing his suspect. After Bucky fled, the officer calmly radioed the pursuit, confident that nearly a dozen cars would respond immediately.

Bucky drove at a high rate of speed and went into a hard sideways slide as he turned onto the first road he came to. He sped down Hatch Road with the deputy in hot pursuit when suddenly he hit a patch of loose gravel and went into an uncontrollable spin. The car stopped hard when it plowed nose first into the embankment of a deep ditch. Bucky was momentarily stunned but recovered enough to jump from the vehicle and flee into the woods. Bucky managed to get away, but police found a loaded 9-millimeter handgun, a portable radio, a flashlight, and a baseball cap on the front seat.

In less than an hour Bucky had acquired another car and made his way back into New York. But after five months the state police had nearly all of Bucky's moves committed to memory. They had enough manpower and had scattered so much technology on land, sea, and air that a local deputy observed that Manning could hear a frog fart anywhere in the search area at 3:00 a.m. Sure enough, a pair of New York state troopers spied a car speeding along a remote stretch of road near the Pennsylvania border at 2:30 a.m. The driver refused to pull over and the troopers gave chase. They rounded a bend just in time to see the occupant jump from the vehicle and flee into the woods.

Within minutes of receiving the report of an unidentified suspect taking flight on foot, law enforcement automatically established a containment perimeter around the area. They inserted roving patrols and canine units inside the perimeter and commenced tracking the suspect. Bucky sensed the seriousness of his situation almost immediately. Instead of engaging in hot pursuit, the trackers began a well-coordinated push using canine units in forward positions. Bucky tried moving in a large circle to get behind his trackers, but quickly found staggered lines of searchers deployed behind the forward positions effectively cutting off his flanking movements.

One of the first things Sheriff Joseph Gerace did that Friday morning was to ask Sheriff Larry Kopko to issue a blanket order deputizing all of his New York deputies in Warren County, Pennsylvania. As Sheriff Gerace kept track of the events, he became more concerned as Bucky penetrated further into Pennsylvania. The sheriff had made a major commitment of manpower and material available for the manhunt, and one of his helicopters was actively engaged in the pursuit, but he didn't want to take chances. He realized that if Bucky slipped past the southern tip of the Allegany Reservoir or made it into the Allegany National Forest that he could survive for weeks or even months without seeing a single person.

Sheriff Gerace shared his concerns with Superintendent Wayne Bennett, who requested the US Marshall's Service deputize New York State Police personnel. With the proper authorizations in place, one of the largest deployments of law enforcement personnel ever assembled in

New York State began to push south into Pennsylvania. With cooperation from a large contingent of Pennsylvania State Police and Warren County Deputies, a command post was established near the Cable Hollow Golf Course near Akeley, Pennsylvania. As the push began, a containment perimeter was quickly established around a two-mile square area surrounding the golf course. By 9:00 a.m. Bucky had made his way across the state line and was spotted by a canine handler off Gouldtown Road near Akeley, Pennsylvania. The trooper claimed that Bucky turned toward him and displayed a handgun in his left hand. The trooper immediately opened fire and turned the dog loose.

"I really didn't have a gun in my hand," Bucky told me from the confines of Clinton Correctional Facility. He explained that he had a tightly rolled bundle of dry clothing in his left hand. "I don't blame him; he probably couldn't tell the difference from a distance." Bucky recounted that he responded the instant he spotted the trooper. He said he jumped a small stream and was frantically clawing his way up a steep embankment before he realized he was taking fire. He described the incident as one of the more frightening episodes of the manhunt.

He said his arms were spread wide and that he was digging into the clay embankment with his fingers to grasp a root or a stone or anything to pull his body over the top. He said the dog was almost on top of him and a bullet splattered dirt between his outstretched fingers. "That shot gave me a boost of adrenalin," Bucky smiled. "The next thing I knew I was over the bank and running all out." Bucky continued along the high ridgeline for nearly a mile before penetrating deeper into the woods. Other canine units joined the pursuit, and they all traveled for a quarter mile or more before Bucky found an accessible place to ascend the embankment and continue to press the chase farther into Pennsylvania.

As canine handlers lead the way, heavily armed and highly trained S.W.A.T. teams from the Pennsylvania State Police, the New York State Police, and local law enforcement pushed through the woodlands. The New York State Police, assisted by the NYS National Guard, a Chautauqua County Sheriff's helicopter, and a Pennsylvania State Police helicopter provided uninterrupted air coverage. Bucky had little choice but to keep moving. As the day wore on it became increasingly obvious to Bucky that it would be only a matter of time before he was run to ground. Bucky called his daughter three times that afternoon.

Some people claimed that he wanted to say goodbye because he knew he was going to be shot on sight. Others said he wanted to apologize for being a shitty father. Either could have been true, but they talked for a long time and what they discussed remains sealed in their hearts and minds. The only thing Patrina said afterward was that she didn't want to see her dad killed. Whether the telephone conversations had anything to do with Bucky's subsequent actions remains unclear, but Bucky devised a plan. He would surrender. But he couldn't surrender to the New York State Police. He feared they would shoot him on sight.

He concluded he would have a better chance surrendering to Pennsylvania authorities, but he remained skeptical because of the strong fraternity with the New York State Police. His first option was to surrender to a deputy sheriff, preferably to a Warren County deputy since they were further removed from the events. But that proved to be more difficult than he supposed. As the day progressed, Bucky felt even more cornered. He had to take a hurried piss because the dogs were hot on his tracks. His energy was quickly being depleted; he hadn't eaten since a sandwich the day before and the only water he had was what he could lap up from the stream.

He remembered the advice of his fellow convict, Doc, the physician convicted for murdering his wife, who once advised him on the importance of proper hydration. "Stay hydrated," the aging doctor had told him. "Dehydration can occur quickly." Even under dreadful circumstances, Bucky's recollections of those prison yard dialogues brought a smile to his face. "Disorientation is an early symptom. You can't think straight," Doc told him. "Always," he admonished, "drink a glass of water before you rob a bank." By late afternoon Bucky realized he could only move in ever smaller circles around a patch of woods that bordered a harvested cornfield, and his options were few.

He could race through the open field and most likely be shot before making it to the other side, or he could wait for an opening to dash across one of the three roads that bordered the golf course. He found that Norberg Road to the east of the golf course was heavily patrolled, and he knew Old State Road to the west was cordoned off by a line of troopers. Going south was useless, because Cable Hollow Road at the southern end of the golf course was occupied by a phalanx of armed men and women under orders to stop anyone who tried to cross the road. Bucky thought of another admonition; one often repeated by his father. "Boy, if you're up shit creek without a paddle, steal a car."

Bucky thought of a lot of things. He thought of his mother. She had died too soon, around the age of fifty-three. She just wore out. He couldn't attend her funeral. He was in prison. It was a good thing she was dead, he thought. He wouldn't want her to see this. He thought of his brother Adrian and how joyful he had been in a helpless, frail body. He died young too. He thought about his oldest sister, Elida, who had been living in a home since the death of their mother. She was in good hands. He fondly remembered how he had to change her diapers when he was a young boy. He remembered how happy and playful she was as he performed the dreaded task. She thought it was a game; she was unaware that she had soiled herself. He hoped she was kept from a television for the next several days.

He thought about his younger sister, Armitty. She had created a good life and never deserved the grief he had caused his family. He had deliberately stayed away from her; he hadn't wanted the cops to bother her family. He knew she would at once be saddened and embarrassed by the day's events. He understood that being the sister of Bucky Phillips could not have been the brightest point in her life. He thought about his daughter and his grandchildren. Bucky was proud of Patrina. She was a good mother. "Damn Manning," Bucky uttered aloud.

As the sun sunk lower in the sky, Bucky Phillips continued to probe the perimeter to catch a glimpse of a friendlier figure. The time had come for him to move. He recognized the symptoms. He was becoming disoriented. His mouth was dry like cotton. He was thirsty and exhausted, and he understood that an irrational step at this point would mean certain death. He saw the helicopter overhead, and he saw a figure standing in a clearing with his hands on his hips. Bucky had dropped his pistol somewhere behind him. He took several deep breaths, raised is hands high over his head, and emerged slowly from a cluster of golden rods. As he took his first step into the open, he was emboldened by a nugget of advice, a bit of cautionary wisdom from Doc, his trusted prison yard advisor. "If you can pick the way you die, a gunshot is probably best. You'll never hear the shot that kills you." Ralph Phillips was prepared to die.

The hail of bullets Bucky expected never came. The Warren County deputy didn't even act surprised. He simply strolled toward Bucky and pulled his cuffs from his belt. He routinely, almost casually, cuffed Bucky's hands behind his back and guided him toward the road. Neither man spoke. Bucky was placed in a state police cruiser and transported to the Pennsylvania State Police Command Post nearby in Russell, Pennsylvania. There he was turned over to the US Marshal's Service. A federal magistrate ordered Bucky returned to the Erie County Holding Center to await arraignment on fugitive charges. For 161 days a petty criminal eluded law enforcement and embarrassed New York State's most elite law enforcement agency that was especially created to bring law and order to New York's rural counties. The longest manhunt in the history of New York was over.

EPILOGUE

On November 29, 2006, Ralph James Phillips was sentenced in separate courtrooms nearly two hundred miles apart for the shooting of two New York state troopers and the murder of another. He pled guilty in both instances and was sentenced to a pair of life terms lengthened by two ninety-nine-year sentences. Unless he hits an appeals trifecta, and charges against him are overturned, Ralph James Phillips will die behind the walls of a New York State maximum-security prison. Ralph will not only spend the remainder of his life in prison, but unless a higher authority intervenes, he is likely to serve out his time in solitary confinement.

Ralph Phillips was always aware of the gravity of his crimes. He offered no excuses. He knew he could have brought the manhunt to an abrupt end by walking unannounced into any police station. He was not forced to pull the trigger on Trooper Sean Brown and acknowledged he could have possibly fled the confrontation that led to the death of Trooper Longobardo. Regardless of the circumstances, the death of Trooper Longobardo weighs heavily upon him. A young boy deprived of his father and the loss of a husband, a son, or a brother especially troubles him. But those who believe that society will be made better if Ralph Phillips lives the rest of his days suffering mental and physical torment for his crimes will be disappointed.

Even living under the most punishing conditions available in New York State prisons, Ralph Phillips displays a peculiar characteristic. Although far from euphoric, he readily adapts to conditions as they are. That should not be surprising; here is a man who was conditioned by incarceration since puberty. He is correct when he says he is a career convict instead of a career criminal. He has been consistently incompetent as a career criminal, but he has been remarkably successful as a career convict. Make no mistake, for good or bad, Ralph James Phillips is very much a product of the state.

Despite the reports of a violent background that circulated among related communities of interest, Ralph Phillips had never been punished for an act of violence throughout his lengthy imprisonments, not even a fistfight. He was previously placed in solitary confinement for building a citizen's band radio from scratch with the help of prison officials and has been serving in solitary confinement since his most recent convictions. His present confinement in solitary, a jail within a jail, has nothing to do with his prison behavior. His behavior has been exemplary. He is courteous toward his guards and prison officials and has never posed a threat to other inmates. One prison guard at Clinton Correctional Facility told me that he had Bucky once before and that he was always a model prisoner.

Bucky Phillips may be "as guilty as hell," as he was reported to have responded when asked for his plea on an escape charge, but a jury of his peers has never found Ralph J. Phillips guilty of any crime. Not a single piece of evidence used to convict Bucky has ever been challenged in an adversarial proceeding. The state has never placed evidence before a judge or jury to be challenged by Ralph's defense. In too many instances, police and prosecutors have evoked the potential of prosecution of others to elicit a guilty response from Bucky.

In Chautauqua County there is little doubt that the state police more resembled a military tactical unit than a police force committed to securing the public safety. Local residents were unnecessarily inconvenienced and often treated contemptuously. Residents also wondered why more reliance was not placed on local law enforcement, including the sheriff's department and local police agencies. Locals were also saddened at the death of Trooper Longobardo, but their shock was muted by public utterances from state police officials that seemed to purposely create expectations of violence. However, two related incidents exacerbated the situation; the shooting of Bradley Horton, and the arrest of Ralph's daughter Patrina Wright and the removal of her children by child protective services.

Plainly spoken, many local residents hold state police commanders as responsible for the deaths of Bradley Horton and Trooper Longobardo as they do Bucky Phillips. The story that Trooper Sean Price was forced to shoot Bradley Horton after becoming ensnared on his ATV and being dragged for nearly a mile is incredible to many people. The fact that the trooper had only superficial injuries and reported for work the following day makes even the most casual observer skeptical of the police version of the events. Horton's family and friends remain convinced that the shooting of Bradley Horton was a case of mistaken identity.

The harshest condemnations are from people who remain adamant that state police officials deliberately allowed Mr. Horton to lay unattended in a field for forty-five minutes to bleed to death before he was airlifted to a hospital. The seriousness of the incident moved Chautauqua County District Attorney David Foley to present the Horton case to a grand jury, but there was insufficient evidence to produce an indictment. DA Foley said he would pursue an indictment if new evidence comes forward, but that appears unlikely at this point in time. The Horton family is pressing for Federal Civil Rights prosecution and has filed a wrongful death lawsuit.

After the manhunt, all charges against Patrina Wright and her mother Kasey Crowe were dropped. By almost any standards, the action against Ms. Wright was unnecessary and cruel. Patrina Wright, who may have seen her father fewer than ten days in ten years, was accused of child endangerment by allowing her children to be in Bucky's presence while he was armed. There was little if any reason to believe that Bucky Phillips was ever in the presence, armed or unarmed, of his grandchildren during the manhunt. The entire episode was orchestrated on the fundamentally flawed premise that Bucky Phillips would immediately surrender.

Facing a barrage of criticism from the union representing the state troopers, State Police Superintendent Wayne E. Bennett retired after the manhunt, but one of his final acts was to order an operational review of the proceedings. Preston L. Felton became the Acting Director of the New York State Police, and while he did not press for the retirement of Major Michael Manning, he suggested it would probably be a good idea. If there is to be reform of the Criminal Justice System in New York, or the New York State Police, it must come from the state legislature. But, the governor, the state attorney general, and the state legislature have remained strangely silent.

Innocent victims of the Phillips manhunt litter the landscape. To the extent that it all swirled around one man, Ralph Phillips must ultimately be held responsible. But the story of how a half-breed Seneca son became entangled in a broken justice system requires retelling for as long as it takes for a nation to prize the pursuit of liberty and justice for all. Unfortunately, the story of Bucky Phillips can be written in every county, in every police station, and in every courthouse in fifty states. Police agencies are becoming increasingly militaristic and place too much reliance upon military tactics that short-circuit individual liberties. Prosecutors are more interested in convictions than justice, and judges are either overworked or just plain lazy. They are all too willing to rely upon the flimsiest police reasoning when signing search warrants and appear to be in league with prosecutors. Pick up a newspaper in any city and chances are good there will be a story about the innocent set free. There are too many erroneous lab results, some even manufactured to fit the circumstances, that are readily accepted as evidence.

Few would disagree that Ralph Phillips has vast experience as a convicted criminal, but how much of what he alleges is true? Dare to take Bucky's challenge: Throw out half or more of his claims, and there remains a badly broken justice system. Evoked guilty pleas may be expeditious for courts and convenient for the state, but they represent a glaring fault in our system of justice. Guilty pleas notwithstanding, every scrap of evidence used to convict should be challenged and examined before a judge, if not a jury, and all forensic testing and conclusions should be independently verified. At a time when two million of our citizens are locked in jails, our system is in need of reform.

The system is broken all the way to and including the Supreme Court of the United States, where nine robed justices dare not televise their proceedings much less deliberations. How can the highest court in the land, even using the strictest interpretation of our Constitution, allow the execution of a prisoner who deliberately leaves his apple pie until he returns to his cell after his execution?

Bucky Phillips sat behind the plexiglass barrier and stared for a long time at his hands. He tugged at his fingertips. He seemed to be searching those dark recesses of the mind where individuals seldom venture, in that place where we see ourselves as we really are, in that place where we can never share the image of our vision. Bucky Phillips stood and let his eyes drift toward the door.

"Where are the gate keepers?" He shrugged and placed his hand against my flattened palm on the plexiglass divider. "Thanks for coming. Come again when you can."

Editor's note: As of this printing, Bucky is currently being held at NYSDOC Midstate Correctional Facility in Marcy, New York.

Police Searching For Escaped Convict

Police are conducting an extensive search after a convict escaped from the Erie County Correctional Facility early on Sunday.

Ralph Phillips, 43, convicted of a parole violation, was on work detail at the prison when he escaped at approximately 5 a.m., leaving his orange jumpsuit behind, according to an April 2 press release from the Erie County Sheriff's Office.

An "extensive ground and air search" was then conducted by the Erie County Sheriff's Office, the Genesee County Sheriff's office, State Police, the Lancaster and Depew police departments and other agencies, but have not turned up any information on his whereabouts, the press release said.

Phillips is described as a six-foot-tall American Indian male weighing approximately 240 pounds.

He is also described as being of medium build with black hair, a long ponytail, glasses and a beard. What clothing he changed into after abandoning the jumpsuit is unknown, police said.

The Erie County Sheriff's Office has asked anyone with information on the whereabouts of Phillips to call 667-5201 or 911.

Pioneer High School Student Accused Of Selling Drugs

YORKSHIRE — A 15-year-old Pioneer High School was arrested Wednesday for allegedly selling prescription drugs.

According to the Cattaraugus County Sheriff's Department, the youth had in his possession a prescription bottle peers. The boy was issued an appearance ticket for Family Court.

CLASSIFIED WANT ADS

PHONE 487-1234

DURING BUSINESS HOURS

Police Still Seeking Escapee

ALDEN — Police are still searching for an escaped prisoner from Erie County who has local ties.

According to the Chautauqua County Sheriff's Department, Ralph "Bucky" Phillips, 43, escaped from the Erie County Holding facility in Alden Sunday.

He's described as a Native American, six feet tall, weighing 235 pounds with brown hair tied back in a pony tail.

Phillips has family and friends in the Stockton/Sinclairville area.

RALPH PHILLIPS

AREA NEWS

Id	P/E	Vol	Last	Chg
0	18	5052	62.62	-.37
9	16	12024	28.47	-.53
5	26	4713	29.89	-.36
6	13	25	20.20	
	42	4865	69.80	-1.15
	36	1396	19.98	-.04
6	35	16086	40.60	-.12
2	14	20570	58.14	-.33
8	24	29026	57.81	-.28
	23	110	8.21	+.02
	35	533	8.15	+.32
3	11	9045	22.25	-.38
9	22	220798	24.35	-.30
	11	51317	84.35	+.21
4		4552	38.57	+.69
1	22	10180	39.15	-.56
	12	16886	43.79	-.41
0	19	7285	42.93	-.25
		2344	13.33	-.58
		284758	5.98	+1.10
4	19	4896	36.13	-.23
	4	12799	52.25	-.27
4	16	3737	51.65	-1.00
	58	639	9.79	-.26
2	21	120468	56.49	-.66
8	15	10744	42.03	-.15
	15	6329	102.23	+.20
		5748	10.19	-.18

Police Continue Search For Escapee

Police are still searching for an escaped prisoner from Erie County who has local ties.

According to the Chautauqua County Sheriff's Department, Ralph "Bucky" Phillips, 43, escaped from the Erie County Holding facility in Alden on April 4.

He's described as a Native American, six feet tall, weighing 235 pounds with brown hair tied back in a pony tail.

Phillips has family and friends in the Stockton/Sinclairville area. Anyone with information is asked to call 753-2131.

RALPH PHILLIPS

Pg. B-4

The Post-Journal

www.post-journal.com

FRIDAY

JULY 14, 2006

Upping The Ante

Search For Phillips Continues; Officials Raise Reward To $50,000

By STEVEN YUNGHANS
Special to The Post-Journal

Information leading to the capture and conviction of Ralph "Bucky" Phillips became much more valuable Thursday as an organization which acts to support the New York State Police doubled the pot.

"The New York State Troopers Foundation today added an additional $25,000 to the reward, upping the total amount to $50,000,'' Maj. Michael T. Manning, Troop A Commander, said during an afternoon press conference.

Manning said the foundation is a not-for-profit organization that accepts donations from a number of contributors to support New York State Troopers and their families.

A reward of $25,000 for information leading the arrest and conviction of Ralph "Bucky" Phillips had been in place since June of this year with contributions from the legal firm of Gleason, Walsh, Dunn and O'Shea, the New York State Troopers Police Benevolent Association and the national "Cop Shot" organization which acts to support police officers and their families when an officer is shot or killed.

Phillips has been on the run since his escape from the Alden Correctional Facility in Erie County this past April. State police have narrowed their search to the hills and woodlands in northern Chautauqua County, focusing in a region spanning from the town of Pomfret south to the town of Charlotte.

Manning said Phillips was seen briefly earlier this week but refused to give any further details.

The Troop A commander responded to some of the criticism that has been circulating throughout the region regarding the massive police presence and search for Phillips, saying the primary goal of the state police has always been to bring Phillips back into custody.

"We'd like to get these troopers out of the woods,'' Manning said. "We'd like to get Bucky Phillips back into jail where he belongs.''

Manning also advised residents not to try and take matters into their own hands to help state police.

"We're not looking for people to go out there and be bounty hunters and go look for this individual, that's not what this is about,'' he said.

"We're searching for him to bring him in and arrest him.'' Manning said. "If we were truly trying to hurt him, the first day he came out of the woods and troopers chased him on foot, it would have been done quick.''

Manning hoped that by adding to the reward money available should someone help authorities locate and apprehend Phillips, people who have known his whereabouts and have been reluctant to speak might be encouraged to do so now.

Manning suggested the possibility members of Phillips' own family might choose to turn on the fugitive who has been said to be hiding somewhere in the forest-covered hills of Chautauqua County since June. However, his sister and other family have repeatedly said they have had no

recent contact with Phillips.

Manning also said he would personally guarantee Phillips' safety should he decide to turn himself in, including agreeing to meet Phillips himself to ensure a safe and secure transition back into police custody.

Attention from various media outlets has focused on the public response to the state police presence and their continuing search.

Phillips' escape was profiled on a nationally syndicated television program as well as becoming the subject of a number of radio programs in recent days.

See BUCKY On Page A-3

Prison Escapee Believed To Be In Pennsylvania

A suspect who escaped from the Erie County Correctional Facility April 4 is believed to be in Pennsylvania.

According to Cattaraugus County Sheriff Dennis B. John, Ralph B. Phillips was seen at 9 p.m. Friday at an isolated camp on Hungry Hollow Road in the town of Great Valley. He said Phillips had a brief conservation with the owner of the camp and was last seen traveling on a motorcycle believed to be headed to the Bradford, Pa. area.

Police suspect Phillips has a handgun and should be considered armed and dangerous. He is a Native American, six feet tall and weighs 235 pounds. He has brown hair.

The motorcycle he is believed to be on is described as a black 1983 Suzuki GS75OT with front and rear chrome fenders. It has front and back New York license plates labeled 26EE67.

Phillips has ties in the Stockton/Sinclairville area.

Bucky Sighting

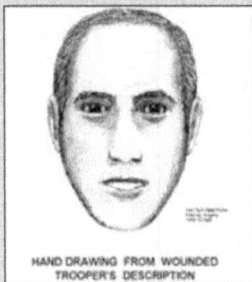

HAND DRAWING FROM WOUNDED TROOPER'S DESCRIPTION

Photo provided by the Erie County Sheriff's Office.

Digitally enhanced photo (removal of facial hair).

Above, Ralph "Bucky" Phillips was spotted near the Tuscarora Indian Reservation in Niagara County. Police would not say whether this picture was taken by a human or by an automatic camera set up at the site.

Photos courtesy of New York State Police

Fugitive Seen In Niagara County

By STEVEN M. SWEENEY

His picture nailed it.

Searchers hunting the fugitive Ralph Phillips looked wearily on in Cattaraugus and Chautauqua counties until Tuesday. That's when they came across a photograph indicating he was 80 miles away.

According to Trooper Rebecca Gibbons of the state police, a camera located near the Tuscarora Indian Reservation in Niagara County captured Phillips' image.

Ms. Gibbons refused to say if the photo was taken by a human or automated sys-tem, who provided the photo to police or its specific location.

"We can't discuss details of our investigation," she said. "Our purpose for releasing the information is to let the public know to be aware. He is thinner this time and wearing a mustache."

Other published photographs of Phillips show him as a pale, medium-built individual. Tan skin, a mustache and bushy hair from the photo taken Tuesday make the fugitive appear much different

See BUCKY SIGHTING on Page A-3

'His Luck Will Run Out'

— Capt. Robert Buchhardt
Cattaraugus County
Sheriff's Department

While the hunt for Ralph "Bucky" Phillips continues, New York State Police are coming up with more reliable clues each time they net an area in their search for the suspect. Troopers set up their command post in the Randolph Junior-Senior High School building Sunday afternoon, reserving parking areas for their marked and un-marked cars and preparing the landing zone for their two helicopters on the practice field behind the bleachers of the football field. Above, one of the two New York State Police helicopters working off the practice field of Randolph Central School.

P-J photo by Jack Berger

Police Scouring Randolph Area After Possible 'Bucky' Sighting

---

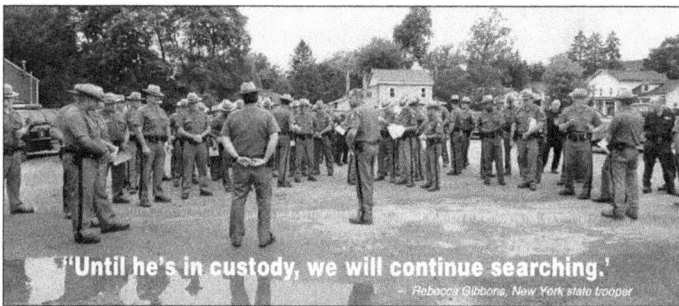

"Until he's in custody, we will continue searching.'
— Rebecca Gibbons, New York state trooper

New York state troopers prepare before a search for Ralph "Bucky" Phillips in Randolph recently.

P-J photo by Jack Berger

Wanted: Bucky

Search For Escaped Con Approaches Four-Month Mark, No End In Sight

By PATRICK L. FANELLI

There's no end in sight as the search for fugitive Ralph "Bucky" Phillips approaches the four-month mark.

What's keeping the manhunt alive appears to be a visible trail Phillips is leav-

information officer assigned to the investigation.

State Police say they'll keep searching for Phillips — wanted for his April 2 escape from the Erie County Corrections Facility and the alleged June 10 shooting of a state trooper

program at the State University at Fredonia, believes this is true — that police will always be searching for Phillips so long as he evades them. However, as leads begin to dry up, police are likely to reduce the number of officers assigned to the search.

An unidentified individual speaks with state police after being stopped at a check point at Webster and Fredonia-Stockton Road south of Fredonia. State police have been maintaining 22 checkpoints around northern Chautauqua County as part of their efforts to catch Ralph "Bucky" Phillips.

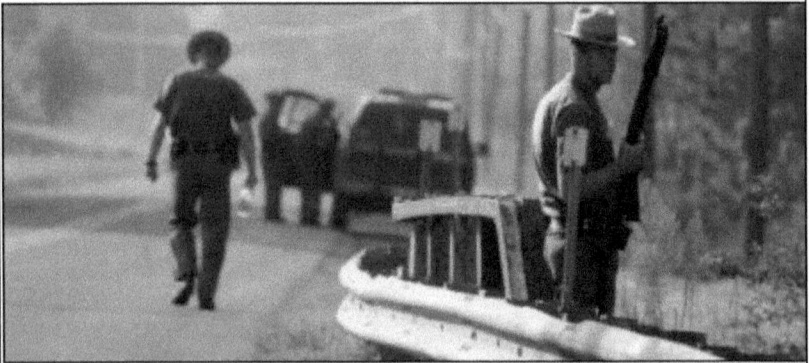

Troopers line the woods on Friday morning in the early part of the final search for fugitive Ralph Phillips on Friday.

The Post-Journal

www.post-journal.com —————— FRIDAY ——————— SEPTEMBER 1, 2006

JAMESTOWN, NY   VOL. 180 NO. 72

"How far does it have to go before the people who think he is a folk hero realize he is anything but?"
— Wayne E. Bennett, New York State Police superintendent

Troopers Shot

Phillips Prime Suspect In Shooting Of Two Officers

By PATRICK L. FANELLI

FREDONIA — Two state troopers are in serious condition after a shooting on Fredonia-Stockton Road late Thursday, and State Police Superintendent Wayne E. Bennett said fugitive Ralph "Bucky" Phillips is the number one suspect.

Joseph Longobardo, 32, and Donald Baker Jr., 38, both state troopers out of Saratoga County, were attacked in what Bennett described as an "ambush" as the pair approached the residence while investigating the fugitive's whereabouts.

"I can't speculate on why someone would do this," Bennett said at a press conference early Friday morning. "I don't call it retaliation. I call it attempted murder."

Now, the manhunt — which Bennett said is the number one priority for

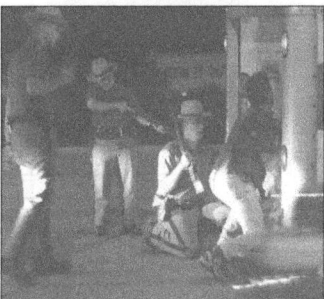

Bachellor Hill Gunfire Intensifies Search

By ALPHA HUSTED

BEAR LAKE — Heavily armed State Troopers and members of the Chautauqua County Sheriff's Department zeroed in on this small lakeside community near the hamlet of Stockton on Thursday night, after reported gunfire on Bachellor Hill Road, possibly involving fugitive Ralph "Bucky" Phillips and the state police.

Roadside patrols and barricades blocked Bachellor Hill Road, which runs from Cassadaga to Bear Lake; also Route 380 between Bear Lake and Stockton was heavily patrolled, as squads of state troopers searched a stretch of woodlands running along Bear Lake's Kelley Hill Road.

Shortly after 7 p.m., Chautauqua County's Starflight helicopter touched down in the Bachellor Road area.

Two state troopers were wounded. Asked to confirm the report at the time, one deputy sheriff said he could not release any information, however he did confirm other reports that Phillips remained on the loose.

Police scanner reports monitored at about 9:30 p.m., indicated police were looking for a red Ford truck, believed to be operated by Phillips in the Brockton area.

According to reports on the police scanner and from several travelers, Chautauqua County roads leading into Pennsylvania were filled with police officers, searching every vehicle crossing the border.

"We're out there looking," a Pennsylvania State Trooper said, though not commenting on the road block situation.

Phillips' Daughter Gets Children Back

By JOAN JOSEPHSON
Special To *The Post-Journal*

CASSADAGA — Ralph "Bucky" Phillips' daughter, Patrina Wright, regained custody of her three children Thursday following an agreement reached in Family Court.

The children were turned over to Child Protection Services after Wright and her boyfriend, Richard Cantanese, were arrested by New York State Police and charged with endangering the welfare of a child for allegedly exposing them to Phillips at a home occupied by Wright's mother on Bachellor Hill Road in Pomfret.

Attorney Sue Evans, who represented Wright in the Family Court hearing Thursday, said she still faces charges of endangering the welfare of a child in both Family and criminal court.

"These charges are still pending," Evans said.

Meanwhile, state troopers are seeking to take Phillips into custody for escaping from the Erie County Holding Center in April, allegedly shooting a trooper near Elmira and for a series of vehicle thefts and break-ins while eluding police capture.

Wounded —

From Page A-3

In addition, estimates of well more than 50 additional state troopers plus members of a number of law enforcement agencies from around the region have been called in to northern Chautauqua County to assist state police. Other resources included a mobile trauma unit from Erie County Medical Center, specialized search teams, helicopters and K-9 units.

State police are also conducting checkpoints throughout the region including Thruway exits in Westfield, Fredonia and Silver Creek.

The New York State Police have been searching for Ralph "Bucky" Phillips, who escaped from the Alden Correctional Facility in Erie County nearly six months ago and has been on the run ever since effectively evading state police and local police agencies while allegedly committing a number of auto thefts and burglaries along the way.

In June, Phillips reportedly wounded a state trooper during a traffic stop near Elmira.

A few days later, he was reported in Chautauqua County where state police descended en masse with traffic stops, blockades, roving patrols, and teams on foot combing through area woodlands.

Bradley Horton, who had been at a fireworks show at the Willow Creek Winery on Sheridan, was shot and killed by a state trooper during a traffic stop June 24 after Horton

Medical units attend to a wounded officer while Starflight prepares to airlift the officer to a hospital.

Troopers —

From Page A-1

"I was on my way to the store to pick up a pizza when they came flying by," said Dan Hornburg of Stockton. "We saw Starflight fly over and land at the firemen's grounds."

The ambulance carrying at least one of the wounded state troopers screamed by soon after, Hornburg said.

By then, police had secured an area a couple miles in diameter, according to Scott Mac-Dowel, chief photographer for Channel 7 News in Buffalo — whose own role turned from observer to participant when he found himself within the enclo-

> ## "Sooner or later, if you're his ticket to freedom, you're going to know what I'm talking about."
> — *Wayne E. Bennett, state police superintendent*

at 12:30 a.m., after most television viewers had already gone to sleep with no official account of what transpired earlier that evening.

Bennett, who travelled to Fredonia from Albany by helicopter, finally arrived and delivered the official statement.

Though two more state troopers have been critically wounded, some still hold out support for the fugitive — who escaped from the Erie County Correctional Facility in April, allegedly shot a state trooper in June, and might have been involved with the theft of 40 assault weapons from a gun shop in

---

both New York and Pennsylvania state police — has intensified, with 75 additional troopers ordered to the area.

"Had anyone reported his presence before tonight, I wouldn't be standing here in front of you telling you I have two very young troopers fighting for their lives," Bennett said. "You will see more of a presence. Our job is to catch this guy."

As of early Thursday, the Fredonia barracks was relatively quiet until reports of the shooting arrived, and hundreds of state troopers arrived from all over the area, reports indicate.

The response in Pomfret was almost immediate.

See TROOPERS on Page A-3

Above, New York State police search vehicles in Fredonia on Thursday. Police are converging on an address in Fredonia, possibly in connection with the search for fugitive Ralph "Bucky" Phillips, who has been on the run since escaping from jail in April and allegedly shooting a state trooper in June. Phillips is also a suspect in two more officer shootings Thursday in Bear Lake. Below left, Trooper Mary Ligammari holds two guns as other officers search a vehicle in Fredonia. At right, Wayne E. Bennett, New York State Police superintendent, speaks to the media Friday morning.

Photos above and at left by The Associated Press
P-J photo at left by Steve Olson

Ralph 'Bucky' Phillips: A Look Back

April 2: Ralph "Bucky" Phillips, convicted of violating his parole, escapes from the Erie County Corrections Facility in Alden with a can opener, leaving an orange jumpsuit behind. The Erie County Sheriff's Department begins the search with the state police assisting.

April-June: During this time, police suspect Phillips is related to several break-ins at hunting cabins in Erie, Allegany and Cattaraugus counties. A pickup truck stolen in Allegany County ends up in Ohio where another vehicle is stolen, and authorities suspect Phillips is involved. Phillips is allegedly spotted by residents in the areas around Sinclairville, Stockton, Randolph, Great Valley and Bradford, Pa.

June 10: State Trooper Sean Brown is shot in the stomach after stopping a Ford Mustang outside Elmira in the early hours. The vehicle is discovered later in the day, and a Chevrolet pickup truck is reported stolen nearby. Police begin searching a "wide radius" around the Elmira-Binghamton area for the vehicle.

June 15: Police continue scouring the Elmira-Binghamton vicinity, but set up checkpoints in Pomfret in Arkwright, since Phillips has significant ties to the area.

June 17: Phillips is featured on Fox's *America's Most Wanted*.

June 21: Phillips is believed to have stolen a Dodge Caravan in the town of Hancock, east of Binghamton.

June 21: Police dismantle their command post in Colesville outside Binghamton.

June 25: Bradley Horton, 25, of Silver Creek, is shot and killed by a state trooper in Sheridan while driving an ATV in the early hours. He allegedly dragged the unidentified state trooper while attempting to flee after a "routine" traffic stop.

June 26: The Dodge Caravan stolen in Hancock is found in the town of Sheridan, and police believe Phillips is on the loose in northern Chautauqua County.

June 29: Police drop a dragnet around Cassadaga.

July 8: A firearm found in the town of Charlotte is linked to the June 10 shooting.

See TIMELINE On Page A-3

ECMC, Hamot Taking Care Of Wounded

By STEVEN YUNGHANS
Special To *The Post-Journal*

Joseph Longobardo, 32, and Donald Baker Jr., 38, both state troopers out of Saratoga County were flown to separate hospitals Thursday after sustaining gunshot wounds.

According to reports from the Fredonia Barracks on Route 60, one of the troopers was taken to Brooks Memorial Hospital in Dunkirk, then flown to Erie County Medical Center for additional treatment. A nursing supervisor said his condition was listed as critical, although she

declined to give any further information.

The other trooper was flown to Hamot Medical Center in Erie, Pa. Both troopers are listed in serious condition, but no other information was available on their condition.

The official word on the condition of the troopers didn't come until after 12:30 a.m. Friday, during a press conference by New York State Police Superintendent Wayne Bennett who flew into the area from Albany.

See WOUNDED on Page A-3

Troopers In Critical Condition After Surgery; Reward Raised

By GREGORY BACON
Special to *The Post-Journal*

FREDONIA — Two troopers shot Thursday night in the town of Pomfret are still alive but in critical condition.

Trooper Joseph Longobardo, 32, was shot in the leg on Bachellor Hill Road on Thursday and sent to the Erie County Medical Center, while Trooper Donald Baker was shot in the back and sent to Hamot Medical Center.

Both men are from the Albany area.

Since the shooting, both have had surgery, yet more is expected in the near future. The two are heavily sedated under medication and have not been interviewed by police.

"Life is a very precious thing," said Wayne Bennett, New York State Police superintendent, during a news briefing Friday.

Bennett said both individuals are married and one of them has a 1-year-old child.

Bennett admitted they currently do not have definitive proof that it was escapee Ralph "Bucky" Phillips, but all things point to him.

"Clearly, he is the prime suspect of these shootings," Bennett said.

Gov. George Pataki issued a statement Friday in support of the shot troopers.

"Our thoughts and prayers are with the families and friends of two New York State Troopers who were shot (Thursday) while looking for fugitive Ralph 'Bucky' Phillips," the gov-ernor said. "I ask anyone about the whereabouts of Ralph 'Bucky' Phillips please call the New York State Police at (716) 679-1520."

See TROOPERS, Page A-3

Inside

- Cassadaga Festival Cancelled,

Page A-3

DONALD BAKER

JOSEPH LONGOBARDO

Cassadaga Stirs With Emotions As Search Heats Up

By ALPHA HUSTED

CASSADAGA — The Village of Cassadaga took on all the surrealism of a Steven Spielberg movie set Friday. There was the drone of helicopters circling above, and the steady rumble of bumper-to-bumper traffic, as heavily armed State Police conducted vehicle checks both inside and outside the community.

With two state troopers shot and critically wounded Thursday evening, on Bachellor Hill Road, the search for fugitive Ralph "Bucky" Phillips is being driven with a new intensity.

Asked to voice their opinions on the ongoing search for Phillips, a number of area residents shared their thoughts with *The Post Journal*.

Nancy Mangine, who was catching up on some shopping, said she just wants "the whole thing to be over."

See CASSADAGA, Page A-3

State Police Superintendent William Bennett addresses members of the media Friday afternoon.

Photo by Gregory Bacon

Crowe's Bail Skyrockets

By DENNIS PHILLIPS

Chautauqua County Judge John Ward on Friday raised bail for Kasey Crowe after the shooting of two New York State Police officers occurred where she resides on Bachelor Hill Road.

Bail was raised from $10,000 cash and $20,000 property bond to $100,000 cash and $200,000 property bond for Crowe, stemming from the ambush of the two New York State troopers — 32-year-old Joseph Longobardo and 38-year-old Donald Baker, Jr. — Thursday outside of Crowe's residence.

Crowe is an acquaintance of Ralph "Bucky" Phillips and together they have a daughter,

See BAIL, Page A-3

"We don't shoot to wound people. That's not the way we're trained."

— Wayne Bennett,
New York State Police
Superintendent

www.post-journal.com

JAMESTOWN, NY

VOL. 180 No. 74

SEPTEMBER 3, 2006

The Sunday Post-Journal

Police Remain On High Alert

Reward Upped Again, Searches Continue

By STEVEN YUNGHANS
Special To *The Post-Journal*

FREDONIA — A $225,000 reward is bringing the New York State Police more leads in the search for Ralph Phillips, but none have yet led troopers to the fugitive.

Despite reports that state troopers are closing in on Phillips, he remained at large Saturday.

Major Michael Manning told reporters in the Fredonia High School auditorium during an evening news conference Saturday that one of the two troopers who was injured Thursday evening in an ambush on Bachellor Hill Road fired his own weapon defensively as 11 shots were fired at him and his partner, both of whom remain in critical condition as of Saturday night.

[See PHILLIPS on Page A-6]

State troopers are shown searching the trunk of a car near Cassadaga on Saturday.

AP photo

Professor Says Shooting Is Change For Phillips

By NICHOLAS L. DEAN

Months on the run and talk of Ralph "Bucky" Phillips as a "folk hero" may have taken its toll on the criminal, making him ripe for muddled thoughts and acts of desperation.

As the prime suspect in the shooting of three state troopers, including two in Pomfret on Thursday, Phillips has again proven he is dangerous. However, according to Dr. Donna Levin, Hilbert College professor and chairperson of psychology, the latest incident marks a significant change in Phillips' state of mind.

"If in fact he is the shooter, it marks a significant change in his sort of 'bravery'," Levin said of the incident. "I don't want to call it 'bravery', but I mean he has become emboldened by talk of him as a 'folk hero'."

[See PSYCHE on Page A-6]

Phillips: Troopers Fired Back

From Page A-1

"We are in error on one bit of information," Manning said. "One of the troopers, and I can't identify which, did discharge a weapon at the scene while being fired upon by a suspect we believe to be Ralph Phillips who fired eleven times at the troopers. The circumstances of being discharged I can't really comment on until we have an opportunity to talk to the two troopers who both remain in critical condition at this time. It is apparent that the troopers did try to defend themselves at the scene."

Manning said Troopers Joseph Longobardo and Donald Baker Jr. were the only troopers at the scene when the shooting began at 6 p.m. Thursday.

State police have maintained surveillance near 4710 Bachellor Hill Road ever since charging Patrina Wright, Kasey Crowe, and Richard Catanese, who had been at the house, with helping Phillips and endangering the welfare of a child.

Manning said the assailant shot the troopers within a close range. "I'll say it was less than a football field, that's close enough," and were taken by surprise. He also said both troopers were behind the house at the time of the shooting.

Close to 300 members of the New York State Police are in northern Chautauqua County, working 12-hour shifts since the night of the shooting either on patrols, at checkpoints performing vehicle searches, searching wooded areas, or investigating evidence from a number of scenes where Phillips or his suspected help have been.

raised to $225,000, Manning also said the New York State Police appreciated the support being offered by area residents.

"The community has been outstanding to us. Their support, on all aspects and the change of hearts I think since the shooting of our two troopers has been just overwhelming form the local community," Manning said. "I can't thank the people of Chautauqua County enough for what I feel is just an overwhelming support for what our troopers are doing."

Manning said there hasn't been any indications that Phillips has fled the area since the shooting, no reports of stolen vehicles, no break-ins and no sightings. He pointed out that the area of northern Chautauqua County which has been a primary focus of the state police search since he was first spotted near Cassadaga in June has

State troopers, with guns drawn, brave the rains brought by Hurricane Ernesto while searching a vehicle Saturday near Cassadaga.

AP photo

'Difficult Day'

Trooper Dies From Gunshot Wounds

By STEVEN YUNGHANS
Special to *The Post-Journal*

New York State Trooper Joseph Longobardo died Sunday afternoon at 3:35 from gunshot wounds suffered during a shooting near 4710 Bachellor Hill Road in the town of Pomfret on Thursday night. He was 32.

The announcement came Sunday night during a press conference held in the Fredonia High School Auditorium from New York State Police Superintendent Wayne Bennett.

"This crime now is elevated to a Class A 1 Felony under New York State Law," Bennett said referring to a charge of aggravated murder of a police officer which carries a mandatory penalty of life in prison without the possibility of parole.

"This has been a very difficult day, and I ask you to communicate to all the people out there in the public that now, more than ever before, the family of Joseph Longobardo needs their prayers."

New York State Troopers and Cheektowaga police officers lift candles to show their support for Troopers Joseph Longobardo and Donald H. Baker, Jr. during a candlelight vigil at the Wesleyan Church of Hamburg Sunday afternoon.

Photo by Tim Latshaw

Trooper: Everyone Is Advised Secure Vehicles, Residences

From Page A-1

"Clearly now, there can be no discussion about the fact that he is a dangerous person and he's a risk to everybody, law enforcement and non-law enforcement alike," Bennett said.

He went on to ask for the public's help in finding Phillips.

"If you see it, report it," Bennett said.

He advised people to secure their vehicles and lock doors on residences.

"That's a very critical thing that you must do because that's how he makes his escape," Bennett said.

Bennett said there were a number of leads the state police responded to Sunday, including a number of sightings which later proved to be false reports.

"We do follow up on every single one of them and we do it immediately," he said. "We still want to encourage the public, please call us, we will follow up on each and every lead, even if they are anonymous."

Superintendent Bennett said state police have noticed a change in the information they have been receiving from the public since reward money for information leading to Phillips' capture had been raised.

"There has been a marked difference in cooperation that we are receiving and I thank those people for coming forward, because they have finally realized that if they were on the fence, there is no more fence now," Bennett said.

With the shooting that occurred Thursday and now the death of one of the troopers that was shot, Bennett believed there should be no question now whether or not Phillips presented a danger to the community for those that had had doubts before.

Bennett also had some new information on the condition of Longobardo's partner who was also shot Thursday.

Trooper Donald Baker Jr. who was shot in the back with a round that penetrated his bullet-resistant vest, is now listed in serious, but stable condition at Hamot Medical Center in Erie, Pa., after a third surgery.

Troopers Longobardo and Baker Jr. were both standing watch at the property where three people had been arrested a week before on charges relating to helping Ralph "Bucky" Phillips elude state police.

Phillips has been a fugitive since his escape from the Alden Correctional Facility in Erie County on April 3 of this year. He has also been connected with forensic evidence to the shooting of a state trooper near Elmira that occurred June 10. Trooper Sean Brown suffered a gunshot wound to the abdomen after stopping to check on a vehicle along a roadway. State police investigators say Phillips was inside that vehicle and shot at the trooper before fleeing the scene. A weapon later recovered in Chautauqua County had been matched to the bullet recovered from Trooper Brown, suggesting a near certain link between Phillips and the shooting.

Phillips has been in and out of Chautauqua County on a five-month odyssey using stolen vehicles, clothing, food and weapons to aid in his bid to avoid being captured by state police.

Phillips has had a history of using parts of the county to hide from police before and seems to be most comfortable hiding out here rather than attempting to leave the area outright.

The reward stands at $225,000 for information leading to the arrest and conviction of Ralph "Bucky" Phillips.

Phillips should not be approached as he is considered armed and dangerous. He has been known to use stolen vehicles, clothing, food and weapons as well as altering his appearance to aid in his flight from police.

Anyone with information on his whereabouts should contact the state police at 679-1520 or contact 911.

The Post-Journal

www.post-journal.com — TUESDAY —

JAMESTOWN, NY

Full Throttle

Police Agencies Converge On County

By STEVEN YUNGHANS
Special to *The Post-Journal*

Additional law enforcement resources continue to pour in to the region as the New York State Police continue the state's largest manhunt in history for fugitive and now suspected cop killer Ralph "Bucky" Phillips.

"We're here today as a group to show the unity we have in the organizations represented that are in the search to arrest Ralph Phillips," Major Michael Manning said Monday afternoon while standing with a group of representatives from the state police, NYS Department of Environmental Conservation Police, the Buffalo Police Department S.W.A.T. team and Chautauqua County Sheriff's Department in front of the Troop A Barracks on Route 60 in Fredonia.

"We have a large contingent of agencies from within Chautauqua County and outside Chautauqua County," Major Manning said. "Whether it be the Sheriff's Department, State Environmental Conservation, Buffalo Police Department, Erie County Sheriff's Department, DEA, FBI, Pennsylvania State Police, and the list goes on."

See COUNTY on Page A-3

The U.S. and New York State flags were lowered to half staff Sunday night after word that Trooper Joseph Longobardo had died as a result of a gunshot wound he suffered Thursday night in the town of Pomfret.

Photos by Steven Yunghans

Cassadaga Feels Effects Of Phillips' Intrusion

By JOAN JOSEPHSON
Special to *The Post-Journal*

CASSADAGA — Windows rattled as a helicopter flew low over the Village of Cassadaga area Monday in a continuing search for fugitive Ralph "Bucky" Phillips who is suspected of shooting three New York State Troopers.

One of these troopers, Joseph Longobardo, 32, died Sunday as the result of the wound he suffered when he was shot while he and his fellow officer, Donald Baker Jr., were keeping the Bachellor Hill home of Phillips' former girlfriend, Kasey Crowe, under surveillance.

Baker also was shot and is listed in critical condition at Hamot Medical Center in Erie, Pa.

The third trooper, Sean Brown, was shot near Elmira in June when he attempted to check on a vehicle allegedly occupied by Phillips. Brown has since been released from the hospital where he was treated for a gun shot wound to the stomach.

When the hunt for "Bucky" first got under way in this area after he escaped from the Erie County Holding Center in Alden in April, any number of local residents treated it as a joke.

See CASSADAGA on Page A-3

U.N Me Isr He

JIDDAH
has mainta
negotiate wi
two soldiers
massive off

But with
— except a
green light t
with the gue

U.N. chic
would appo
the first p
between the
Lebanon en

The anno
of a prison
release, ar
repeatedly r
governmer
domestic mer

The agre
through on
serving the
that ended
fighting. Is
Lebanon af
the two sol
cross-border

The U.N.
the fighting
tional releas
has said it
for Arab pri

"Both s
offices of
resolve this
conference
of Jiddah.
work discre
find a soluti

"The onl
if I'm going

Fredonia Increases School Security Measures

By MICHAEL RUKAVINA
Special to *The Post-Journal*

As the manhunt for fugitive Ralph "Bucky" Phillips continues to escalate, Fredonia Central School is taking the necessary steps to maintain and increase safety for students and faculty for the upcoming school year. Fredonia Central School has been in daily contact with local police agencies to help increase security measures at the Wheelock Primary School and the Main Street Campus.

"Our Police Department will continue to patrol both locations throughout the school day and after normal school hours," said Fredonia Police Chief, Brad Meyers.

In addition, School Resource Officer Robert Tracy will be stationed at the Wheelock Primary School on a daily basis to help provide extra security and supervision. Unlike Wheelock, the Main Street Campus is directly adjacent to the barracks of the New York State Troopers on Route 60. The State Troopers have immediate access to the Main Street Campus at all times and are currently using the High School Auditorium as a meeting and press conference location.

See FREDONIA on Page A-3

CHAUTAUQUA COUNTY SHERIFF JOSEPH GERACE

Lives On Hold

Search For Escaped Convict Continues

FREDONIA (AP) — The first day of school for kids in rural Western New York meant recess in the classroom, no outdoor sports practice and armed state troopers continuing to search vehicles at nearly two dozen checkpoints.

The normal rhythms of life in this sleepy corner of the state have been radically jolted as hundreds of police scour the woods for Ralph Phillips, the escaped convict suspected of killing one trooper and wounding two others during five months on the run.

For some, the search for Phillips threatens their beloved hunting season. One village lost out on summer's last hurrah, canceling Labor Day festivities because of safety concerns.

"They're trying to do their job but it's annoying," said Fred Mead of Silver Creek, outside an auto parts store across from a media camp that has sprung up.

Phillips, 44, broke out of the Erie County jail

Greg Edwards, Chautauqua County Executive, speaks as Dave Foley, Chautauqua County district attorney; and state Sen. Catharine Young, look on.

Photo by Steven Yunghans

Phillips Among Most Wanted; Reward Upped

By **MICHAEL RUKAVINA**
Special to *The Post-Journal*

FREDONIA — The reward for Ralph Phillips is approaching the half-million mark.

Laurie Bennett, FBI special agent in charge, joined with New York State Police Superintendent Wayne Bennett at a press conference Thursday to announce the reward for the fugitive has been upped to $450,000.

The increase is due to his placement on the FBI's Top Ten Most Wanted List, which includes a reward of $100,000. Phillips is the 483rd person to be placed on that exclusive list, which has led to the capture of 453 fugitives, 147 thanks to citizen cooperation.

This recent turn of events has re-established the FBI as a primary resource to the already agency-filled manhunt.

"Our role in this matter is to bring our resources to the New York State Police that they deem appropriate in their investigation. We will work in tandem with our law enforcement partners that you see here today to assist the New York State Police in our law enforcement mission," said the FBI's Bennett.

See REWARD on Page A-3

"This miserable creature will suffer for the rest of his life"

— Wayne Bennett,
New York State Police superintendent

Phillips Caught

Manhunt Ends With Stunning Silence

By **DEAN WELLS**
Special to *The Post-Journal*

AKELEY, Pa. — Instead of gunfire, it ended in applause.

The manhunt for escaped convict Ralph Phillips ended Friday when the fugitive, who vowed to go down fighting, a "suicide by cop," walked out of the woods on the hill above Akeley with his hands in the air and surrendered to authorities.

Police confirmed at 7:56 p.m. that Phillips was in custody. Several minutes

Above, law enforcement officers transport Ralph Phillips, center, after he was captured in Akeley, Pa. on Friday. Below, A law enforcement officer takes part in the search for Ralph Phillips in Carroll on Friday.
Photo above by The Associated Press

The End
Of The Line

Sept. 8, 2006

1:55 a.m.
Stolen car reported, two Warren County Sheriff's Deputies pursue. Car crashes and man escapes into woods.

2:30 a.m.
Another car stolen, man jumps from moving vehicle and escapes into the woods.

7:30 a.m.
Perimeter set up from Frewsburg to Akeley.

9:10 a.m.
A New York trooper and dog tracked Phillips down and fire several shots.

Ralph Phillips is shown walking into court for his arraignment Saturday.
AP photo

Ralph Phillips has a variety of facial hair arrangements throughout his tenure as a fugitive.

Hello Ray

①

August 27

Received your letter and excerpt.

First. I don't believe your really
  trying to "screw" me out of
money!
      But I really don't know what
your up to, either.

Second, you really don't know
what is going on with me, Ray.
Yes, I did plead guilty. Am
  I guilty? Int depends on who
you speak to. 99% of the
  county probably has no clue
of the truth.
      However- that is of no
import to me.
      What is is my getting my
case reversed.
      You have a book which could
become something - but not as it
stands.
      The only thing you'll do by
publishing that book is
      fuck my strategy up. And
I wont give what you want
until my ass is out of the
fryin' pan.
      Third, I will be back!

I know the troopers think they have it licked and I'm all done. I was pretty stupid for many years and I never knew squat about the law.

For two years I've been on my job and guess what? What those assholes did will come back to bite them. Only a matter of time.

I will be filing a collateral attack shortly to vacate my conviction. I expect it to take a couple years because it has to go through county court (they'll deny it outright) then the Appellate Division and likely to the Court of Appeals.

But I am going to come back for trial.

Imagine the publicity, Ray. Your book will be very much desired then. And I'll help you then. However. You understand the ramifications if I do so now— it will come back to haunt me.

My freedom is more valuable to me than being known.

I read the piece you sent. Its

a nice piece of fiction. ☺
I will say you've captured
a part of my personality.
   Your a good writer, I give
you that.
   But there no substitute for
facts.
      My dad wasn't one to
have "patients" to teach me
   much. "Buck", not Bucky,
learned his lessons of life alone.
   And   the blizzard of '77
I   was in Butta, N.Y. in
   a   "group home" shoveling
snow   out of folks yards
   for money.
The learn to came later. ☺

The single shot .22 was a
   "savage" ad the knife was
a Buck.

   Goodnight.

         Take Care

And when you see   Buck
my "friends" with
the big heads -
tell 'em "we ain't
done yet." Not
by a long "shot."

BIBLIOGRAPHY

Butterfield, Fox. *All God's Children: The Bosket Family and the Tradition of Violence.* Harper Perennial, 1996.

Dionne, E. J., Jr. "Only Politicians Have Found Easy Answers to Youth Crime." *New York Times*, July 9, 1978.

Goldin, Davidson. "Prosecutor Says Troopers Block Fake-Evidence Inquiry." *New York Times,* February 14, 1995.

Mayo, Katherine. *Justice to All: The Story of the Pennsylvania State Police.* Houghton Mifflin Company, 1920.

Perez-Pena, Richard. "Supervision of Troopers Faulted in Evidence-Tampering Scandal." *New York Times,* February 4, 1997.

Phillips Manhunt Operational Review. New York State Police, 2007.

Stewart, Daniel L., Frederick C. Lamy, and Frances T. Sullivan. *In the Matter of the Escape of Ralph Phillips an Inmate of the Erie County Correctional Facility.* New York State Commission of Correction, 2006.

Treaster, Joseph B. "State Delinquent Center: No Punishment or Reform." *New York Times*, March 2, 1976.

ABOUT THE AUTHOR

Ray Hall, a graduate of Jamestown Community College, was a veteran of the U.S. Air Force who went on to run several businesses throughout his lifetime. He had been employed by the former Jamestown Telephone Company and was past president of the telephone workers union. Ray had worked for the Norvell Reed Farm, where he bought, sold, and auctioned cattle. He was the Clerk of the Chautauqua County Legislature from 1980 until 1983. During his retirement years, he hosted a talk radio show on WJTN called *The Hall Closet* and wrote a blog for the *Post Journal*. Ray had a lifelong passion for politics and served as Chairman of the Jamestown Democratic Party for several years. Ray completed writing *Killer on the Run* prior to his passing on December 20, 2011.